CHALLENGING
ISLAMIC TRADITIONS

Published by William Carey Library
1605 E. Elizabeth St.
Pasadena, CA 91104 | www.missionbooks.org

Melissa Hicks, editor
Cheryl Warner, copyeditor
Alyssa E. Force, graphic design
Jeremy Lind, indexer

William Carey Library is a ministry of
Frontier Ventures
www.frontierventures.org

Printed in the United States of America
20 19 18 17 16   5 4 3 2 1 BP

Library of Congress Cataloging-in-Publication Data
Power, Bernie.
    Challenging Islamic traditions : searching questions about the Hadith from a Christian perspective / Dr. Bernie Power.
        pages cm
    Includes bibliographical references and index.
    ISBN 978-0-87808-489-0 -- ISBN 0-87808-489-4 1. Hadith. 2. Christianity and other religions--Islam. 3. Islam--Relations--Christianity. I. Title.
    BP135.P69 2015
    297.1'2516--dc23

                                                                    2015022505

CHALLENGING
ISLAMIC TRADITIONS

Searching Questions about the Hadith
from a Christian Perspective

BERNIE POWER

WILLIAM CAREY
LIBRARY

CONTENTS

I

CRITICAL ISSUES

II

CONTRASTS WITH BIBLICAL TEACHING

III
CHALLENGES FROM OTHER PERSPECTIVES

IV
PRACTICAL IMPLICATIONS

TRANSLITERATION TABLE

CONSONANTS								
b	=	ب	z	=	ز	f	=	ف
t	=	ت	s	=	س	q	=	ق
th	=	ث	sh	=	ش	k	=	ك
j	=	ج	ṣ	=	ص	l	=	ل
ḥ	=	ح	ḍ	=	ض	m	=	م
kh	=	خ	ṭ	=	ط	n	=	ن
d	=	د	ẓ	=	ظ	h	=	ه
dh	=	ذ	'	=	ع	w	=	و
r	=	ر	gh	=	غ	y	=	ي

VOWELS			
SHORT	a = ´	i = ِ	u = ُ
LONG	ā = ا	ī = ي	ū = و
DIPHTONG	ay = اَيْ	aw = اَوْ	

ILLUSTRATIONS

SIDEBARS

TABLES

INTRODUCTION

ISLAM IS OFTEN IN THE HEADLINES for all the wrong reasons. The attacks in New York and Washington on September 11, 2001, with the subsequent war in Afghanistan, the ongoing violence in Iraq and Israel/Palestine, Iran's nuclear ambitions, political unrest in the Middle East, almost daily suicide bombings in various locations around the world, and the continuing threat of terror from Islamic jihadists, dominate the international scene. In Western countries, social and political issues concerning Muslim immigrants and multiculturalism have assured Islam recurring, and often negative, coverage in the media.

Internally, Islam faces many problems. Among the fifty-two Muslim majority countries, it is rare to find participative democracies, widespread human rights, or comprehensive progress and development. Within and among these countries there are massive disparities of wealth and education. Islamic nations include some of the richest countries in the world, and also many of the poorest. Corruption at almost every level of government and business is often the norm. Former President of Pakistan Pervaz Musharraf bemoaned Islam's current state: "We are the poorest, we are the most illiterate, we are the most backward, we are the most unhealthy, indeed, we are the most unenlightened, the most deprived and the weakest of the human race today. To top all this, we are involved in strife and fratricide within and perceived to be terrorists outside."[1]

Yet Islam makes prodigious assertions about itself and its followers. Muslims are told that they are "the best of peoples ever evolved for mankind"[2] and that they have been chosen by Allah.[3] Islam is the only acceptable religion,[4] and it will be superior or prevail over all other religions.[5] "Islam is the answer" has become a common catch-cry for Muslims in the West and elsewhere.

Muslims claim that Islam is a comprehensive religion, covering every part of life. The important scholar Sayyid Qutb made the following declaration: "Islam … is intended to penetrate into the veins and arteries of a vital society and to be a concrete organized movement." Islam is not "merely a belief, so that it is enough merely to preach it." It is "a way of life" that "takes practical steps to organize a movement for freeing man. Other societies do not give it any opportunity to organize its followers according to its own method, and hence it is the duty of Islam to annihilate all such systems, as they are obstacles in the way of universal freedom."[6]

The key text of Islam is the Qur'an. Muslims hold it to be the literal word of God. At Muhammad's death, the divine revelation for Muslims ceased. However the Qur'an, when it was eventually compiled, lacked important details. There is little easily identifiable information about the life of Muhammad. There is no prescription, for example, for entry into the Muslim community, the *shahāda* (Islamic confession of faith) does not exist in its full form in the Qur'an,[7] and circumcision is not mentioned at all. Key Islamic theological terms such as *tawḥīd* (oneness) are not found in the Qur'an. Nor are significant rituals outlined, such as when and how to perform the five daily prayers. The amount for the *zakāt* (almsgiving) is not specified. So the Qur'an cannot stand by itself—extra information is needed.

This gap is filled by the Hadith,[8] a collection of traditions about Muhammad and the early Muslims. The Hadith are crucial to an understanding of the Qur'an. Each hadith, or account, consists of an *isnād*, or chain of witnesses, usually back to Muhammad, and a *matn*, or content, sometimes just a sentence long, or perhaps running into several pages. The matn is usually a saying, action, or some information about Muhammad and/or the early Muslims. The behavior described in the Hadith is called the *sunnah*[9] or tradition of the Prophet, and it is important for Muslims today.

The important writer Mohammed Nāsir-ul-Dīn al-Albāni states: "There is no way to understand the Qur'an correctly except in association with the interpretation of the Sunnah."[10] Another Muslim scholar comments that "it is almost impossible to understand or explain the meaning of a large number of Qur'anic verses if the Traditions are rejected as useless and inauthentic."[11] The connection between Qur'an and Hadith cannot be riven.

"The Qur'an is both the foundation and fountain of faith and, among the fundamentals of Divine Law, the Shari'ah, its place is unique. Its purpose however is only to lay down the principles. Its elaboration and interpretation are left to the Sunnah and the Hadith…. The believer is religiously bound to accept as true both the Prophet's interpretation and elucidation of the Qur'anic verses as well as the "wisdom" revealed to him by Allah."[12]

The Hadith, as important as they are to Muslims, are often found to present a message that is not acceptable to non-Muslims. This book aims to contrast the ideas from the most important collection of the Hadith (that of al-Bukhāri)[13] with the teaching of the Bible and with commonly accepted norms found in other societies. This may go some way to understanding why Islam has failed to deliver on its promises resulting in the current predicament in which Muslims find themselves. Knowledge of the Hadith will also help Christians and others comprehend some of the reasons behind Islamic violence, its lack of progress, and the so-called "clash of civilizations" with the West and with other countries.

NOTES

1   Source: http://news.bbc.co.uk/2/hi/south_asia/1824455.stm (accessed July 7, 2013).

2   Q.3:110. Qur'anic verses are denoted by e.g. Q.5:3, which denotes the fifth chapter and the third verse of the Qur'an. The English translation in this study will be taken from al-Hilali and Khan, *Noble Qur'an,* unless otherwise noted.

3   Q.22:78; 27:59.

4   Q.3:85.

5   Q.61:9; 48:28,29; 9:33.

6   Qutb, *Milestones*, 12.

7   The two phrases which make up the *shahāda* are present, the first in Q.37:35 and the second in Q.48:29, but never in the same sentence. Muhammad's name is found only four times (Q.3:138; 23:40; 47:2; 48:29).

8   The term "Hadith" will be used in this book as both an individual and collective noun, following standard academic practice. Occasionally the plural "hadiths" will be used. The Arabic word *hadīth* is singular, and its plural is *ahādīth*. Since it is a commonly accepted term in English, like the words *Muhammad, Islam,* and *Qur'an,* it will not be transliterated.

9   The plural of *sunnah* is *sunan*. Some Hadith collections have this title.

10 Source: www.ilaam.net/Articles/StatusOfSunnah.html (cited July 7, 2013).

11 Azami, *The Sunnah in Islam*, 29-31. Despite such frequent assertions about the necessity of the Hadith, there is a long history of Muslim opinion which regards the Hadith as unreliable. This will be detailed in chapter 2.

12 Azami, *The Sunnah in Islam*, 8, 16.

13 The Hadith pericopes (individual accounts) will be referred to by their number, e.g., B.1:37, which refers to al-Bukhari vol. 1, Hadith account no. 37. al-Bukhāri's collection has nine volumes, with the number of pericopes varying from 582 (vol. 6) to 895 (vol. 3).

I

CRITICAL ISSUES

The Hadith have not been without their detractors. Critics have noted that there are a variety of collections of the Hadith, with significant variation and even contradiction between them. Scholars, both Muslim and non-Muslim have challenged the whole concept of the Hadith for a variety of different reasons. They note that there was a lack of consistency about the Hadith from the very earliest days of Islam. Furthermore the relationship between the Qur'an and the Hadith is convoluted and confusing. Serious questions have been raised about the manner in which the Hadith were compiled. This first section deals with these issues and some others besides.

THE CHALLENGES OF IDENTIFYING THE HADITH

1. COMPARING TEXTS

This book begins with a comparison between the Islamic Hadith and the Bible, taken from a Christian perspective. Working with the texts of another religious tradition needs to be carried out perceptively. Any religious tradition will internally present a range of beliefs. These could be displayed on a continuum (see Illustration 1),[1] from agreement, i.e., concepts that the tradition strongly asserts or affirms, to disagreement, i.e., concepts that it negates or refutes.[2] In the middle of the continuum will be aspects on which the religion's teaching is uncertain or undefined.

ILLUSTRATION 1: Affirmation/Refutation Continuum

An example may illustrate this. Muslims clearly assert that "there is only one God" (Q.112:1). They would oppose the statement that "Jesus Christ is the Son of God" (c.f. Q.9:30). Muslims, however, disagree among themselves about the meaning of the term "seeking His face" as applied to Allah (Q.18:28). Their theologians have come up with a wide variety of interpretations of this phrase. The Qur'an itself admits that some of its verses are "not entirely clear" (Q.3:7, Hilali and Khan translation).[3] Even for Muslims, it is not always easy to identify what they all hold in common.

But when another religion or spiritual tradition is brought in, the picture becomes even more complicated. No two religious traditions are identical: when their teachings are overlaid on each other, patterns emerge and possible responses become evident. (See Illustration 2.)

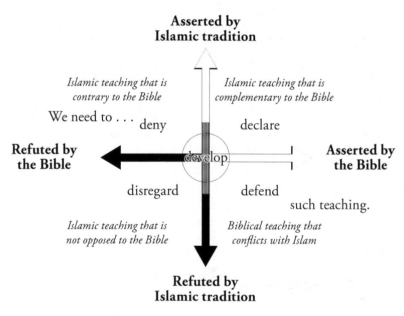

ILLUSTRATION 2: Responses to Affirmation/Negation

If an Islamic Hadith is *complementary*, that is, it agrees with the revelation found in Christian Scripture, there should be no difficulty in a Christian affirming or publicly declaring such information.[4] Some of the material in the Hadith will be *contradictory*. It will refute biblical teaching. Christians are called to "contend for the faith"[5] and deny such teaching. Some will be *conflicting*, i.e., it will disallow what Scripture affirms. This calls for a defensive apologetic.[6] Paul states that "we demolish arguments and every pretension that sets itself up against the knowledge of God."[7]

Material which is *contrary* to or not dealt with by both traditions can generally be ignored,[8] for it generally adds little to the common understanding. Some material will be *supplementary*—it may not be found in Scripture, but it does not contradict biblical revelation. This can be explored and even developed. Paul takes this approach when debating with the Greek philosophers on the Areopagus.[9] Paul notes that "we take captive every thought to make it obedient to Christ."[10] Throughout this study, certain propositions and ideas found in the Hadith will be challenged and denied, significant differences will be unveiled, and the teaching of the Bible will be presented as an alternative.

Problems within the Hadith that raise substantial issues can be identified. As a matter of integrity, these problems cannot be ignored. These are roadblocks or barriers which must be uncovered and inspected. Erroneous accounts must be exposed and corrected, and Christian teaching which is under attack should be defended. Honesty and frankness are required, as well as sensitivity and respect.

2. THE EARLIEST COLLECTIONS OF HADITH

After Muhammad and the early Muslims had died, Muslims began to write historical accounts of their lives. Some of the earliest collections of these writings are listed in table 1.[11] Generally they followed a less rigorous methodology than the later collections (e.g., they lacked complete *isnāds*) giving them a lower status in the eyes of later Muslims. Although earlier anthologies than these may have existed, there are "no authentic remains of any compilation of an earlier date than the middle or end of the second century of the Hijra."[12] The *Hijra* was the migration of Muhammad and his followers from Mecca to Medina in AD 622. It signifies the beginning of the Muslim community.

	NAME OF COLLECTION	NAME OF COMPILER	DATE OF COMPILER	NO. OF HADITHS
1	Muwaṭṭa'	Mālik b. Anas	d.179/795	1,823
2	*Minhat al-maʿbud fi tartīb Musnad al-Ṭayālisi Abi Dāwūd*	Abu Dāwūd al-Ṭayālisi	d.203-4/ 819-20	2,767
3	*Muṣannaf* (lit. 'classified')	Abd al-Razzāq	d.211/826	21,033
4	Musannaf	Abu Bakr b. Abi Shayba	d.235/849	37,943
5	*Sunan* (lit. 'paths'. sing. *Sunnah*)	'Abdallah b. Abd al-Rahmān al-Darīmi	d.255/869	3,503

TABLE 1: List of Earliest Anthologies[a]

Some terms should be explained. A musnad classified Hadiths according to the name of the transmitter closest to Muhammad, e.g., "Abu Hurayra," whereas a *muṣannaf* classified them by topical headings, e.g., "prayer" or "fasting."

But a problem soon arose. As Muslim scholars gathered the accounts of Muhammad's life and early Islamic history, they found that discerning real traditions from fictitious accounts was no straightforward task. "In the first two centuries after Muhammad's death the number of Hadiths increased in direct proportion to the demand. Whenever the community faced a new issue each party concerned would seek authority for its view in a Hadith....

---

a   Dates will be given in the format : Hijri/Gregorian e.g. 179/795.
       Dates after 1500 AD will only be given in Gregorian format.

This became a flourishing industry."[13] One man, 'Abd al-Karīm Abū 'l-'Auja, when sentenced to death for apostasy and atheism, confessed to fabricating 4,000 Hadiths which he attributed to the Prophet. He was executed by crucifixion in 104/722 by Muhammad b. Sulaimān b. 'Ali, governor of Basrah.[14]

By the beginning of the third century after Muhammad, there were many Hadiths in circulation.[15] Margoliouth claims that al-Bukhāri had heard 90,000 of them.[16] Guillaume quotes a figure of 600,000 but notes that "these figures must be taken with a grain of salt."[17] This larger figure has been questioned by Kamali:

> It may be that these figures consisted mainly of the number of reports and reporters rather than of actual *aHadith*.... If we were to eliminate repetition and reduce all of this to the actual number of Hadith, we would have a much smaller number of *aHadith* left, that may or may not exceed ten thousand in number.

However he does admit this springs from his concern that "citing figures in the order of hundreds of thousands of Hadiths ... overshadowed and minisculed the significance of the earlier collections."[18]

Abbott, on the other hand, finds the numbers quite acceptable, because

> using geometric progression, we find that one to two thousand Companions and senior Successors transmitting two to five traditions each would bring us well within the range of the total number of traditions credited to the exhaustive collections of the third century. Once it is realised that the *isnād* did, indeed, initiate a chain reaction that resulted in an explosive increase in the number of traditions, the huge numbers that are credited to Ibn Hanbal, Muslim and Bukhāri seem not so fantastic after all.[19]

3. THE SIX ACCEPTED COLLECTIONS

Methods for identifying the "'authentic" *(ṣaḥīḥ)* Hadiths from those that were simply "good" *(ḥasan)* or "weak" *(ḍa'if)* were developed. This led to six collections being accepted as authoritative by most Muslims. They are the following (see Table 2):

COMMON NAME OF THE COLLECTION	NAME OF COMPILER	DATES OF COMPILER[b]	NUMBER OF HADITHS	NUMBER WITHOUT REPETITION	NUMBER OF HADITHS CONSIDERED
ṣaḥīḥ al-Bukhāri	Muhammad b. Isma'il **al-Bukhāri**	b.194/810–d.256/870	7,275[c]	2,602[d]	300,000 or 600,000[e]
ṣaḥīḥ Muslim	**Muslim** b. al-Hajjaj	b.202/817–d.261/875	7,190	3,030	300,000
Sunan Abu Dawud	**Abu Dawud** Sulayman b. al-Ash'ath al-Sijistani	d.275/889	5,274	4,800	500,000
Kitab al-sunan al-kubra	Ahmad b. Shu'ayb **Al-Nasa'i**	d.303/915	5,000		
Al-Jami' al-ṣaḥīḥ	Muhammad b. Isa **Al-Tirmidhi**	d.279/892	3,956	3,873	
Sunan Ibn Maja	**Ibn Maja** al-Qazwini	d.273/886	4,341	1,339	

TABLE 2: The Six Accepted Collections

b   All dates will be given in the form: Hijri/Gregorian e.g. 194 AH/810 AD. http://www.islamicfinder.org/Hcal/index.php is a website which changes dates from Hijri (Islamic) to Gregorian (Western) calendar.

c   Guillaume, *The Traditions of Islam*, 28, recognises that other authorities give figures of 7,295 and 7,397.

d   Guillaume, *The Traditions of Islam,* 28, citing Houdas. Kutty "The Six Authentic Books of Hadith," 20, gives a figure of 2,762.

e   Guillaume, *The Traditions of Islam,* 28.

Voll notes the shortcomings of these anthologies:

> These great collections are not, however, canonical. No institution has ever officially accepted them, and the verifying community has been the general consensus of the community, which is flexible. The six collections contain contradictory material, and Muslims, from time to time, go outside of the body of *Hadiths* contained in these collections for authoritative opinion.[20]

In fact, some scholars claim that the sixth collection should be the *Muwaṭṭa'* of Mālik b.'Anas instead of the *Sunan* of Ibn Mājah. Neo-Sufi thinkers like the Indian Naqshbandiyya scholar Shāh Wālī Allāh al-Dihlāwī (AD 1702-1762) "did not accept the standard ninth-century *Hadith* as infallible or not open to question and analysis." He gave precedence to the *Muwaṭṭa'* over the standard ninth-century compilations.[21]

Although all of the Hadiths in al-Bukhāri are claimed to be ṣaḥīḥ, not all scholars are agreed.[22] Nor have these collections come down in a single unchallenged edition. al-Bukhāri's text, for example, "exists in several 'narrations' (*riwāyāt*), of which the version handed down by al-Kushmayhani (d.389) on the authority of Bukhari's pupil al-Firabri is the one most frequently accepted by the ulema."[23]

4. COMPREHENSIVENESS OF THESE COLLECTIONS

When first published, the so-called "authentic" collections were challenged by a group of early Muslims, the *ahl-al-hadīth* ("people of the hadith"), who strongly supported the use of all of the Hadith. Their concern was that any writings which drew on hadiths not listed in these collections would be scoffed at by another group of Muslims, the *ahl-al-ra'y* ("people of the opinion"), who felt human reasoning was a key element in discerning Islamic teachings. Unlisted hadiths could be easily dismissed with the charge, "That is not in the ṣaḥīḥ!"

But a ready answer to this charge existed: the collectors admitted that they had been selective in their choices. "Under fire from such critics, al-Bukhāri and Muslim defended themselves by saying that their books did not include *all* the ṣaḥīḥ hadiths in circulation. Al-Bukhāri only selected ṣaḥīḥ traditions useful for his legal discussions, and Muslim had limited his book to hadiths whose authenticity he believed was agreed to by all."[24]

Al-Hākim al-Naysābūrī (d.405/1014) in his *al-Mustadrak* compiled a list of 8,800 hadiths which he considered ṣaḥīḥ but had been omitted from the ṣaḥīḥayn (the two most authoritative collections, i.e., al-Bukhāri and Muslim). Both Abū al-Ḥasan al-Dāraqutnī (d.385/995) and Abū Dharr al-Harawī (d.430/1038) had earlier compiled one volume called *Ilzāmāt* (*Addendums*) with similar lists.[25] Clearly the "six collections" were never, in the early days at least, seen to be the only authorized lists of authentic Hadiths.

5. POLITICAL BIAS IN THE HADITH

These compilations also exhibit a clear political bias, reflecting the pragmatic realities of scholarly life under the Baghdadi ʿAbbāsid dynasty (AD 750-1100) which had deposed the ʿUmayyad rulers based in Syria (AD 661-750). Guillaume contrasts these "canonical" collections with the *musnad* work of their older contemporary Aḥmad ibn Hanbāl (d.241/855) who "suffered considerably under the ʿAbbāsid order."[26]

> Whereas the two great works of al-Bukhāri and Muslim may be searched in vain for any generous recognition of the merits of the Umayyads, Aḥmad, who forsooth had little to thank their successors for, preserves many of the numerous traditions extolling the glories of the Banu Umayya which must at one time have been current in Syria. A similar liberal attitude is adopted towards the Hadith which support the claims of the Shiʾas.[27]

It raises the question of whether political endorsement at the highest level allowed and even promoted the public dispersal and acceptance of these "six books." Siddiqui denies any positive encouragement from the Abbasids: "None of the compilers of the important and authoritative collections of *Hadith* received any post, purse or privilege from the caliphs or their officials."[28] Brown, however, cites Goldziher, who finds evidence of court patronage by both the 'Umayyads and 'Abbāsids for the hadith collectors and even hadith fabricators. Here are two examples. When their enemy 'Abdallāh b. al-Zubayr (d.73/692) controlled Mecca and the pilgrimage routes, the Umayyads, claimed Goldziher, circulated the hadith that urged Muslims not "to remove the saddles from their mounts [in other words, "to visit"] except at three mosques." This enabled the Umayyads to establish an alternative pilgrimage location to Jerusalem which was conveniently located in Umayyad-controlled Palestine. Their agents also fabricated a hadith claiming Muhammad gave his Friday sermons while seated, allowing the Umayyad rulers to do so and thus to appear more majestic before their congregations. "The Umayyads were able to forge and circulate these hadiths successfully, Goldziher argues, because they patronized and sponsored the early collection of hadiths.... The study of hadiths on a large scale occurred *because* of Umayyad interest in political propaganda."[29]

6. SHI'A COLLECTIONS OF THE HADITH

Other Muslims reject the six collections for historical reasons. Due to their different assessment of early Islamic history, Shi'a Muslims do not recognize the primacy of the Sunni collections.

> Since the Shi'a denied the legitimacy of the Sunni succession of Caliphs, Abū Bakr and 'Umar, though companions of the Prophet, could no longer be accepted as authoritative sources of Muslim religious teaching. An independent Hadith and law in which 'Ali was the prime authority was necessary. Thus the Shi'a elaborated their own Hadith and law, differing from the Sunni versions only in matters of detail and

in chains of transmission. The Hadiths of the imams, and especially the Hadiths attributed to 'Ali ... are central teachings of Shi'ism.[30]

Any Hadith transmitted by Aisha, the greatest single contributor to al-Bukhāri's collection, are rejected by Shi'as. The major Shi'i collections are detailed in Table 3.[31]

	NAME OF COLLECTION	NAME OF COMPILER	DATE OF COMPILER	NUMBER OF HADITH
1	*Masnad* 'Supported collection'	Zaid bin Ali	d. 120/740	
2	*Al-Kāfi fi 'ilm al-din'* Sufficiency in Religious Knowledge'	Abu Ja'far Muhammad b. Ya'qub al-Kulayni	d.328/939	15,176
3	*Kitab man-lā-yastahzirahu 'I-Faqīh* 'Non-conjectural Book of Jurisprudence'	Shaikh Ali al-Babuya al-Kummi	d.381/991	
4	*Al-tahzīb* 'Cultural Education'	Shaikh Abu Ja'far Muhammad ibn Ali ibn Husain al-Tusi	d.459/1067 or d.460/1068	13,590
5	*Al-istibsār* 'Seeking Insight'	Shaikh Abu Ja'far Muhammad ibn Ali ibn Husain al-Tusi	d.459/1067 or d.460/1068	5,511
6	*Najhu al-balāghah* 'The Peak of Excellence'	Sayyid ar-Razi	d.406/1015	
7	*Bihar al-anwar* 'The Ocean of Lights'	Muhammad Baqir al-Majlisi	d.1110/1700	110 volumes

TABLE 3: Shi'a Collections of the Hadith

7. COMMENTARIES ON AL-BUKHĀRĪ'S HADITH

Al-Bukhārī's collection of the Hadith has attracted many significant commentators who felt the need to elucidate and expand on its content. More than twenty commentaries have been written. The more important ones are listed in Table 4.

These works will be referred to as appropriate at different points in this book.

NAME OF COMMENTARY	AUTHOR	DATES
Sharh Ibn Battaal 'Ibn Battāl's Commentary'	Abu al-Hasan 'Ali ibn Khalaf ibn 'Abd al-Malik (10 vols)	d.449/1057
Al-Kawākib al-Darāri fi Sharh al-Bukhārī 'The Flowing Stars Commentary on al-Bukhārī'	Shams al-dīn al-Kirmānī	d.786/1384
Fath al-bārī Sharh ṣaḥīḥ al-Bukhārī 'Victory of the Creator's Commentary on al-Bukhārī'	Ibn Hajar al-'Asqalānī (96 vols)	d.852/1448
Umdah al Qari fi Sharh ṣaḥīḥ al Bukhari 'Main Subject Reader Commentary on al-Bukhārī'	Badr al-Dīn al-'Ayni (25 vols)	d.855/1451
Irshad al-Sari 'Guidance of the Traveller'	Ahmad ibn Muhammad al-Qastalani (15 vols)	d.923/1517
Hāmisha ṣaḥīḥ al-Bukhārī 'Sidenotes on al-Bukhārī'	Imam al-Sindi (4 vols)	d.c.1163/ 1750
Manār al-Qārī Sharh mukhtasar ṣaḥīḥ al-Bukhārī 'Reader's Lighthouse Abridged Commentary on al-Bukhārī'	Hamzah Muhammad Qāsim (5 vols)	Published 1410/1990

TABLE 4: Commentaries on al-Bukhārī's Hadith Collection

The Hadith collections, then, have been disputed territory from the earliest days. Some of the first collections of the Hadith suffered from a lack of clear *isnāds* back to the prophet and were rejected by succeeding generations. Later collections included complete *isnāds*, but with the passing of time it became easier to fabricate such links. The vast majority of the accounts that came to light were rejected for various reasons. None of the "authentic" collections claims to be totally comprehensive, and there is evidence of some political tampering, or at least, patronage. Even the collections which are currently considered the most authentic have been challenged by Muslim scholars, both Sunni and Shi'a, at different times. Later scholars have taken it upon themselves to write commentaries on the Hadith, to clarify the meanings, and to add what might have been missing. The Hadith always have been and continue to be a topic of debate in the Muslim community.

NOTES

1 All diagrams in this book are original unless noted otherwise. The author is aware of the shortcomings of diagrams and models. They are structured representations of reality, not reality itself. The diagrams, like the words we use, are simplified attempts to denote multifaceted entities and relationships. Their value lies in the extent to which they help us to further grasp the complex reality of the world in which we live. An observation by Albert Einstein regarding mathematics may also apply to these diagrams and models: "Insofar as the statements of mathematics are certain, they make no contact with reality; insofar as they make contact with reality, they are not certain" (quoted in Weston, "Gospel," 39).

2 An analogy of this concept would be the Muslim attitude toward actions which fall into five classifications:
(1) obligatory or enjoined *al-wājib* or *fard;* (2) recommended or praiseworthy, but not compulsory *al-mustahabb* or *mandūb;* (3) permitted or legally indifferent *al-halāl* or *jā'iz;* (4) disliked or deprecated, but not forbidden, *al-makrūh;* (5) forbidden *harām* or *al-muharram* (Doi, *Introduction,* 10).

3 The Qur'an hints at this within its own corpus, with the statement, "In it are Verses that are entirely clear, they are the foundations of the Book ... and others not entirely clear ... but none knows its hidden meanings save Allah" (Q.3:7, Al-Hilali and Khan, *Noble Qur'an,* 67). The term "not entirely clear" *mutashābihāt* is translated by others as "allegorical" (Ali, *Holy Qur'an: Text, Translation and Commentary,*

1273) or "unspecific" (Saheeh, *Qur'an*, 45). Aly, commenting on this verse, states: "The Qur'an itself admits to its ambiguity" (Aly, *People Like Us*, 217). In a later edition of Ali, the word "allegorical" is replaced by "not entirely clear," thus conforming to al-Hilali and Khan's translation (Ali, *The Holy Qur'ān: English Translation of the Meanings and Commentary,* 140).

4   C.f. Titus 1:12,13. This concept is further developed in my book *Engaging Muslim Traditions.*

5   Jude 3.

6   E.g., Titus 1:9.

7   2 Cor 10:5.

8   E.g., Titus 1:14.

9   Acts 17:23.

10 2 Cor 10:5.

11 An earlier account of Muhammad's life, the *Sira* (biography), was written by Ibn Ishaq.

12 Sir William Muir cited in Guillaume, *The Traditions of Islam*, 19.

13 Hitti, *Islam: A Way of Life*, 42.

14 According to www.muslimaccess.com/sunnah/hadeeth/scienceofhadith/asb7.html (accessed July 7, 2013). Also recorded in Ibn Al-Athir *Al-Kāmil fi al-tarīkh* (Beirut, Dār al-kutub al-'ilmiyah, 1994), vol. 5, 207.

15 Fischer and Abedi, *Debating Muslims*, 470, claim that Malik's *Muwatta* contained 1,700 Hadiths chosen from 10,000 that were considered.

16 Margoliouth, *Mohammed*, 12.

17 Guillaume, *Traditions of Islam*, 28.

18 Kamali, *A Textbook of Hadith Studies*, 26.

19 N. Abbott, *Studies In Arabic Literary Papyri,* Volume II (Qur'anic Commentary & Tradition), 1967, The University of Chicago Press, 62, cited in /www.islamic-awareness.org/Hadith/exisnad.html (accessed February 25, 2009).

20 Voll, *Islam*, 24.

21 Voll, *Islam*, 62,66.

22 See ch. 2, part 2.

23 Abdal Hakim Murad, "*Fath al-Bari*: Commentary on ṣaḥīḥ al-Bukhāri," http://sunnah.org/history/Scholars/fath_al_bari.htm, (accessed July 30, 2011).

24   Brown, *Hadith*, 38.

25   Brown, *Hadith*, 42.

26   Siddiqui, *Hadith Literature*, 90.

27   Guillaume, *Traditions*, 24. He lists some these "Syria-honoring" Hadiths preserved by al-Tirmidhi and others on pages 47–50.

28   Siddiqui, *Hadith Literature*, 89.

29   Brown, *Hadith,* 206–10 (italics his).

30   Lapidus, *History*, 115–16.

31   Hughes, *Dictionary*, 643 and Robson "Hadith," vol. 3, 24.

2

ATTITUDES OF SCHOLARS
TOWARD THE HADITH

SCHOLARS HAVE ARTICULATED a wide range of attitudes toward the Hadith.

1. NON-MUSLIM SCHOLARS

The generally accepted Hadith collections were not compiled until two hundred or more years after the death of Muhammad.[1] Earlier versions did exist, but they are usually discounted due to the unacceptable methodology of their collectors.[2] Anderson uses Islam's late adoption of the Hadith as grounds to cast doubt on them. "The greater part of the alleged sayings and doings of the Prophet must be regarded as fictions which mirror the history of the theology, politics and jurisprudence of early Islam."[3] Jewish researchers Nevo and Koren make the following observation:

Non-contemporary literary sources are, in our opinion, inadmissible as historical evidence. If one has no source of knowledge of the seventh century except texts written in the ninth century or later, one cannot know anything about the seventh century: one can only know what people in the ninth century or later believed about the seventh.[4]

Schacht is quite clear:

> It is generally conceded that the criticism of traditions as practiced by the Muhammadan scholars is inadequate and that, however many forgeries may have been eliminated from it, even the classical corpus contains a great many traditions that cannot possibly be authentic.... Goldziher ... has shown positively that the great majority of traditions from the Prophet are the documents not of the time to which they belong, but of the successive stages of development of doctrines during the first centuries of Islam.[5]

H. A. R. Gibb concurs, even identifying some of the specific groups and doctrines which constructed the Hadith as their battleground. "It is possible to trace in *hadiths* the struggle between the supporters of the Umayyads and the Medinan opposition, the growth of Shiism and the divisions between its sects ... the rise of theological controversies, and the beginnings of the mystical doctrines of the Sufis."[6]

These conclusions are typical of most non-Muslim scholars. Extensive critical work has been carried out by more recent scholars.[7] "Many are highly dismissive of the Hadith. Goldziher and Schacht began this trend, and were followed by the revisionists Wansbrough, Crone, and Cook. Juynboll's criticisms are based mainly in his assessments of the *isnāds*."[8]

> Others are less dismissive. Schoeler, for example, "questions the traditional European positing of huge gap between the transmitters and the compilers."[9] Nabia Abbott wrote that "the traditions of Muhammad as transmitted by his Companions and their Successors were, as a rule, scrupulously scrutinised at each step of the transmission."[10] Madelung notes that work with the narrative sources, both those that have been available to historians for a long time and others which have been published recently, made it plain that through their use of them a much more reliable and accurate portrait of the period can be drawn than has so far been realized.[11]

Non-Muslim scholars can be categorized along a continuum according to their attitudes toward the Hadith.[12] The vast majority of non-Muslim scholars express serious doubts about the historical validity of most of the Hadith (see Illustration 3).

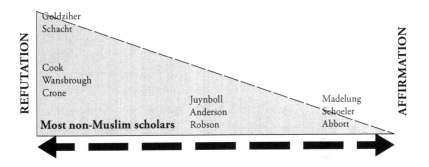

ILLUSTRATION 3: Attitudes of Non-Muslim Scholars toward the Hadith

2. MUSLIM SCHOLARS

A similar schema applied to Muslim researchers gives the opposite result (see Illustration 4). The vast majority of Muslim scholars accept the Hadith collections without question and defend their authenticity. Like the eighth and ninth century *ahl al-ḥadīth* ("Partisans of the Hadith"), most followers of Muhammad believe that "the isnād is part of religion" and if anyone "impugns reports from the early community or denies anything from the hadiths of the Messenger of God, then doubt his Islam."[13]

Other Muslims, however, express some reservations. Despite their pivotal role and position within Islam, the Hadith have not been without detractors. There is much within the Hadith that raises serious questions, and significant assaults have been mounted from within the household of Islam. Abū al-Ḥassan al-Dāraquṭni (d.385/966) in his kitāb al-tatabbuʻ "Book of Succession" challenged seventy-eight of al-Bukhāri's hadiths on the basis of their isnāds.[14] Abū al-Faraj Ibn Al-Jawzi (d.597/1200) found one *mawḍū* (forged) hadith in al-Bukhāri.[15]

Sayyid Ahmad Khan (1817–1898) may have been the earliest modern Muslim Hadith-doubter, for he "questioned the historicity and authenticity of many, if not most, traditions, much as Ignaz Goldziher and Joseph Schacht would later do. He advocated a critical reexamination of the *hadith*, including those in the two major collections of Muslim and Bukhari, and the acceptance of only those that could be traced directly to the Prophet himself."[16] Chiragh Ali (1844–1895) "anticipated Goldziher in his skepticism concerning the authenticity of even the classical collections."[17] In 1885, this Indian scholar referred to the Hadith or "traditions" as

> the inventions of a playful fantasy ... not deserving of confidence ... very few of which are genuine reports.... a chaotic sea. Truth and error, fact and fable mingled together in an indistinguishable confusion ... I am seldom inclined to quote traditions having little or no belief in their genuineness, as generally they are unauthentic, unsupported, and one-sided.[18]

His cynicism was shared by Mahmoud Abu Rayyah (1889–1970), who "adduced many arguments from different sources to undermine the position of Hadith literature. The result of his research was a book which ... tore the Hadith literature to pieces." He concluded that "the entire Tradition literature should be submitted anew to an extensive examination as to its textual reliability."[19]

Equally unconvinced was Rashid Rida (1865–1935), who believed that "many Hadiths of sound *isnād* should be submitted to criticism of their contents.... He rejected Hadiths if they appeared to him to be rationally or theologically objectionable, or if they conflicted with broad principles of the Shari'ah." Asghar Ali Engineer criticizes the reliability of the Hadith on the grounds of their late compilation, their anti-women statements, and their conflict with "the clear teaching of the Qur'an."[20]

The Pakistani scholar Ghulam Ahmed Parvez (1903–1986) was one of the most controversial religious figures of the subcontinent in the last century. With Sir Syed Aḥmad Khān he is accused by mainstream Islamic scholars of bringing heterodox freethinking into the fold of Islam in the subcontinent. He held a critical view of the Hadiths, denying the existence of jinn and angels and had different views on the miracles described in the Qur'an. For his openness toward full reinterpretation of all Qur'anic verses and his controversial ideas, many traditional Muslim 'ulamā' (scholars) declared him a kāfir (infidel). He based the name of his organization on the title of a poem ("Dawn [or Resurgence] of Islam) by Mohammed Iqbāl, who in turn was openly criticized by Sayyid Qutb. The Palestinian Professor Suliman Bashear (1947–1991) wrote that "serious doubts could easily be cast not only against traditions attributed to the Prophet and Companions but a great deal of those bearing the names of successors too."[21]

Most recent attacks by Muslims have been based on the matn of the Hadiths. Kamali notes that "critics have identified about 210 aḥādīth in the weak category in al-Bukhārī and Muslim. Out of this 32 appear in both, another 75 appear in al-Bukhārī and the rest … in Muslim."[22] Although he accepts the majority of the Hadith as valid, Israr Khan claims that "if any component of the … hadith contrasts with the Qur'an, the tradition may be forthrightly rejected as unacceptable."[23] He takes a razor to all the collections of the Hadith, including al-Bukhāri and Muslim. Dissecting pericopes, he excises individual words, phrases, or whole accounts which do not fit with his interpretation of the material based on modern criteria of reasoning, human rights, and scientific knowledge.[24] Feminist theologian Riffat Hassan dismisses any Hadith, including some from al-Bukhārī, which denigrate women. "It is gratifying to know that these ahadith cannot be the words of the Prophet of Islam … regardless of how male chauvinist Muslims project their androcentrism and misogyny on their Prophet."[25] Fazlur Rahman reveals significant doubt when he agrees with the conclusion of Western researches on the Sunnah, that in content it is composed of continued tribal customs and the free-thinking activity of early jurist…. Whatever original Prophetic content there was in the Sunnah, it was neither large, nor specific.[26]

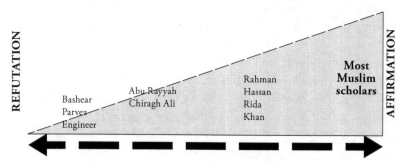

ILLUSTRATION 4: Attitudes of Muslim Scholars toward the Hadith

The highest profile assault on the Hadith came from Libya's Colonel Mu'ammar Qaddafi in July 1977. He pointed out irreconcilable contradictions within the Hadith. These included Muhammad's advice to "take half of your religion from [Aisha]" contrasting with the Prophet's claim that "women are deficient in mind and religion."[27] Of particular concern was Muhammad's statement that "when two Muslims fight (meet) each other with their swords, both the murderer as well as the murdered will go to the Hell-fire."[28] Qaddafi took this to mean that Ali would go to hell for fighting against Mu'āwiya over the Caliphate. He was also concerned about the two hundred-year time gap between event and compilation, so he pronounced the Qur'an as the only real source of God's word.[29] When a meeting with Hizb utTahrir delegates proved ineffective,[30] a committee of scholars, led by Al-Azhar University's Sheikh Muhammad al-Gazoly, visited him, pointing out the dangers of such a stance. These included being branded as an infidel and renegade. Qaddafi recanted, and the committee announced his repentance to the Muslim world.[31]

He was not the only Muslim leader to question the Hadith. Ayatollah Khomeini wrote on jurisprudence and quoted a Hadith in support of his view. Other versions of the same Hadith differ from the one he quoted, thus undermining his point, so he set forth various explanations. Possibilities include that Muhammad's companions "misquoted the original statements of the prophet," that a phrase "was added to the Hadith or … the phrase was in fact there but was dropped," that it was accurately relayed but "was dropped by the scribes," or that the original hearer "forgot it."[32] Kamali realizes

the implications, noting that "the presence of [weak and even fabricated hadith ... in the hadith collections] tends to undermine
confidence in the veracity of the larger corpus of hadith."[33]

Increasingly, questions about the Hadith are arising from inside
the Islamic camp. Several Muslim groups are now taking a guarded
view toward the Hadith or even openly repudiating it. One organization, calling itself "The Quranist Path," states:

> We believe solely in the Quran, as all that was descended
> upon all the prophets and messengers of God mentioned in
> the Quran. While we do consider the Hadith and all other
> holy texts to be often essential in explaining and highlight-
> ing some points in the Quran, we do not however take them
> to be indisputable words of God. The Quran alone, as it has
> directly descended to us from God, is what we regard as the
> source of all Islamic teachings. We therefore can look to the
> Hadith from a critical point of view, agreeing and disagree-
> ing with its constituents whenever we see necessary.[34]

In 2008, Turkey's Department of Religious Affairs commissioned a
team of theologians at Ankara University to carry out "a fundamental review of the Hadith," to bring them up to date with modern
conditions. Professor Mehmet Gormez illustrated this from the
Prophetic command requiring women to travel with a *mahram* or
male relative as a chaperone.[35] "But this isn't a religious ban. It came
about because in the Prophet's time it simply wasn't safe for a woman
to travel alone like that. But as time has passed, people have made
permanent what was only supposed to be a temporary ban for safety
reasons."[36] More conservative Muslims have questioned or dismissed
this wording of "a fundamental review," noting that one of theologians on the review panel is a Jesuit priest.[37]

3. REASONS GIVEN BY MUSLIMS
WHO REJECT ALL THE HADITH

Some Muslims claim that the Hadith have no authoritative role for
the following reasons.

(a) The Hadith imply the insufficiency of the Qur'an as a revelation[38]

Some Muslims have questioned the concept of the Hadith, believing that it implies the inadequacy of the Qur'an. Indian scholars 'Abdallah Chakrāwali (d.1930) and Khwāja Aḥmad Dīn Amritsari (d.1936) wrote articles and books claiming that Islamic law could be gleaned from the Qur'an alone.[39]

The very existence of the Hadith implies that the Qur'an suffers from certain deficiencies. This is contrary to the Qur'an's self-description of its comprehensive nature. The verbs describing the process of revelation (awḥa, anzal, nazzal) are found 328 times in the Qur'an. There are over 60 titles of the Qur'an occurring in 520 verses.[40] Added to the multiple occurrences of āyā/t (which can mean "verses," "signs," or "miracles") and sūra (chapter), the Qur'an and its processes are mentioned 1,091 times in its 6,200 verses.

The Qur'an's claims about itself are summarized in this table below.

PERSPICUOUS: A clear book/Qur'an	Q.5:15, 12:1; 15:1; 26:2, 195; 27:1; 28:2; 36:69; 43:2; 44:2
with clear verses	Q.22:16; 24:34; 66:11; 24:46; 57:9
in a clear Arabic tongue	Q.16:103; 26:195; 20:113; 39:28; 41:3,44; 42:7
so you may understand	Q.2:242; Q.12:2; 43:3
INERRANT: It has no contradictions, falsehood or crookedness	Q.4:82; 41:42; 18:1; 39:28
COMPREHENSIVE: It is detailed and explained by Allah	Q.6:114; 12:111; 16:89; 17:12; 7:52; 20:113; 17:89; 18:54; 11:1
Allah neglected or omitted nothing	Q.6:38; 30:58; 39:27
Allah made the Qur'an easy to remember	Q.54:17,22,32, 40; 44:58; 19:97; 44:58
Muhammad was to convey it in a clear way	Q.16:82; 14:1
SUFFICIENT: Allah could have supplied other books if needed	Q.18:109
UNIQUE: The pagans & jinn are challenged to bring a book or Suras like it	Q.28:49; 37:157; 2:23; 10:38; 11:13; 17:88; 28:86,87

TABLE 5: The Qur'an's claims about itself

These expansive references and claims cause Wild to suggest that "the Qur'an is the most meta-textual, most self-referential holy text known in the history of world religions."[41]

The presence of the Hadith, however, casts doubt on the comprehensibility, perspicuity, and sufficiency of the Qur'an. If the Qur'an is as complete, clear, and adequate as it claims to be, why should any other writings, like the Hadith, be needed?

One Muslim group makes the following assertion:

> The Prophet's sole mission was to deliver Quran, the whole Quran, and nothing but Quran (3:20; 5:48-50, 92, 99; 6:19; 13:40; 16:35, 82; 24:54; 29:18; 42:48; 64:12). Delivering the Quran was such a momentous and noble mission that the Prophet did not have any time to do anything else. Moreover, the Prophet was enjoined in the strongest words from issuing any religious teachings besides the Quran (69:38-47). He was even enjoined from explaining the Quran (75:15-19) - God is the only teacher of the Quran (55:1-2) and the Quran is the best Hadith (39:23 & 45:6).[42]

(b) The Qur'an's negative attitude to the word "Hadith"

Recognizing the many prohibitions and permissions found in the Hadith, its detractors from within the Muslim community note the following verse: "Say, "Did you note how God sends down to you all kinds of provisions, then you render some of them unlawful, and some lawful?" Say, "Did God give you permission to do this? Or, do you fabricate lies and attribute them to God?"[43] Even Muhammad could not do this. When the Prophet tried to do so, God admonished him: "O Prophet! Why do you make something unlawful, which Allah has made lawful to you in seeking to please your wives?" [44] The responsibility of adding to or subtracting from the divine revelation belonged to God alone.[45] Nothing Muhammad could do or say even when he was in "revelatory mode" could have any impact on the Qur'an, according to this view. One Hadith appears to deny the authoritative nature of its own corpus with the statement that Muhammad "did not leave anything except what is between the two bindings (of the Qur'an)."[46]

(c) The unreliability of the Hadith as historical records

The scholarly attacks on the Hadith outlined above began to make an impact. Dr. Muḥammad Tawfīq (d.1920) wrote an article entitled al-islām huwa al-Qur'ān *waḥdahu* ("Islam is the Qur'an alone") in a 1906 issue of the magazine Al-Manar ("The Lighthouse"). "The Prophet did not explicitly order the recording of his Sunna, and indeed hadiths were not set down in any lasting or reliable form for over a century after Muhammad's death. How could God ever allow his religion to depend on such a dubious source?"[47] Since then, many others have joined the Qur'an-only movement.[48]

(d) Other models besides Muhammad in the Qur'an

In the light of the common view that Muhammad was the best example of humanity, it may be asked: Was Muhammad meant to be the only example to follow? The Qur'an provides other models for emulation besides Muhammad. Jesus had been sent as an example to the people of Israel.[49] To the readers of the Qur'an, "an excellent pattern for you to follow" was to be found in Abraham and those who were with him.[50] The people of Abraham had been given "the Book and Wisdom,"[51] just as Muhammad had.[52] So had Yahya (John the Baptist),[53] Jesus,[54] and the prophets before him.[55] The revelatory combination of book-plus-wisdom was not unique to Muhammad nor to Islam. An interesting choice of someone to follow was an unnamed non-Arab pagan woman: "Allah sets forth the wife of Pharaoh as an example to those who believe."[56] Clearly Muhammad is not the only one put forward in the Qur'an as a model for imitation.

(e) Are Muslims required to be carbon copies of Muhammad?

Other Muslims doubt the normative nature of the life of Muhammad and ask whether he was ever intended to be the mold for all believers for all areas of life for all time. A telling factor is the almost total absence of the mention of *sunnah* in Muhammad's early biography recorded by Ibn Ishaq. The word *sunnah* is found only five times in this monumental work, and then in relation to two particular incidents in early Islamic history.[57] In one incident, the redactor Ibn

Hisham removes this reference altogether.[58] The Mu'tazila scholar Aḥmad Ibn Ḥa'it (d.230/845) criticized the Prophet for all his marriages, believing that there was "no need to regard either him or his revelation as normative, or any more than inspirational."[59] A century ago, Muhammad Tawfiq Sidqi (1881–1920) suggested that Muhammad's life was never intended to be imitated in tiny detail.[60] The Pakistani scholar Fazlur Rahman believed that Muhammad was not concerned with small details. "The Prophet did not lay down rules for the minutiae of life, and so it follows that he intervened in events in a way which can only be seen as normative in a general sense."[61] Some Shia thinkers who believe that the gate of *ijtihād* (personal interpretation) is still open can countenance the possibility of change due to a different context. Former Iranian president Ali Akbar Hashemi Rafsanjani noted:

> Islam which developed 1400 years ago on the Arabian peninsula—a settlement where the people were fundamentally nomads—*was a legal code specific to that society*.... Now the legal code, which was executed *in those days for that particular nation* aspires to become the code for a world in which humanity has plunged the depths of the earth ... competed in space to conquer Mars.... *At this very moment millions of people are engaged in legal research to better human society*. The Islam which was revealed some 1400 years ago *for the limited society of that time*, now desires to become the fulcrum of [modern] social administration."[62]

A modern Syrian writer suggests that Muhammad was not a unique exemplar for imitation:

> The Prophet is a model to us in the sense that he observed God's limits, not in the sense that we must make the same choices that he made. The life of the Prophet is the first historical variant of how the rules of Islam can be applied to a tribal society of the time. But it is the first variant, not the only one or the last one.[63]

4. A MUSLIM RESPONSE TO THESE ISSUES

Other Muslims would decry any rejection or revision of the Hadith. They note that criticism of the Hadith was foreseen by the Prophet himself. When asked about the evil to come, Muhammad replied: "(There will be) some people who will guide others not according to my tradition. You will approve of some of their deeds and disapprove of some others . . . They will be from our own people and will speak our language."[64] This questioning of the Prophet's behavior as normative would, according to this saying, come from within the Muslim community itself. When someone suggested to Imrān bin Husayn, a Companion of the Prophet, that the Hadith was unnecessary, his reply was sharp: "Indeed you are an idiot, do you find in the Book of God prayer explained!? Do you find in it fasting explained!? Indeed the Quran ordains this, but the Sunna explains it."[65]

So how then is the Hadith related to the Qur'an?

NOTES

1   See ch. 1, part 3.

2   See ch.1, part 2.

3   Anderson, *Islam in the Modern World*, 4.

4   Nevo and Koren, *Crossroads*, 9.

5   Cited in Warraq, "Aspects of the History of Koranic Criticism," 232.

6   Gibb, *Mohammedanism*, 86.

7   E.g., Wansbrough, *Quranic Studies*; Crone, *Meccan Trade*; and Cook, *Muhammad*.

8   Gregor Schoeler, *The Oral and the Written in Early Islam*, trans. Uwe Vegelpohl, ed. James E. Montgomery (London and New York: Routledge, 2006), cited in G. F. Haddad "Enduring Myths of Orientalism" from http://mac.abc.se/home/onesr/d/myor_e.pdf cited on August 2, 2011.

9   These categories were compiled from a variety of sources, including Siddiqui, *Hadith Literature*, 124–35, and Juynboll, *Muslim tradition*, 2–6.

10   Abbott, *Studies*, Volume 2, 2.

11   Madelung, *Succession*, xi.

12   The positions of these scholars are mostly taken from Wael Hallaq, "The authenticity of Prophetic Hadith: A Pseudo-problem," *Studia Islamica* 99 (1999),75–90 cited in www.globalwebpost.com/farooqm/ study_res/islam/ fiqh/hallaq_Hadith.html (accessed July 7, 2013).

13   Brown, *Hadith,* 174.

14   Khan, *Authentication,* 37; and G. F. Haddad, "Weak Hadiths in ṣaḥīḥ al-Bukhārī?" www.livingislam.org/k/whb_e.html (accessed July 7, 2013).

15   Kamali, *Textbook,* 203.

16   Esposito, *Islam,* 138.

17   Juynboll, *Muslim tradition,* 2.

18   Cited in Guillaume, *Traditions,* 95–97.

19   Mohsen Haredy, "Hadith Textual Criticism: A Reconsideration" in *Al-Baiyyinah* Apr-Jun 2008, 34–40, www.witness-pioneer.org/ VMagazine/v8i1/April-June2008_v8i1.pdf. (accessed July 4, 2013).

20   Asghar Ali Engineer,"Qur'an, Hadith and Women" in *Dawn,* September 25, 2009. www.dawn.com/wps/wcm/connect/ dawn-content-library/dawn/the-newspaper/editorial/quran,-Hadith-women-599 (accessed December 4, 2009).

21   Suliman Bashear, "Abraham's Sacrifice of His Son and Related Issues," 277, cited in Warraq, "Aspects of the History of Koranic Criticism," 238, n. 58. For his nonconformist views, Bashear was killed by his students in An-Najah National University in Nablus.

22   Amali, *Textbook,* 247 n. 2.

23   Khan, *Authentication,* 47.

24   Khan, *Authentication,* passim.

25   Hassan, "Made from Adam's Rib," 124.

26   M. Yahya Birt, "The Message of Fazlur Rahman," www.global-webpost.com/farooqm/study_res/fazlur_rahman/birt_fazlur.html (accessed December 4, 2009).

27   http://islamicsystem.blogspot.com/2009/02/understanding-Hadith.html (accessed July 8, 2013). See also "Studies in Usul ul Fiqh" in www-personal.umd.umich.edu/~etarmoom (accessed July 7, 2013).

28   al-Bukhārī 1:30; 9:204, 205.

29   St John, *Libya and the United States*, 96.

30   http://islamicsystem.blogspot.com/2007/11/refutation-of-gadaffi-others-who-reject.html (accessed July 7, 2013).

31   Gabriel, *Islam and Terrorism*, 60.

32   Khomeini, *Islamic Government*, 44.

33   Kamali, *Textbook*, 203.

34   Source: http://pressthat.wordpress.com/statement-of-belief/ (accessed July 7, 2013).

35   B.2:192, 193, 194, 288; 3:85, 87, 215.

36   http://news.bbc.co.uk/1/hi/world/europe/7264903.stm (accessed July 7, 2013).

37   http://muslimmatters.org/2008/03/03/authority-of-sunnah-hadi-threvelation/ (accessed July 7, 2013).

38   Most of this material was adapted from http://submission.org/Critical_View_Overview.html (accessed July 7, 2013).

39   Brown, *Rethinking*, 38–39.

40   Hughes, *Dictionary*, 484 lists many of these.

41   Stefan Wild, *The Qur'an as Text* quoted in McAuliffe, "Introduction," 2.

42   Source: www.submission.info/quran/appendices/appendix12.html (accessed July 7, 2013). This group is by no means orthodox, making remarkable claims for itself and its founder, Rashad Khalifa.

43   Q.10:59.

44   Q.66:1 (Malik translation).

45   Q.2:106.

46   B.6:537.

47   Brown, *Hadith*, 245.

48   Current examples of such "Qur'an-only" Muslim groups which reject the Hadith are Free Minds, www.free-minds.org/, and United Submitters International, http://submission.org/index.html. Others, such as Bazm-e-Tolu-e-Islam ("Resurgence of Islam") www.tol-ueislam.com, will accept the Hadith to the extent that they do not contradict the Qur'an. These tend to be fringe groups within the Muslim fold, but the potential challenge they raise to mainstream Islam is significant.

49   Q.43:59.

50   Q.60:4,6.

51   Q. 2:129; 4:54.

52   Q.2:129; 3:164.

53   Q.19:12.

54   Q.3:48; 5:110.

55   Q.3:81

56 Q.66:11. The term used for Abraham as a "good pattern" *uswa(t) hasana(t)* is identical to that used for Muhammad in Q.33:21. For Jesus and the Pharoah's wife, the term is "example" *mathal.*

57 See Ibn Ishaq, *Sira*, 645–46, 684. Ibn Ishaq did, however, edit another work called *Sunan,* which is no longer extant.

58 Ibn Ishaq, *Sira*, 645, n. 2.

59 Thomas, *Anti-Christian polemic*, 7.

60 www.aboutquran.com (accessed July 29, 2010).

61 M. Yahya Birt, "The Message of Fazlur Rahman," www.freerepublic.com/focus/fr/531762/posts (accessed July 8, 2013).

62 Catherwood, *Islamic Rage*, 184–85 (emphasis mine).

63 Mohammad Shahrour, "The Divine Text and Pluralism in Muslim Societies" in www.quran.org/shahroor.htm (accessed November 12, 2007). One commentator refers to Shahrur's book *The Book and the Qur'ān: A Contemporary Reading* as "a Copernican revolution in Muslim exegesis." Wild, "Political interpretation of the Qur'ān," 284.

64 B.4:803; 9:206.

65 Abū Sa'd al-Sam'ānī *Adba al-imlā' wa al-istimlā'* 4, cited by Brown, *Hadith*, 150.

3

THE RELATIONSHIPS BETWEEN QUR'AN AND HADITH

THE RELATIONSHIPS BETWEEN the Qur'an and the Hadith are complex and fluid. When he was alive, Muhammad was performing actions (which then became sunnah) and receiving inspiration (*waḥī*) from Allah at the same time. These two modes sometimes contradicted each other.

Muhammad occasionally preempted the divine revelation by his speech and actions, resulting in a later backdown. The classic example is the case of the "Satanic verses," where Muhammad recited a verse describing three Meccan idols as "exalted swans whose intercession is approved." Unfortunately this "revelation," although popular with the pagans of Mecca and winning their support for Muhammad, did not come from Allah.[1] Later it was explained to Muhammad that Satan had also slipped false revelations into the mouths of other prophets.[2] The wife of Abū Lahab[3] believed that all of Muhammad's revelations had a demonic source. When the inspiration ceased for a time, she told him: "I think your Satan has deserted you."[4]

At other times, Muhammad lagged behind the revelation by not fully implementing a command he had received. Allah chides Muhammad for his fear of public opinion: "But you did hide in yourself (i.e. what Allah has already made known to you that He will give her to you in marriage) that which Allah will make manifest, you did fear the people (i.e., Muhammad SAW married the divorced wife of his manumitted slave) whereas Allah had a better right that you should fear Him."[5]

Moreover, the Companions and Successors made statements after Muhammad's death, and these sometimes differed from or reinterpreted both *sunnah* and *waḥī*.[6] The principle of "abrogation," where a newer verse cancels (*nāsikh*) a previous verse which then becomes obsolete (*mansūkh*), had been outlined in the Qur'an.[7] Abrogation has also been applied to the Hadith, and to the interplay between Qur'an and Hadith. There are a variety of ways in which this occurred.

1.QUR'ANIC VERSES WERE CANCELED BY HADITH AND REMOVED

Anas noted about the purported statement of the seventy martyrs of Banī Salim: "Allah revealed a Qur'anic Verse to His Prophet regarding those who had been killed, i.e. the Muslims killed at Bir Ma'una, and we recited the Verse till later it was canceled. (The Verse was:) 'Inform our people that we have met our Lord, and He is pleased with us, and we are pleased with Him.'"[8] This verse was then removed from the Qur'anic corpus.

2. A QUR'ANIC VERSE ABROGATED ANOTHER QUR'ANIC VERSE

Some Qur'anic verses are proclaimed in the Hadith to be abrogated by other verses (see Table 6).[9]

VERSE	ABROGATED BY	CONCEPT	HADITH REFERENCE
Q.2:284	Q.2:285	Concealing or disclosing what is in your minds	B.6:68,69
Q.2:234	Q.2:240	Maintenance bequeathed to widows (1)	B.6:53,54,60
Q.2:240	Q.4:12	Maintenance bequeathed to widows (2)	B.6:55[f]
Q.8:65	Q.8:66	Numbers of enemy troops to be fought	B.6:175,176
Q.25:68	Q.4:93	Punishment for killing another believer	B.6:285

TABLE 6: Qur'anic Verses Abrogated by other Verses in the Hadith

3. LOST QUR'ANIC VERSES WERE REINSTATED BY THE HADITH

When 'Umar bin al-Khaṭṭab was Caliph, he recalled three verses which had been recited by Muhammad as inspired but were no longer found in the written editions of the Qur'an.[10] He announced to the people:

> Allah sent Muhammad with the Truth and revealed the Holy Book to him, and among what Allah revealed, was the Verse of the Rajam (the stoning of married person (male & female) who commits illegal sexual intercourse, and we did recite this Verse and understood and memorized it. Allah's Apostle did carry out the punishment of stoning and so did we after him. I am afraid that after a long time has passed, somebody will say, "By Allah, we do not find the Verse of the Rajam in Allah's Book," and thus they will go astray by

f   This Hadith does not identify the verse, but a reference in al-Hilali and Khan, *Translation of the meanings of the Noble Qur'an in the English Language*, 53, n. 2 does.

leaving an obligation which Allah has revealed. And the punishment of the Rajam is to be inflicted to any married person (male & female), who commits illegal sexual intercourse, if the required evidence is available or there is conception or confession. And then we used to recite among the Verses in Allah's Book: "O people! Do not claim to be the offspring of other than your fathers, as it is disbelief (unthankfulness) on your part that you claim to be the offspring of other than your real father." Then Allah's Apostle said, "Do not praise me excessively as Jesus, son of Mary was praised, but call me Allah's Slave and His Apostle."[11]

Aisha claimed a similar uncertainty in the procedures preventing a couple from marrying if they had shared the same wet-nurse as babies. "It had been revealed in the Qur'an that ten clear sucklings make the marriage unlawful, then it was abrogated (and substituted) by five sucklings and Allah's Apostle (peace be upon him) died and it was before that time (found) in the Qur'an (and recited by the Muslims)."[12]

Juynboll notes that

Al-Suyuti (*Itqān*, iii, 72–75) has … listed some assorted verses, including the famous stoning verse … that were, as several Companions tell us, allegedly revealed to Muhammad, but were never incorporated in [the Qur'an] … [giving] the impression that there were more such fragments floating about which never made it into what later came to be called the "Uthmanic codex.[13]

4. HADITH REVELATIONS
NOT INCLUDED IN THE QUR'AN

Some revelations recorded in the Hadith were not included in the Qur'an. When his wives were challenged by 'Umar for going outside to attend to toiletry needs, the Divine Inspiration was revealed to Muhammad and when that state was over, he (the Prophet) was saying: "O women! You have been allowed by Allah to go out for your needs."[14] Yet one searches the current Qur'an in vain for this verse. Likewise, when a man asked Muhammad about assuming *Ihrām* (the prescribed dress for pilgrimage) after perfuming himself, the Prophet went into inspirational mode, accompanied by a red face and heavy breathing. Afterwards, he called the man and gave the ruling: "As regards the scent which you perfumed your body with, you must wash it off thrice, and as for your cloak, you must take it off; and then perform in your 'Umra [minor pilgrimage] all those things which you perform in Hajj."[15] However, no such verses are recorded in the Qur'an. In fact, all of the *Hadith qudsi* would fall into this category. It is difficult to comprehend why some first-person statements by Allah, recorded as coming from the mouth of the Prophet, should have been included as part of the Qur'anic text, and other similar statements were omitted.

5. VERSES ABROGATED BY THE HADITH YET REMAIN IN THE QUR'AN

A revealed verse, although still found in the Qur'anic corpus, may be abrogated by a Hadith describing prophetic *sunnah*. For example, the Qur'an seems to allow owners to use slave girls for prostitution unless the girl "desires chastity,"[16] but Muhammad forbade owners taking money earned from the prostitution of their slave girls.[17] According to one Qur'anic edition, the verse describing the punishment for adultery (where flogging is decreed) has been abrogated by the *sunnah* of stoning.[18] Commenting on the view of the exegete al-Ṭabarī, Burton comments: "As far as he was concerned, the Sunnah in this instance undoubtedly had superseded the ruling of the Qur'an."[19] Ibn 'Umar likewise declared that the Qur'anic option of feeding a poor person instead of fasting[20] was canceled by the Hadith.[21]

6. VERSES AND SUNNAH
ABROGATED BY THE HADITH

Qur'anic verses and prophetic *sunnah* may both be abrogated by the Hadith. The Qur'an permitted marriage to Jewish and Christian women by Muslim men, [22] but ibn 'Umar declared it unlawful. [23] This was a remarkable ruling, since Muhammad had married both Jewish and Christian women. However, since it is recorded in al-Bukhāri's collection of the Hadith, ibn 'Umar's ruling is taken seriously by the legal jurists and has resulted in a division among the orthodox Sunni schools. The Ḥanafi school forbids a Muslim man marrying a "Jewish or Christian woman" (*kitābiyya*) if the couple lives outside of Islamic territory in the "House of War" *(dār al-ḥarb)*. However, the Maliki school both allows and disapproves of such a marriage. [24]

7. ABROGATED VERSES
REINSTATED BY THE HADITH

Some verses believed to be abrogated were reinstated by the Hadith. The validity of verses relating to the provision for orphans and the poor[25] and the killing of believers[26] had been challenged by some Muslims, but were declared unabrogated in the Hadith. [27] Yahya b. Abī Kathīr (d.129/747) stated that "the Sunna came to rule over the Quran, it is not the Quran that rules over the Sunna." [28]

8. A LATER QUR'ANIC VERSE MAY
ABROGATE AN EARLIER HADITH

At times, a Hadith, in the form of the *sunnah* of the Prophet, was abrogated by a later revelation. Muhammad, for example, based on a revelation,[29] prayed at the graveside of a polytheist, thereby establishing a precedent for all Muslims to follow,[30] but then a revelation came forbidding this practice. [31] In the early days of Islam, Muhammad's wives were permitted to attend the mosque for prayers[32] until the verse "O wives of the Prophet, ... stay in your houses"[33] came down.

9. AN EARLIER QUR'ANIC VERSE MAY
ABROGATE A LATER HADITH

This principle of Qur'an abrogating *sunnah* was even applied retrospectively.

> During the Prophet's time, in a clearly attested Sunnah, the booty of conquered tribes who did not peacefully surrender, was to be redistributed as booty. 'Umar forbade the extension of this to the conquered territories of Iraq and Egypt on the basis of the general Qur'anic injunction towards justice (59:10) ... which could not permit the neglect of these populations and future generations, for the short-term gain of the Arabs.[34]

Since some of the actions and sayings of Muhammad's successors, the four rightly-guided Caliphs, were recorded in the Hadith, they became a component in the construction of later *shari'a* law. They felt free to overrule or act contrary to a deed of Muhammad because they had seen him do the same thing when his own actions were apparently inconsistent.[35] Other theologians applied the same principle. The founder of the Ḥanifi school, Abū Ḥanifa (d.767) "rejected the Hadith that exempted the death penalty for the death of a non-Muslim by a Muslim based on the fact that in the Quran all human life is treated equally."[36] Muhammad's statement in the Hadith[37] was seen as less significant than the earlier verse.[38]

10. ONE HADITH MAY ABROGATE
ANOTHER HADITH

Earlier Hadith are sometimes stated as abrogated by later Hadith. These included rulings about ritual matters such as ablutions after sex[39] which were later canceled[40] as well as instructions about sexual discharges[41] or *coitus interruptus*,[42] prayers led by a sitting person,[43] and fasting on the day of Ashura.[44] *Mut'ah* or temporary marriage was initially allowed,[45] based on the Qur'anic permission,[46] but later it was forbidden.[47] Several works were penned listing hadiths which were abrogated by other hadiths. These included *Nāsikh al-ḥadīth wa mansūkhuhu* ("Abrogating and Abrogated Hadiths") Abū Bakr Aḥmad al-Athram (d.261/875) as well as the large and widely studied works of Ibn Shāhīn (d.385/986) and Abū Bakr al-Hāzimī (584/1188).[48]

11. A CURRENT QUR'ANIC VERSE WILL BE ABROGATED WHEN A HADITH IS FULFILLED

The payment of a "protection tax" by Christians and Jews (*Jizya*) is mandated in the Qur'an.[49] However, the Hadith point to a time when this will be abolished at the return of Christ,[50] indicating that it is a temporary injunction.

The various relationships between Qur'an and Hadith are summarized in Table 7.

	TYPE OF RELATIONSHIP BETWEEN QUR'AN AND HADITH	EXAMPLES FROM THE HADITH
1	Qur'anic verse cancelled by Hadith and removed	B.4:57
2	Qur'anic verse abrogated by another Qur'anic verse	B.6:53,54,55,60, 68, 69,175,176,285
3	Verses omitted from later Qur'anic editions	B.8:817
4	Some revelations recorded in the Hadith were not included in the Qur'an	B.3:17; 6:508; 7:164
5	Qur'anic verse abrogated by Hadith	B.3:170; 6:338,805
6	Qur'anic verse and prophetic *sunnah* abrogated by Hadith	B.7:209
7	'Abrogated' verses reinstated by Hadith	B.6:100,114,289
8	Hadith abrogated by Qur'anic verse	B.2:359; 1:824 (Q.33.33)
9	An earlier Qur'anic verse may abrogate a later Hadith	B.1:111
10	Hadith abrogated by another Hadith	B.7:562; 1:180; 5:172
11	Qur'anic verse will be abrogated by a Hadith	B.3:425, 656; 4:657

TABLE 7: List of Relationships between Qur'an and Hadith

These complex relationships resulted in friction within the Muslim community. Ubayy, the best Qur'an reciter of 'Umar's period, was sometimes discounted because he would not omit abrogated verses from his recitations.[51] The Caliph Uthmān bin 'Affan, seeking to collect a single authoritative edition of the Qur'an, came under pressure to leave out abrogated verses, which he refused to do.[52] Many Hadiths report Muhammad's interdiction about eating donkey meat, including its context.[53] Several contemporaries confirmed this ruling. However, when questioned about it, "Ibn 'Abbās, the great religious learned man, refused to give a final verdict and recited: 'Say: I find not in that which has been inspired to me anything forbidden to be eaten by one who wishes to eat it, unless it be carrion, blood poured forth or the flesh of swine' (Q.6.145)."[54] Clearly for him the revelation found in the Qur'an was more significant than the prophetic *sunnah* found in the Hadith.

In other places, the Hadith explain Qur'anic verses, outlining the *asbāb ul-nuzūl*, or occasions of revelation. There are over 300 verses or passages of the Qur'an which are mentioned (see the Appendix). The Hadith thus stands in judgment to the Qur'an by elucidating on it. The classical commentaries *(tafāsīr)* have their own sets of explanations of how and why certain verses were revealed, but the earliest complete extant list is that of al-Wāhīdi (d.467/1075). Firestone, for one, is unconvinced of the value of such *asbāb ul-nuzūl* works. "The problem with relying on them is that they seldom agree and often contradict one another."[55] An example would be the verse describing those who seek gain at the cost of Allah's covenant.[56] It is claimed to have been revealed in response to a dispute between two cousins about a well.[57] However. the next Hadith declares that it came because a man in the market made false claims about his merchandise.[58]

Despite their intertwined content, there are differences in the ways that the two revelations can be used and handled. Unlike the Qur'an, the Hadith are not suitable for recitation during prayers, and Hadith texts can be touched and read by those who are ritually unclean, including menstruating women and mothers in the post-childbirth period.[59] The Hadith are not considered inimitable, and those who repudiate the Hadith are not deemed guilty of unbelief.[60]

The relationship between the Qur'an, with its sketchy outline, and the Hadith's more comprehensive minutiae has been likened to "an architect's master plan and the detailed instructions of the builder."[61] Along with the Qur'an, the Hadith represents a major source of Islamic teaching which is believed to cover every aspect of life. Siddiqi proposes that the Hadith literature "played a decisive role in establishing a common cultural framework for the whole Islamic world, and continues to wield substantial influence on the minds of the Muslim community."[62] Muslims learn many of the Hadith by heart, having been taught them in school. Part of the attraction of the Hadith literature is the human interest factor—the mention of names, places, and events. The Hadith relate to the common person and deal with everyday topics. The Qur'an, by contrast, with its lofty poetic style, seems far removed from ordinary experience. It often speaks in abstractions. Details of time, place, and actors are absent. Even when it does involve narrative, the language of the Qur'an, in both vocabulary and syntax, is difficult for the unscholarly to fathom.

Notwithstanding these high claims, some of the Hadith remain a mystery. There are enigmatic sayings, given without a context or any clue as to what they mean, such as "The Prophet said, 'This and this are the same.' He meant the little finger and the thumb."[63] Often they preserve mundane details which would seem to have little practical application.[64] Some meanings have been lost in time, speaking to situations which are no longer known. Abū Bakr said to the delegate of Buzakha, "Follow the tails of the camels till Allah shows the Caliph (successor) of His Prophet and Al-Muhajirin (emigrants) something because of which you may excuse yourselves."[65] The Hadith also contain historical information from fifty years after Muhammad died.[66] This includes the gruesome account of a Muslim in AD 680 playing with the freshly severed head of al-Husain, Muhammad's grandson, as it lay on a tray.[67] It is hard to imagine why such an event should be recorded, except to further inflame Sunni-Shia relations.

The interchange between Qur'an and Hadith is multifarious and intricate, suggesting that the eighth-century aphorism, "the Sunnah decides upon the Qur'an, the Qur'an does not decide upon the Sunnah,"[68] could be an oversimplification. However, this saying was clearly widespread, cited by al-Darimī (d.255/869), al-Shaibāni (d.189/805), and al-Shāfiʿī (d.204 /820).[69]

Firestone attributes these complex relationships to the changing circumstances of the early Muslim community:

> There is no reason to expect that Muḥammad's own inter-
> pretation of the divine revelations should have always been
> consistent, since the needs of the day varied during his pro-
> phetic career. Some of this prophetic interpretive material
> also entered into the public domain of the early Muslim
> community but probably at a level that was different from
> what was remembered as the official scriptural recitation.
> There was, therefore, a certain fluidity to both the "published
> text" of the oral Qur'an and to its interpretation during the
> lifetime of the Prophet.[70]

Muhammad's own actions contributed to this fluidity, as the next chapter shows.

NOTES

1   Ibn Ishāq, *Sira,* 165, 166.

2   Q.22:52.

3   Mentioned in Q.111:4, 5.

4   B.6:475, 467, 506.

5   Q.33:37, Al-Hilali and Khan, *Translation,* 568 (parenthesis theirs).

6   See ch. 6.

7   Q.2:106. How frequently this occurs is a matter of some dispute.
     "Jalalu'd-Din in his 'Itqan' gives a list of 20 verses, which are acknowl-
     edged by all commentators to be abrogated. But he notes that there
     may be as many as 500 verses affected by abrogation. The Sword verse
     Q.9:5 was said to abrogate 124 other verses, the last of which was
     Q.109:6" (Hughes, *Dictionary,* 520). There are numerous collec-
     tions of *nāsikh wa-mansūkh*—the earliest one is apparently that by
     Abū ʿUbayd al-Qāsim b. Sallām (d.224/838) (Juynboll, "Hadith and
     the Qur'an," vol. 2, 389). There are 137 verses commonly listed as
     abrogated (Sachedina, "The Qur'ān and other religions," 299).

8   B.5:421; also 5:416, 417; 4:57. A similar concept, although not
    identical wording, is found in Q.5:119; 9:100; 98:8.

9   Although a later verse usually abrogates an earlier verse, Suyuti in his
    al-Iqtan maintains that Q.33:52, which did not permit Muhammad
    to take more wives, was abrogated by the earlier Q.33:49, which
    allowed him to marry more women. Dashti, *Thirty Three Years*, 95.

10 Muhammad's wives Aisha (al-Muwaṭṭaʾ 8:26) and Hafsa
    (al-Muwaṭṭaʾ 8:27) noted other phrases recited by Muhammad
    which were no longer in the written Qur'an. References from
    CD-ROM "The Islamic Scholar" Hadith/Muwatta.

11 B.8:817; also 8:816 and 8:804, 809, 816, 824, 825.

12 Reported in Muslim *Book 8, Number 3421* from CD-ROM "The
    Islamic Scholar," Hadith/Muslim.

13 Juynboll, "Hadith and the Qur'an," vol. 2, 385.

14 B.7:164.

15 B.6:508; also 3:17.

16 Q.24:33.

17 B.3:439, 440, 482, 483; 7:258, 259, 260, 656, 845.

18 Al-Hilali and Khan, *Translation of the Meanings of the Noble Qur'an*,
    108, 466, contrasting Q.24:2 and B.8:805.

19 Burton, *Collection of the Qur'ān*, 106.

20 As outlined in Q.2:184 and 2:196.

21 B.3:170; 6:33. This abrogation is denied in B.6:32, where the change
    is described as a concession for the aged.

22 Q.2:221. The verse states: "Do not marry unbelieving woman (sic)
    until they believe." Yusuf Ali's footnote designates the meaning of
    "unbelieving" *(almushrikāt)* as "Literally 'pagan" (Yusuf Ali, *The Holy
    Qur'ān: English Translation of the Meanings and Commentary*, 94 n.
    245-A).

23 B.7:209.

24 Source: www.bismikaallahuma.org/archives/2005/marriage-with-the-
    people-of-the-book/ (accessed June 26, 2011).

25 Q.4:8.

26 Q.4:93.

27 B.6:100 and 6:114, 289.

28 *Sunan al-Darimi* cited in Brown, *Hadith,* 150.

29 Q.9:80.

30 B.6:192, 193, 194.

31 Q.9:84, outlined in B.2:359; 6:193, 194.

32 B.1:824; 2:22,23.

33 Q.33.33. Aisha suggests that this came from the discovery that Jewish women were not allowed to attend the synagogue (B.1:828).

34 M Yahya Birt, "The Message of Fazlur Rahman," www.freerepublic.com/focus/fr/531762/posts (accessed July 8, 2013).

35 See ch. 4.

36 Rami Bailony "Finding the spirit of Muhammad," www.toledomuslims.com/criterion/Article.asp?ID=199 (accessed February 15, 2008).

37 Recorded in B.1:111.

38 Found in Q.5:32.

39 B.1:291.

40 B.1:180.

41 B.1:179.

42 B.1:291, 292.

43 B.7:562.

44 B.5:172.

45 B.7:52.

46 Q.4:24.

47 B.7:50,52, 432; 5:527.

48 Brown, *Hadith,* 162.

49 Q.9:29.

50 B.3:425, 656; 4:657. Jizya may, of course, be abolished because all the Jews and Christians have become Muslims.

51 B.6:8.

52 B.6:53.

53 E.g., B.7:429, 430, 431, 433, 434, 435.1, 436.

54 B.7:437.

55 Firestone, *Jihad,* 49.

56 Q.3:77.

57 B.6:72; 3:692.

58 B.6:73.

59 Based on Q.56:79.

60 Ibrahim and Johnson-Davies, *Forty Hadith Qudsi,* 9.

61 Vouwzee, "Islamic Philosophy," vol. 2, 763.

62   Siddiqui, *Hadith Literature,* xiii.

63   B.9:33, 34.

64   E.g. B.3:66.

65   B.9:328.

66   E.g. B.4:342.

67   B.5:91.

68   Cited in Yahya M. Birt, "The Message of Fazlur Rahman," www.
      freerepublic.com/focus/fr/531762/posts (accessed July 8, 2013).

69   Guillaume, *Traditions,* 43.

70   Firestone, *Jihad,* 44–45.

4

MUHAMMAD'S VARIANT BEHAVIOR

SOME HADITH APPEAR TO CONTRADICT OTHERS, suggesting either an inconsistency on the part of Muhammad or a variety of irreconcilable sources. The existence of such discrepancies within the matn of the Hadith has generated a branch of Islamic scholarship called *mushkil al-Hadīth* (lit. "difficult (things) in the Hadith") or sometimes *mukhtalif al-Hadīth* (lit. "conflict in the Hadith").[1]

1. MUHAMMAD'S WORDS AND ACTIONS

(a) Conflicting actions

Muhammad's actions were subject to change (see Table 8).

Muhammad tore down a curtain decorated with pictures B.8:130	He reclined on the same material when it was turned into cushions B.3:659; 7:838
He said: "You should not long for death." B.9:339,340,341	He set out to commit suicide several times B.9:111
He wore a silk shirt during prayers B.1:372; 7:693	Then he violently removed it saying: "This (garment) does not befit those who fear Allah!" B.1:372; 7:693
He wore a gold ring B.9:401	He threw it away when others copied him, B.9:401 Then he began to wear a silver ring B.7:755,756
Sometimes he assumed ihrām with his hair oiled and parted B.2:611	Sometimes his hair was matted B.2:613

TABLE 8: Muhammad's Variant Personal Behavior

The ambiguity extended to religious aspects. Muslim martyrs were buried with funeral prayers[2] and also without them.[3] After the move to Medina, the number of prescribed *rakats,* "bowings," during ritual prayer, *salat,* was doubled.[4] He performed ablutions by washing his body parts "only once" according to Ibn 'Abbās,[5] but "twice" according to 'Abdullah bin Zaid.[6] Muhammad's practice of *al-Qunūt* (extempore prayers including ritual curses on one's enemies) after bowing during the ritual prayer, instead of before it, lasted for only one month, when it changed back again.[7] Of course, these differences may be the results of mere variations in Muhammad's behavior or of uncertain reporting by the transmitters and collectors, but the result will be the same lack of lucidity for a Muslim looking for a clear model to follow.

There were times when Muhammad spoke and acted as a prophet, and others when he spoke and acted only as an imperfect human being. On his deathbed, Muhammad requested a pen and paper to write something important, but his companions ignored this request,[8] thinking that the Prophet was delirious.[9] In such extreme situations, Muhammad was not a suitable model for emulation.

Some Muslim scholars readily admit this. The former head of the Australian Federation of Islamic Councils, Dr. Ameer Ali, admitted that Muhammad was not the "perfect model" as most Muslims believed. Asked if the prophet had character flaws, he said: "Of course—you must look at him as a human being also."[10] Following outcries from other Muslim leaders, Dr. Ali issued a statement two days later explaining his comments:

> There are two dimensions to the Prophet's life; a human dimension and a prophetic dimension. The human dimension is the model of reality while the prophetic dimension is a model for reality…. I alluded to the incident about the blind man who came to visit the Prophet and was ignored by him because the Prophet was engaged with other matters. Later, Allah rebuked the Prophet for this behaviour [Q.80:1-12]. I said that this was a manifestation of the human element of the Prophet which was later corrected by Allah. And I said humans are fallible, and only Allah is

infallible. If we ignore the human dimension of the Prophet, we are in danger of elevating him as equal to Allah in terms of infallibility, which is shirk.[11]

Since the revelation was progressive, Muhammad was constantly being updated on the appropriate ways to act. After observing a Hajj (pilgrimage to Mecca), he admitted that he had some new insights, saying: "If I had formerly known what I came to know lately, I would not have driven the *Hadi* [camel for sacrifice] with me and would have finished the state of *Ihram* [ritual purity] along with the people when they finished it."[12]

Despite this, Muhammad criticized his followers for not copying him enough. "The Prophet did something as it was allowed from the religious point of view but some people refrained from it. When the Prophet heard of that, he ... said, "Why do some people refrain from doing something which I do? By Allah, I know Allah more than they."[13]

(b) "Do as I say, not as I do" or "Do as I do, not as I say"?

It was not only in his personal actions that such uncertainty prevailed. It extended to his commands. Muhammad fasted while traveling, including during hot days,[14] yet told his men that "It is not righteousness that you fast on a journey."[15] The Muslim attack on Hunain occurred during the month of Ramadan.

Some of Muhammad's troops were fasting and some were not. So he took a container of milk or water and drank it in front of them, and "those who were not fasting told those who were fasting, to break their fast (i.e. as the Prophet had done so)."[16] However, even this did not solve the problem forever. Ibn 'Abbās noted: "Allah's Apostle fasted and sometimes did not fast while traveling, so one may fast or may not (on journeys)."[17] He forbade al-Wiṣāl (fasting continuously without breaking one's fast in the evening or eating before the following dawn) for his supporters, but practiced it himself, claiming a special divine provision.[18] With pressure from others who wanted to emulate him, Muhammad avoided doing good deeds lest his actions be considered compulsory for all.[19]

The result must have been diminished communal standards of behavior, falling to the lowest common denominator.

Although polygyny was allowed by the Qur'an[20] and practiced by Muhammad himself,[21] he refused to let his son-in-law 'Ali bin Abi Ṭālib marry another woman unless Ali first divorced Muhammad's daughter Fāṭima, because the presence of a second wife in her household would "hurt" Fatima and she "hated" it.[22] This has been taken to mean that a man cannot marry another wife without consulting his current wife or wives. Yet Muhammad apparently did not consult his own wives, since he married the Jewish captive Ṣafīya bint Ḥuyay before returning to Medina after the attack on Khaybar.[23] Any Muslim desiring to take another wife has two opposing prophetic precedents to contend with: whether to obtain the permission of his current wife or not.

The "oath cluster" construction, involving swearing on created things, occurs in seventy-three verses in the Qur'an.[24] Yet Muhammad contradicted such an action with his dictum: "If anybody has to take an oath, he should only by Allah."[25]

There are other examples of Muhammad acting differently from the rules he gave to others (see Table 9).

He forbade Muslims to answer the call of nature with their face or back towards a holy place - B.1:146,147	Muhammad himself did so - B.1:150,151
He commanded others to respond to greetings B. 2:331; 7:753; 8:241 - and to answer him during their prayers - B.6:1,170,528	He did not respond to their greetings during his prayers - B.5:215; 2:308
He ordered Muslims to do the opposite of Jews and Christians by dyeing their hair and beards - B.4:668; 7:786	Some of his followers claimed that he dyed his hair - B.1:167; 4:747; 7:784, 785, but others denied it - B.4:750; 7:782,783
He allowed his followers to eat garlic B. 1:814; 9:458 except before prayers B.1:815; 7:362,363	But he did not eat garlic because he spoke to angels - B.1:814; 9:458
Making a will was mandatory for others B.4:3; 5:737; 6:540	He did not make a will himself, except for the Qur'an - B.4:3; 5:737; 6:540

Muhammad gave Ali a silk suit - B.7:731,279	He became angry when Ali wore it B.7:731,279
Musical instruments were declared unlawful (along with illicit sexual intercourse, the wearing of silk and consumption of alcohol B.7:494.2 [g]	Musical instruments were allowed in the Prophet's own house B.2:70,72,103: 4:155; 5:268, and as a lamentation for fallen warriors B.5:336; 7:77

TABLE 9: Muhammad's Commands or Permissions which Differed from His Actions

Some followers responded by applying Muhammad's restrictions even more stringently than he did. "I heard 'Abdullah bin Abi Aufa saying, 'The Prophet forbade the use of green jars.' I said, 'Shall we drink out of white jars?' He said, 'No.'"[26]

At other times Muhammad was ambivalent. He announced: "This is the day of 'Ashura.' Allah has not enjoined its fasting on you but I am fasting in it. You have the choice either to fast or not to fast (on this day)."[27] Even choosing to fast might not produce the hopedfor outcome. On one particularly hot and difficult military campaign, some opted to fast. "Those who fasted did not do any work and those who did not fast served the camels and brought the water on them and treated the sick and (wounded). So, the Prophet said, 'Today, those who were not fasting took (all) the reward.'"[28]

(c) Conflicting advice to others

Despite encouraging his court-poet Ḥassan bin Thābit to lampoon Islam's enemies[29] and commending Amir bin Al-Aqwa' for his verse supporting the Muslims,[30] Muhammad said: "It is better for a man to fill the inside of his body with pus than to fill it with poetry."[31]

---

g   Any case against singing and music based on the Qur'an is rather thin, for they are not mentioned at all. Two passages are cited Q.31:6 and Q.53:59-61, where 'idle talk' *lahw alhadīth,* and 'amusements' *ismad lana* are criticised. Many of the classical commentators equate these terms with singing. The four orthodox schools consider "singing" *ghinaa* as "sinful," according to Abu Eid, "Islamic ruling concerning music," 5.

When he arrived in Medina and found the Jews fasting on the day of 'Ashura, Muhammad ordered his followers to do the same, saying, "I am closer to Moses than [the Jews]." However this ruling was eventually rescinded, for it passed through several stages, as

- initially, obligatory [32]
- then, recommended [33]
- then, semi-optional [34]
- then, optional [35]
- finally, abandoned, when fasting
  in Ramadan took its place [36]

At times, he presented a ruling, then backed away from it. "The Prophet said, 'Pray before the Maghrib (compulsory) prayer.' He (said it thrice) and in the third time, he said, 'Whoever wants to offer it can do so.' He said so because he did not like the people to take it as a tradition."[37]

He once gave his troops an order, but on reflection modified how they were to carry it out. "Allah's Apostle sent us in a mission (i.e. an army-unit) and said, 'If you find so-and-so and so-and-so, burn both of them with fire.' When we intended to depart, Allah's Apostle said, 'I have ordered you to burn so-and-so and so-and-so, and it is none but Allah Who punishes with fire, so, if you find them, kill them.'"[38] Even in the Qur'an, Muhammad was criticized by Allah for allowing his gentleness to cloud his judgment when he gave in to those who refused to fight.[39] The challenge for Muslims, then and now, is in discerning whether their Prophet was acting or speaking in a mode worthy of emulation or not.

2. REASONS FOR THESE CONFLICTING ACTIONS AND COMMANDS

Al-Shāfi'ī was unequivocal that "no two reliable hadiths can be contradictory, since it is impossible for the Prophet to have an inconsistent Sunna."[40] However, a variety of reasons may account for the variant ways in which Muhammad spoke and acted throughout the Hadith accounts.

(a) Inaccurate methodology of Hadith collectors

Some Muslim scholars have suggested that any inconsistencies are the fault of the collectors of the stories. Kamali claims that Hadith methodology was in the early stages of development when the accepted *al-kutub al-sitta* ("six collections") came into existence. "It may therefore not come as a surprise to note that that both *al-Bukhāri* and *Muslim* contain ḥadīth that were subsequently identified as weak *(Da'īf)* or which did not fulfil some of the prerequisites of authenticity for a ṣaḥīḥ ḥadīth."[41] Most Muslims, however, reject this stance and consider all of al-Bukhāri's accounts as "authentic" ṣaḥīḥ, so other reasons must be sought beyond an inadequate methodology by the collectors.

(b) Different cultural inputs

Some legal rulings were based, positively or negatively, on foreign practices and experience. Once Muhammad said: "I intended to prohibit cohabitation with the suckling women, but I considered the Greeks and Persians, and saw that they suckle their children and this thing (cohabitation) does not do any harm to them (to the suckling women)."[42] Consequently this behavior was not banned. On the other hand he forbade the use of fingernails in slaughtering animals because they "are the tools used by the Ethiopians (whom we should not imitate for they are infidels)."[43]

Muhammad also adopted pre-Islamic pagan customs. The Hajj custom of running between the mountains of Safa and Marwa was eschewed by some early Muslims as part of a ritual performed to worship the pagan idol Manat, but Muhammad directed that it be continued.[44] Despite this, he told his listeners that one of the most hated to Allah was "a person who seeks that the traditions of the Pre-Islamic Period of Ignorance should remain in Islam."[45]

His personal behavior sometimes demonstrated no clear pattern. On occasion Muhammad imitated non-Muslims, but at other times he forbade this. "The Prophet used to copy the people of the Scriptures in matters in which there was no order from Allah. The people of the Scripture used to let their hair hang down while the pagans used to part their hair. So the Prophet let his hair hang down first, but later on he parted it,"[46] even though he told his followers to "do the opposite of what the pagans do."[47] A prophetic *sunnah* would be difficult to establish under such circumstances.

(c) Variant classifications

When Muhammad made a snap ruling, such as forbidding donkey meat while his hungry troops were cooking it on the fire, his motivation was debated by his followers. "We then thought that the Prophet had prohibited such food because the *Khumus*[48] had not been taken out of it. Some others said, "He prohibited the meat of donkeys from the point of view of principle, because donkeys used to eat dirty things."[49] A man applied the same logic and refused to eat a chicken because "I have seen it eating something dirty,"[50] but he was challenged about this because Muhammad used to eat chicken.[51] It would be hard for his followers to find a pattern vis-à-vis acceptable food:

- Cows could be eaten but not ridden[52]
- Donkeys could be ridden but not eaten[53]
- Horses and camels could be both ridden and eaten[54]
- Onagers, the wild ass and cousin of the donkey, were ḥalāl as food[55]
- Domestic donkeys were ḥarām as food[56]

A variety of theories were proposed for the latter ruling: "I do not know whether the Prophet forbade the eating of donkey-meat (temporarily)[57] because they were the beasts of burden for the people, and he disliked that their means of transportation should be lost, or he forbade it on the day of Khaibar permanently."[58]

(d) Responding to group pressure, or simply taking good advice?

Whatever Muhammad's reasons for banning donkey meat as food, he quickly compromised on the pots used for cooking it. "The Prophet said, 'Throw away the meat and break the pots!' Some man said, 'O Allah's Apostle! Shall we throw away the meat and wash the pots instead?' He said, '(Yes, you can do) that too.'"[59]

Other prophetic rulings were just as quickly and easily overturned. "Allah's Apostle forbade the use of (certain) containers, but the Ansar [Medinan Muslims] said, "We cannot dispense with them." The Prophet then said, "If so, then use them."[60] His command to "avoid sitting on the roads" was replaced by guidelines for roadside etiquette when the people objected to this decree.[61]

He knew he was not infallible. He admitted that he occasionally fell victim to articulate speakers, resulting in unjust judgments, so these judgments should be ignored.

"Once Allah's Apostle said, 'You people present your cases to me and some of you may be more eloquent and persuasive in presenting their argument. So, if I give some one's right to another (wrongly) because of the latter's (tricky) presentation of the case, I am really giving him a piece of fire; so he should not take it.'"[62]

(e) Pragmatism

Occasionally Muhammad seemed to deem anything that his followers were doing as acceptable. Sometimes a change needed a divine revelation to endorse it (see Figure 33). At other times a lack of patience sufficed. After facing a series of questions on the order of activities for the Hajj, he had apparently reached his emotional limit. "The Prophet said, 'Do, and there is no harm,' concerning all those matters on that day. And so, on that day, whatever question he was asked, he said, 'Do it, do it, and there is no harm therein.'"[63]

Other rulings were modified when the circumstances changed. Sacrifice meat prohibited one year, for example, was pronounced acceptable the next year for economic reasons,[64] "for in that year the people were having a hard time."[65] When some Muslims were unsure if meat given to them had Allah's name mentioned over it during its slaughter (thus making it *haram*), Muhammad simply instructed them: "Mention Allah's Name on it and eat."[66] If making all food Islamically acceptable could be dealt with this simply, it would seem to nullify the need for today's lucrative *halal* industry.

It was becoming clear that the rules were flexible if the situation altered. Siddiqui notes: "There is no doubt that a large number of *Hadiths* contradict one another.... For it is a natural thing for the leader of a fast-developing movement to change the instructions he issues to his followers, in order to respond to a changing situation."[67] This general tenet does not account for the significant number of apparently random rule revisions instituted by the Prophet.

(f) A development in the law

Some changes or fresh understandings came as a result of new revelations (see Sidebar *Change By Revelations*).

At times these changes reveal a development in the law. The Hadith openly admits such cases. "Allah's Apostle sent for an Ansari man who came with water dropping from his head. The Prophet said, 'Perhaps we have forced you to hurry up, haven't we?' The Ansari replied, 'Yes.' Allah's Apostle further said, 'If you are forced to hurry up (during intercourse) or you do not discharge then ablution is due on you' (This order was canceled later on, i.e. one has to take a bath)."[69] Note the final sentence in parentheses. Although the new requirement of *ghusl* (full body wash) after intercourse, instead of the *wuḍu'* (normal ablutions), may seem a minor change, it had significant implications. Muslims who did not fulfill all requirements of ritual purity would be praying in a state of defilement, and their prayers would be unacceptable to Allah.

CHANGE BY REVELATIONS

Altering the qibla from Jerusalem to Mecca raised an issue: the legitimacy of the prayers previously offered toward the Jewish and Christian holy city. This problem was resolved with a revelation: "Before we changed our direction towards the Ka'ba (Mecca) in prayers, some Muslims had died or had been killed and we did not know what to say about them (regarding their prayers). Allah then revealed: 'And Allah would never make your faith (prayers) to be lost (i.e. the prayers of those Muslims were valid).' (Q.2.143)" [68]

He told his followers: "If the wife of anyone of you asks permission to go to the mosque, he should not forbid her,"[70] and he allowed his own wives to attend for prayers.[71] But then the verse "O wives of the Prophet, ... stay in your houses"[72] came down. This creates a tension for those seeking to imitate Muhammad's way. Is his universal permission and initial practice still valid, or has the specific revelation regarding his own wives (which becomes *sunnah*) now revoked it for all women?

(g) Limited and transitory nature of some commands

Some of Muhammad's commands were specific and temporary, not applicable for all time, while others were meant to be obeyed by all Muslims in perpetuity. Following a ruling about sacrifice during the Hajj, "Suraqa bin Malik stood up and asked 'O Allah's Apostle! Is this permission for us only or is it forever?' The Prophet replied, 'It is forever.'"[73] When a man asked about forgiveness for kissing a woman: "Is this instruction for me only?" The Prophet said, 'It is for all those of my followers who encounter a similar situation.'"[74] Sometimes Muhammad made an exception for a single instance. When a man did not fulfill the normal requirements for slaughtering at Eid, he asked: "Will that be sufficient as a sacrifice for me?" The Prophet replied, "Yes. But it will not be sufficient for anyone else (as a sacrifice), after you."[75]

Although bewailing the dead by Muslim women was forbidden, one woman was allowed to make the pledge of allegiance to Islam and then wail at a funeral afterwards because she owed a lamentation to another woman.[76] Initially Muhammad had refused to offer the funeral prayer for any Muslim who left behind unpaid debts, presumably because this might make the Prophet responsible for these debts or indicate an implied condoning of borrowing and usury. However, "When Allah made the Prophet wealthy through conquests," Muhammad declared: 'I am closer to the Believers than themselves, so if one of the Believers dies in debt, I will repay it.'"[77] When asked if women and children could be killed in battles, he replied, "They (i.e. women and children) are from them (i.e. pagans),"[78] but at another time he disapproved of[79] and then forbade[80] such killing, thus condoning their deaths.

(h) Muhammad operating outside his area of expertise

There were times when Muhammad's attempted grasp exceeded his reach. He was a trader, not a farmer, but once he advised agriculturalists against pollination or grafting of the date-palms. The farmers found their yields decreased. He later said of those who followed his faulty guidance: "If there is any use of it, then they should do it, for it was just a personal opinion of mine, and do not go after my personal opinion, but when I say to you anything on behalf of Allah, then do accept it, for I do not attribute lies to Allah, the Exalted and Glorious."[81]

In another version of this hadith, he stated: "I am a human being, so when I command you about a thing pertaining to religion, do accept it, and when I command you about a thing out of my personal opinion, keep it in mind that I am a human being."[82]

Here is the first seed of a separation between sacred and secular. Muhammad was discriminating between his spiritual teaching, which must be followed, and his worldly teaching, which might be ignored or even disobeyed.

(i) Forgetfulness

Islam's Prophet was open about his own shortcomings, which might lead to error. He told his followers: "I am a human being like you and liable to forget like you."[83]

Even though Gabriel used to meet him every night in Ramadan to teach him the Qur'an (see Illustration 5),[84] Muhammad forgot some of the divine revelation and needed to be reminded,[85] just as the Qur'an had foreseen that he would: "We shall make you to recite (the Qur'an), so you shall not forget (it), *except what Allah may will.*"[86] Some of his companions admitted to forgetting the contents of his sermons on important issues,[87] and many of the transmitters of the Hadith confessed that they could not recall some details of the accounts they were passing on.[88] Although it is Allah who causes people to forget verses,[89] Muhammad told those who forgot Qur'anic verses to practice and keep reciting them.[90] They may have wondered about the value of this, since the divine will might cause them to forget once again.

The disquiet of his followers must have been compounded by the apparently arbitrary changes that Muhammad at times made to the prayers,[91] while simply forgetting to perform them correctly at others.[92] Some such as Qāḍī 'Ayyāḍ bin Musa (d. 544/1149), in his book al-Shifa' bi Aḥwāl al-Muṣṭafa

ILLUSTRATION 5: The Angel Gabriel Meeting with Muhammad [h]

("Healing by news of the chosen one"), have suggested that Muhammad's "forgetting" was deliberate, to teach believers how to act when they had made similar mistakes.[93]

(j) Conflicting Hadiths placed together as a model for others

It was not only forgetfulness that could be used in this way. The Hadith redactors seemed to place accounts of contradictory advice and actions alongside or near to each other. Mernissi claims that this was intentional, turning it into an editorial principle for organizing the Hadith material. "The rule was to give one or more contradictory versions in order to show readers conflicting points of view, and thus permit them to be sufficiently well informed to decide for themselves about practices that were the subject of dispute."[94] Armstrong uses the same argument: "They did not promote one theory or interpretation of events at the expense of others. Sometimes they put two quite different versions of an incident side by side, and gave equal weight to each account, so that readers could make up their own minds."[95] This might not be helpful to future jurors who would attempt to advise others facing the same situations that Muhammad encountered.

The punishment for drinking alcohol illustrates this in a group of Hadith accounts which are clustered together. Several describe how

---

h   "Archangel Gabriel talking to the prophet Muhammad," http://angels. about.com/od/AngelsReligiousTexts/f/How-Does-Archangel-Gabriel-Quiz-Muhammad-In-The-Hadith.htm.

Muhammad ordered "all the men in the house" to beat an intoxicat-
ed man named an-Nu'man, and they used their hands, shoes, twisted
garments and palm-tree stalks to do so. He ordered a man named
Abdullah to be lashed, but no number was specified. By Abū Bakr's
caliphate, the punishment became forty lashes, which was increased
to eighty in 'Umar's rule. But Ali as Caliph proclaimed that "no fixed
punishment has been ordered by Allah's Apostle for the drunk."[96]

The prohibited consumption of ṣadaqa (charitable gifts)[97] was in
the next account redefined and sanctioned.[98] Definitions were occasionally modified. All picture makers were cursed,[99] for angels do not
enter a house with pictures in it.[100] However, sometimes only images
of creatures which have souls were forbidden.[101]

SUMMARY

Muhammad's actions sometimes conflicted with each other. He
admitted that he was learning new things and so he changed his
behavior for the context. He sometimes ordered his followers to do
things which he did not do himself, or forbade them from copying
his actions. At other times he was ambivalent, giving his followers the choice of whether to imitate him or not, and occasionally
his advice was conflicting. Several reasons have been suggested for
these inconsistent sayings and deeds. The Hadith may have been
inaccurately recorded, or the result of input from different cultures.
Muhammad may have been using a system of classification which
was consistent in his own mind but is no longer clear to us. He may
have been responding to group pressure or good advice, or simply
may have been pragmatic. Muhammad's rulings may have reflected
a development in the law, or simply been a unique directive for one
person for one time. Sometimes these discrepancies may have been
due to deficiencies in Muhammad himself. He told farmers not to
pollinate or graft their date-palms, but when production dropped,
he said that this had just been his personal opinion and that he
was simply a human being. He also forgot some of his commands
and revelations, and asked to be reminded of them. Some scholars
suggest that the conflicting commands were given and recorded to
provide a dialectical model for future lawmaking.

NOTES

1 See Kamali, *Textbook,* 108–12.

2 B.2:428.

3 B.2:427.

4 B.5:272.

5 B.1:159.

6 B.1:160.

7 B.5:422.

8 B.1:114, also 5:716; 7:573.

9 B.4:393.

10 In *The Australian,* October 4, 2006, www.theaustralian.news.com.au/story/0,20867,20521646-601,00.html (accessed January 21, 2007).

11 Source: http://islcsydney.com/story.php?id=2909 (accessed January 21, 2007).

12 B.9:335, 336.

13 B.9:404; 8:123.

14 B.3:165, 166.

15 B.3:167.

16 B.5:575.

17 B.5:576.

18 B.3:182–188.

19 B.2:228, 271, 273, 275.1.

20 Q.4:3.

21 B.7:142.

22 B.7:157.

23 B.1:367.

24 E.g., Q.36:2; 37:1–3; 38:1; 43:2; 44:2; 50:1; 51:1–4; 52:1–6; 68:1; 74:32–34; 75:1,2; 77:1–5; 79:1–5; 81:15–18; 84:16–18; 85:1–3; 86:1,11,12; 89:1–4; 90:1; 91:1–7; 92:1–3; 93:1,2; 95:1–3; 100:1–5; 103:1.

25 B.5:177; 8:129, 641, 642, 643; 9:498.

26 B.7:501.

27 B.3:221.

28 B.4:140.

29 B.8:171, 173, 174.

30 B.8:169.

31 B.8:175, 176.

32 B.4:609; 5:278, 279; 6:202, 261.

33 B.3:223.

34 E.g. B.3:147, 181; 9:370.

35 B.2:662; 3:117.

36 B.3:116; 6:30.

37 B.2:277; 9:465.

38 B.4:259.

39 Q.9:43.

40 Brown, *Hadith*, 164.

41 Kamali, *Textbook,* 202.

42 *Muslim 8:3392* from CD-ROM "The Islamic Scholar," Hadith/
    Muslim.

43 B.3:668.

44 B.2:706; 3:18.

45 B.9:21.

46 B.7:799 also 5:280.

47 B.7:780.

48 The one-fifth of all war booty which was due to the Prophet himself
    (B.1:50). This seems to have been the issue when Muhammad gave
    the same order concerning camel and sheep meat (B.7:406).

49 B.5:531.

50 B.7:427; 8:712.

51 B.7:427, 429, 430, 431, 433, 434, 435.1, 436.

52 B.3:517.

53 B.5:529.

54 B.5:530; 7:418.

55 B.3:49.

56 E.g., B.7:405.

57 This bracketed term is an interpolation from Khan, *The Translation of
    the Meanings of ṣaḥīḥ Al-Bukhāri*. According to others it was perma-
    nent: "He did not allow us to eat it later on" (B.5:535).

58 B.5:536.

59 B.5:509; 7:405; 8:169, 343. Breaking or washing pots featured in the
    Levitical sacrifice procedures (Lev 6:28).

60   B.7:496.

61   B.3:645; 8.248.

62   B.3:845,638; 9:97, 281, 292, 295.

63   B.8:658, 659.

64   B.1:39.

65   B.7:476, 477.

66   B.7:415.

67   Siddiqui, *Hadith Literature*, 127.

68   B.5:332.

69   B.1:180.

70   B.7:165.

71   B.1:824; 2:22, 23.

72   Q.33.33.

73   B.3:683; 9:336.

74   B.6:209.

75   B.2:99; also 7:453, 454.

76   B.6:415.

77   B.3:495; 7:284.

78   B.4:256.

79   B.4:257.

80   B.4:258.

81   Muslim 30:5830 from CD-ROM "The Islamic Scholar," Hadith/
     Muslim.

82   Ibid.

83   B.1:394.

84   B.1:5.

85   B.3:823; 6: 556, 557, 558, 562; 8:347.

86   Q.87:6–7 (italics mine).

87   B.8:601.

88   See ch. 7, part 2.

89   B.6:559.

90   B.6:550.

91   B.1:792, 793.

92   B.1:394, 398, 469.

93   Brown, *Hadith*, 10.

94   Mernissi, "Women's Rights in Islam," 123.

95   Armstrong, *Muhammad* (2006), 15.

96   B.8:764–772.

97   B.3:750.

98   B.3:751 also 2:571; 3:753.

99   B.3:751 also 2:571; 3:753.

100   B.3:318; 4:447, 449, 570; 5:337, 338; 7:110; 840, 841, 844.

101   B.5:338.

5

RESULTS OF
CONTRADICTORY HADITHS

THE CONSTANT CHANGES in Muhammad's actions and commands outlined in the last chapter evoked a series of responses in his followers.

1. UNCERTAINTY

When Muhammad ordered that the dead "hypocrite," 'Abdullah bin Ubai bin Salul, be exhumed from his grave, his followers were mystified. They were even more amazed when the Prophet laid the corpse in his own lap, placed his saliva on him, and clothed the erstwhile traitor in his own shirt before reburying him. The comment by the narrator was, "Allah knows better (why he did so)," although a possible explanation was proposed.[1]

Even when Muhammad asked simple questions, like, "What day, or month, or town is this?" his followers dared not answer because they "thought he might give it another name."[2] He had created an atmosphere of insecurity with potential arbitrary change.

Occasionally the information from Muhammad was incomplete or unclear. Abū Hurayra reported that the Prophet said, "'Between the two blowing [sic] of the trumpet there will be forty.' The people said, 'O Abu Hurayra! Forty days?' I refused to reply. They said, 'Forty years?' I refused to reply."[3] Once he enigmatically proclaimed to his followers: "Do not believe the people of the Book, nor disbelieve them, but say, 'We believe in Allah and whatever is revealed to us, and whatever is revealed to you.'"[4]

In a remarkable admission, Muhammad claimed that his sayings might be understood better secondhand by others who were not in attendance than by those actually listening to him. He told a group of followers that "it is incumbent upon those who are present to convey it (this message of mine) to those who are absent because the informed one might comprehend what I have said better than the present audience who will convey it to him."[5]

Observing a man who worshiped in the mosque, Muhammad sent him back three times, saying: "You have not prayed."[6] Apparently the man had rushed his prayers, for he was told to prostrate, bow, and sit "until you feel at ease." This implies that accurate performance of the rite with the purest intention is not sufficient: prayer is validated by a subjective emotional element.[7] Improper prayers annulled their whole identification with Islam and placed their eternal destiny in jeopardy: "Hudhaifa saw a person who was not performing the bowing and prostration perfectly. He said to him, "You have not prayed and if you should die you would die on [sic] a religion other than that of Muhammad."[8]

Ultimately Muhammad himself became the focus of trust for Muslims: "They can have no faith until they make you [i.e. Muhammad] judge in all disputes between them, and find in themselves no resistance against your decisions, and accept [them] with full submission."[9] This created an atmosphere of acquiescence.

2. A CULTURE OF APPARENT RANDOMNESS

With the lack of clarity came a decrease in balance and perspective. Among the fifteen criteria used by early Hadith scholars for assessing authenticity, As-Sibāʿi listed that the Hadith "should not promise large rewards or grave punishments for insignificant acts."[10] Shāh

'Abdul 'Azīz rejected any tradition which "includes severe penalty for a minor misdeed, or too great a reward for an ordinary act."[11] Some Hadith appear to defy these standards. One small action might have eternal positive ramifications. In recounting the story of a man who gave water to a thirsty dog, Muhammad commented: "Allah approved of his deed and made him to enter Paradise,"[12] and "Allah thanked him for his (good) deed and forgave him."[13] A Jewish prostitute was forgiven by performing the same deed.[14]

Likewise, a single act could have eternally negative results. A woman was sent to hell for locking up a cat which died of starvation.[15] As punishment, the cat was lacerating the woman with its claws.[16] Muhammad's slave Mud'ab, despite being martyred at Khaybar, went to the hell-fire for taking a sheet before the distribution of booty.[17] Another inhabitant of the fire was 'Amr bin Luhai "who started the tradition of freeing animals … in the name of idols."[18] Soiling himself with urine earned one unfortunate man torture in the grave,[19] by contrast a man who deliberately urinated in the mosque was allowed to continue.[20]

Orders promulgated at one time might be later reversed. The *muhājirs*, immigrants from Mecca, were given land by the *Anṣār*, Medinans who supported Muhammad's cause, in return for half of the yearly yield.[21] Muhammad's directive against the practice of renting out land in exchange for some of its crop may have come later, when the economic situation of the new Islamic colony had stabilized.[22] It was ultimately obeyed when the Jewish town of Khaybar was conquered, and half their annual produce was taken by the Muslims.[23] Even to his contemporaries, the distribution of war booty among his tribal warriors seemed totally arbitrary. "'Uthmān bin 'Affān and I went to the Prophet and said, 'You had given Banu Al-Muttalib from the Khumūs [one-fifth of all plunder claimed by Muhammad] of Khaibar's booty and left us in spite of the fact that we and Banū Al-Muṭṭalib are similarly related to you.' The Prophet said, 'Banū Hāshim and Banū Al-Muṭṭalib only are one and the same.' So the Prophet did not give anything to Banū 'Abd Shams and Banū Nawfal."[24] One disgruntled soldier claimed that "in this division Allah's Countenance has not been sought," and this charge made Muhammad angry.[25]

His followers must have been perplexed. At one time, virgin girls and menstruating women were ordered to stand behind men for prayers for purification from sins,[26] but at another time menstruating women were told to keep away from the "prayer room" *(muṣalla)*.[27] Eating an *onager* (wild desert ass) while in state of *muḥrim* (purification) was allowed,[28] but also forbidden.[29] Exchanging fresh fruits for dried dates was initially banned, but later permitted.[30] Sometimes an identical incident is given different explanations. When a man remained asleep in bed during the time for prayers, Muhammad announced that "the devil urinated in his ears."[31] However, when the Prophet and his companions overslept, missing their prayers, the same explanation was not given. Instead the rationalization was: "Allah captured your souls (made you sleep) when He willed, and returned them (to your bodies) when He willed."[32] Exceptions to prophetic *sunnah* were frequently made, such as for the sacrifice for Eid al-Adha.[33] It resulted in an indecisiveness in later times. When Muʿāwiya, a later Caliph, offered an incorrect prayer, the response was: "Leave him, for he was in the company of Allah's Apostle."[34] Other companions differed in their memories of what Muhammad said. When Maḥmūd bin al-Rabīʿ Al-Anṣāri's memory of the Prophet's saying was challenged by Abū Aiyūb, Maḥmūd traveled back to Medina to have the saying verified by Itbān bin Mālik.[35]

3. FEAR OF MUHAMMAD'S ANGER DUE TO QUESTIONING

A potentially negative ruling from Muhammad seemed to intimidate his companions. Even the normally unflustered ʿUmar bin al-Khaṭṭāb fled from the Prophet when Muhammad did not answer a question that ʿUmar had asked. "I made my camel run faster and went ahead of the people, and I was afraid that some Qur'anic Verses might be revealed about me."[36] A verse which forbid upsetting the Prophet had been revealed: "Surely those who annoy Allah and His Messenger, are cursed by Allah in this world and in the hereafter. He has prepared for them a humiliating punishment."[37]

Trepidation about an adverse revelation even affected social relations between husbands and wives. Ibn 'Umar reported: "During the lifetime of the Prophet we used to avoid chatting leisurely and freely with our wives lest some Divine inspiration might be revealed concerning us. But when the Prophet had died, we started chatting leisurely and freely (with them)."[38]

People's queries often attracted Muhammad's ire. "Once the people started asking Allah's Apostle questions, and they asked so many questions that he became angry."[39] It was not only the frequency of questions but also their content that precipitated his fury. "The Prophet was asked about things which he did not like, but when the questioners insisted, the Prophet got angry."[40] His emotions became apparent. When someone asked:

> ## SOME VERSES IN THE QUR'AN SEEM TO DISCOURAGE OPEN INQUIRY
>
> The Qur'an states: "He [i.e. Allah] cannot be questioned for His acts but they [i.e. the unbelievers] will be questioned (for theirs)" (Q.21:23). In fact, some queries were potentially dangerous. "O you who believe! Ask not questions about things which if made plain to you may cause you trouble.... Some people before you did ask such questions and on that account lost their faith" (Q.5:101,102). Muhammad demanded total compliance: "It is not for a believer, man or woman, when Allah and His messenger have decreed a matter that they should have any option in their decision. And whoever disobeys Allah and His messenger, he had indeed strayed into a plain error. (Q.33:36).

"What about a lost camel?" ... the face of the Prophet became red (with anger)."[41] He made no attempt to hide his displeasure. "Allah's Apostle became angry and it was apparent on his face."[42] This expressive reaction was recorded many times in the Hadith: "Allah's Apostle got angry and his cheeks or face became red."[43] "On that the color of the face of Allah's Apostle changed (because of anger)."[44] When one unfortunate man asked about his eternal fate during such a session, Muhammad retorted angrily: "You will go to the Fire."[45] He announced to his followers: "Allah has hated you for ... asking too many questions,[46] so Muhammad forbade it.[47] He told them:

"The most sinful person among the Muslims is the one who asked about something which had not been prohibited, but was prohibited because of his asking."[48] The clear subtext was: it is better not to ask at all (see Sidebar *Some Verses in the Qur'an...*).

Even his closest companions did not feel free to inquire about his unclear actions. When Muhammad skipped some prayers, "Abu Bakr and 'Umar were also present among the people on that day but dared not talk to him (about his unfinished prayer). And the hasty people went away, wondering. 'Has the prayer been shortened?'"[49] (As it turned out, Muhammad had simply forgotten.) Muhammad's labile emotions intimidated his followers into silence. "When 'Umar saw the signs of anger on the face of Allah's Apostle, he said, 'We repent to Allah.'"[50]

The fear of incurring divine disfavor via a prophetic revelation due to their queries led to insecurity among his followers. On one journey, they debated over whether he was fasting or not, until an insightful woman sent him a bowl of milk which he drank, ending their doubt.[51] Eventually some began to apologize before making inquiries, in order to allay Muhammad's irritation. One man said: "I want to ask you something and will be hard in questioning. So do not get angry."[52] A more open and inquisitive atmosphere might have prevented some of the conflict and lack of coherence which arose among those trying to imitate him.

At other times, Muhammad was quite open to any interrogation. "I am here to answer your questions," he told one man.[53] His inconsistency must have added to the consternation of his followers.

4. BEATINGS

Muhammad's variable prayer life brought some strange outcomes. One time he did not perform the extra two *raka'āt* (bowings) for 'aṣr (afternoon) prayer, so the story went around that he had forbidden these prayers. Some of his followers treated the nonconformists with violence. Ibn Abbas reported: "I and 'Umar used to beat the people for performing them." When one of Muhammad's wives sent her slave girl to ask him about the omission of these prayers, the

Prophet's answer was simple: "Some people from the tribe of 'Abdul Qā'is came to me to embrace Islam and busied me so much that I did not offer the two Rakat which were offered after Zuhr [midday] compulsory prayer, and these two Rakat (you have seen me offering) make up for those."[54] A simple instance of non-communication led to Muslim leaders misguidedly striking their followers for praying too much.

Others could be thrashed for not praying enough. Muhammad gave the following advice about bringing up children: "Order your children for *ṣalat* (prayers) at the age of seven and beat them (about it) at the age of ten."[55]

5. FRUSTRATION

Muhammad started praying at night, but ceased when copied by increasing numbers of his followers. He explained: "I saw what you were doing and nothing but the fear that it (i.e. the prayer) might be enjoined on you, stopped me from coming to you."[56] The early Muslims were frustrated with Muhammad's attempts to lighten their loads, claiming that his past and future sins were already forgiven, so presumably he did not need to generate as much religious merit as they did. The Prophet became angry at their protests, saying: "I am the most Allah fearing, and know Allah better than all of you do."[57]

6. DIVISION

Because of instances such as this, Muhammad's contemporaries were emboldened to criticize his decisions, and he was sometimes forced to justify his choices, including the selection of military commanders.[58] As he ordered his men to set up camp before the battle of Badr, al-Ḥabāb b. al-Mundhir asked him: "Is this a place which God has ordered you to occupy, so that we can neither advance nor withdraw from it, or is it a matter of opinion and military tactics?"[59] The Prophet admitted that it was the latter, and the campsite was changed to a better location on al-Ḥabāb's advice. The overall outcome must have been a confused and confusing picture to those who sought to emulate him in every detail. If the supreme model for Muslims was likely to change his mind, then how could the detail of his actions be a model for everyone to pursue? The Swiss scholar Tariq Ramadhan claims that Muhammad took a contextual approach. "When he was asked about matters of spirituality, faith, education, or doubt, he would often offer *different answers to the same questions*, taking into account the psychological makeup, experience, and intelligence of the listener."[60] Unfortunately Muhammad did not endow the same privilege of flexibility on future generations of Muslims. He told them: "Recite (and study) the Quran as long as you are in agreement as to its interpretation and meanings, but when you have differences regarding its interpretation and meanings, then you should stop reciting it (for the time being.)"[61]

7. DISCOURAGING INNOVATION AND EXPERIMENTATION

One of Islam's strengths is its comprehensive nature. The seminal thinker Abul Ala Mawdudi claimed that "the sharia is a complete scheme of life and an all embracing social order."[62] Due to the breadth of topics and detail found in the Hadith, Islam claims to have a ruling or example to cover every imaginable situation. "It is this ideal of the *imitatio Muhammadi* [imitation of Muhammad] that has provided Muslims from Morocco to Indonesia with such a uniformity of action: wherever one may be, one knows how to behave when entering a house, which formulas of greeting to employ, what to avoid in good company, how to eat, how to travel. For centuries Muslim children have been brought up in these ways."[63] Unfortunately this has its downside in limiting Muslim expression to that which Muhammad personally experienced. The nineteenth-century Indian reformer Sayyid Ahmad Khan, for example, refused to eat mangoes since the Prophet had never touched this favorite fruit of India, and the mystic Bayezid Bistami avoided watermelons for sixty years, as he was unsure how Muhammad would have cut them.[64]

These mundane examples are symptoms of a wider malaise which can afflict Islam and Muslims—an unwillingness to experiment or to consider new options. An intimidating punishment for experimentation was outlined: "whoever innovates in [Medina] an heresy (something new in religion) … or gives shelter to such an innovator, will incur the curse of Allah, the angels and all the people, and none of his compulsory or optional good deeds will be accepted on the Day of Resurrection."[65] One Muslim commentator suggests an impact on successive generations that "gave the traditional, inherited legacy a sacred aspect, even though it is the product of human interpretation. Thus, it became a dogma that people had to accept and apply literally. Over time, this approach reinforced itself, so that the original message was covered by human heritage. As a result, Islamic culture became petrified."[66]

How this has played out in the political and economic systems in Muslim societies throughout history has been documented. Professor Timur Kuran, in his book *The Long Divergence: How Islamic Law Held Back the Middle East,* points out that "the role of classical Islamic law in blocking organizational modernization and stultifying Middle Eastern, and particularly Muslim, enterprise, is hardly understood…. Not even the typical Islamist appreciates the limitations of Islamic law (generally known as the *shari'a*) as a basis for social, economic, and political order in the twenty-first century."[67] Sharia law often presents itself as negative, offering more a list of "don'ts" rather than a positive approach to life (see Illustration 6).

ILLUSTRATION 6: Sharia Often Presents Itself as Negative[i]

i   http://www.raymondpronk.wordpress.com.

Tariq Ramadhan perceptively observes that "Revelation is both a gift and a burden."[68] The Hadith can present a mixed blessing to individuals who seek to live wholly according to their teaching, because they "constitute an open rather than a prescriptive text. The range of specific issues and advice is so great that whatever a Muslim believes and does there are infinite aspects of the Hadith that elude him. There is an endless tension among precepts fulfilled, precepts neglected, and precepts not understood."[69] If there is a "best" way that one should act in every circumstance, much freedom, creativity, and spontaneity is stifled.

8. DISREGARDING MUHAMMAD'S ADVICE

A result of the inconsistencies outlined above was that Muhammad's advice was not always followed even by his own companions. His troops acquired women as plunder following the raid on Bani Mustaliq. They wanted to resell them as slaves, for they said "we are interested in their prices."[70] However, the men complained that "the long separation from our wives was pressing us"[71] and that "we desired women, and celibacy became hard on us."[72] They asked Muhammad about using *coitus interruptus* with the captive women, for they "intended to have sexual relation with them without impregnating them,"[73] presumably because pregnancy would reduce their resale value. Although Muhammad had advised against it on theological grounds, saying, "It is better for you not to do so,"[74] Jābir reported that *coitus interruptus* was practiced by his men during the Prophet's lifetime.[75]

Another time his plan was challenged and then vetoed by his followers. During the Battle of the Trench, Muhammad offered one-third of the Medinan date crop to the attacking Ghaṭafān tribe to induce them to withdraw. When the leaders of the Muslim 'Aws and Khazraj tribes in Medina heard about this, they asked if this idea was a divine revelation or Muhammad's "personal choice."[76] When Muhammad told them it was the latter, they retorted angrily: "After God has honoured and guided us to Islam and made us famous by you, are we to *give* them our property? We certainly will not. We will give them nothing but the sword." Muhammad's proposed treaty was then destroyed.[77]

Following Muhammad's death, there were even more opportunities for the new leaders to disregard his example and teachings. The next chapter deals with this phenomenon.

NOTES

1   B.2:433.

2   B.2:797; 5:688; 7:458; 9:539.

3   B.6:338.

4   B.9:460.

5   B.9:119.

6   B.1:759; 8:268, 269, 660.

7   It is interesting that it was an external observer, Muhammad, not the praying man himself, who was the judge of the man's feelings of ease.

8   B.1:757, 772.

9   Q.4:65.

10 As-Sibā'i, *As-Sunnah wa makanatuha fi at-Tashri` al-Islami*, 250–251, quoted in Mohsen Haredy, *"Hadith Matn Criticism: A Reconsideration of Orientalists' and Some Muslim Scholars' Views"* (MA. Thesis, Leiden, 2001) from www.islamOnline.net, cited on August 24, 2011.

11 From *Al-Ujula An-Nafi'a* (A Helpful Report) cited in Tabbarah, *The Doctrine of Islam*, 477. Ibn al-Qayyim (d.751 AH) included this among his five criteria for authenticating hadiths. Khan, *Authentication*, 39.

12 B.1:174; 3:551, 646; 8:38.

13 B.3: 646, 551.

14 B.4:673.

15 B.3:553.

16 B.1:712; 3:552.

17 B.5:541.

18 B.2:303.

19 B.2:443, 460; 8:78, 81. Caner and Caner, *Unveiling Islam*, 38 n. 2, find this incongruent with Muhammad's advice to drink camel's urine mixed with milk as a medicine, as found in B.7:590.

20 B.8:54, 149.

21 B.3:799.

22 B.3:532, 533, 801, 802.

23 B.3:521, 522, 524, 531.

24 B.5:538 also 5:540.

25 B.8:306.

26 B.2:88.

27 B.2:91.

28 B3:47, 48, 49, 50, 744; 4:106, 163; 7:318, 398, 400.

29 B3:51, 747, 768.

30 B.3:389.

31 B.2: 245; 4:492.

32 B.1:569; 9:563.

33 B.2:75, compared with B.2:71.

34 B. 5:108.

35 B.2:279.

36 B.6:357.

37 Q.33:57.

38 B.7:115.

39 B.8:373.

40 B.1:92; 9:394.

41 B.3:609, 615, 618.

42 B.1:19.

43 B.1:91, 92, 93, 469; 3:615; 6:109; 7:214; 8:133, 306.

44 B.3:548, 871; 6:416, 626; 8:348.

45 B.9:397.

46 B.2:555 also 3:591, 8:6, 480.

47 B.9:395.

48 B.9:392.

49 B.8:77.

50 B.9:394.

51 B.2:723; 3:209; 7:509.

52 B.1:63.

53 B.1:63.

54 B.5:656.

55 Hadith Abū Dawud 195, 196 cited in Al-Hilali and Khan,

Translation of the Meanings of the Noble Qur'an, .3 n. 2(a).

56 B.2:229.

57 B.1:19.

58 E.g., B.5:77.

59 Ibn Ishaq, *Sira,* 296–97.

60 Ramadhan, *The Messenger,* 114 (italics mine).

61 B.9:466,467; 6:581.

62 Maududi *The Islamic Law and Constitution,* 5.

63 Cited in Schimmel, "The Prophet Muhammad as a Centre of Muslim Life and Thought," 55.

64 Schimmel, *Islam: An Introduction,* 54.

65 B.8:747; 3:91, 94, 861; 4:497, 404; 9:403, 409.

66 Mohammad Shahrour, "The Divine Text and Pluralism in Muslim Societies," www.quran.org/shahroor.htm, cited September 15, 2008.

67 Kuran, *The Long Divergence,* 301–2.

68 Ramadhan, *The Messenger,* 41.

69 Lapidus, *A History of Islamic Societies,* 102.

70 B.3:432.

71 B.3:718.

72 B.5:459.

73 B.8:600; 9:506.

74 B.3:432.

75 B.7.135, 136.

76 Ramadhan, *The Messenger,* 142–43.

77 Ibn Ishaq, *Sira,,* 454 (italics his).

6

THE NEXT GENERATIONS

FROM THE EARLIEST DAYS after Muhammad's death, the Muslim leadership did not present a univocal perspective. The Prophet's example and his orders to others had revealed a fair amount of elasticity, and his immediate successors exhibited a freedom to sometimes move in completely different directions. The early caliphs did not always follow Muhammad's practice. This may have been due to Muhammad's inconsistency, where a variety of modes of behavior were presented. Alternatively it may have been a recognition that they were facing different challenges to those that Muhammad faced and so they needed to make different choices than he did.

1. ABŪ BAKR (R.10/632–12/634)

Muhammad's immediate successor signaled a change in policy in his use of finances. When Abū Bakr al-Ṣiddīq was chosen Caliph, he said, "My people know that my profession was not incapable of providing substance to my family. And as I will be busy serving the Muslim nation, my family will eat from the National Treasury of Muslims, and I will practice the profession of serving the Muslims."[1] There may be an implied criticism of Abū Bakr's radical action by the Hadith collectors, who sandwiched this account between reports of the indigence of Muhammad's household[2] and the sweaty manual labor of Muhammad's Companions which necessitated a bath.[3] Exaggerated claims were being made about the Prophet. 'Anas bin Mālik asserted that Muhammad's poverty was such that he "never saw a roasted sheep with his eyes."[4] However, other Hadiths speak of him sharing a roasted sheep with 130 men[5] and eating from a poisoned roasted sheep in Khaybar.[6] Both the Qur'an and the Hadith speak of how Allah had made Muhammad "rich."[7] Clearly he was not the penurious prophet that is sometimes presented by Muslims.

Abū Bakr's rules of war differed from Muhammad's practices (see Sidebar *Abu Bakr's Environmental Policy*).

The first Caliph instructed his general Yazīd bin Abu Sufyān as follows: "Do not kill women or children or an aged, infirm person."[12] Although Muhammad had sometimes expressed a dislike for and forbade killing women,[13] he did ask his men to assassinate the poetess 'Aṣma' bint Marwān,[14] Fartana, and another unnamed singing slave girl belonging to 'Abdullah b. Khatal,[15] and Sāra, a freed slave girl who "had insulted him in Mecca."[16] When a Jewish woman was strangled and a slave woman stabbed for slandering him, Muhammad declared that no recompense was payable for their blood.[17] At the order of Zayd bin Ḥāritha, Muhammad's freed slave and erstwhile adopted son, the "very old woman" Um Qirfa was cruelly killed, according to al-Ṭabari "by putting a rope to her two legs and to two camels and driving them until they rent her in two."[18] Likewise, the 120-year-old Jew Abū 'Afak was murdered at the Prophet's request.[19] Clearly women and the aged were not exempt from

---

ABU BAKR'S ENVIRONMENTAL POLICY

Abū Bakr's environmental policy differed from Muhammad's. Muslim troops under the command of the Prophet burnt and cut down the palm trees of Banū al-Nadīr during a siege,[8] and received divine permission for this action.[9] Muhammad then commanded his troops to cut down the vineyards of Thaqif during the siege of Tā'if.[10] However, Caliph Abū Bakr later ordered his army commander Yazīd: "Do not destroy or burn palm trees. Do not cut down fruit-bearing trees."[11]

violent attack during Muhammad's reign, but Abū Bakr reversed this policy.

At other times, Muhammad's successor held to convention. When Fāṭima requested her father's inheritance, Abū Bakr refused, saying: "I will not leave anything Allah's Apostle used to do, because I am afraid that if I left something from the Prophet's tradition, then I would go astray."[20]

2. 'UMAR BIN AL-KHAṬṬĀB (R.12/634–AD 23/644)

The above ruling on Fāṭima's inheritance was reversed by the second Caliph, 'Umar bin al-Khaṭṭāb, who gave the Prophet's property (of sadaqa) at Medina to 'Ali and 'Abbās.[21] This action should not be seen as surprising: during the Prophet's lifetime, 'Umar had openly disputed Muhammad's decisions, such as signing the treaty of Hudaibiya. He even sought support from others against Muhammad.[22]

As Caliph, 'Umar continued to question the reasons behind Muhammad's actions. He addressed the Black Stone embedded in the corner of the Ka'ba: "By Allah! I know that you are a stone and can neither benefit nor harm. Had I not seen the Prophet touching (and kissing) you, I would never have touched (and kissed) you." More damaging was his explanation of the reasoning behind some Islamic rituals: "There is no reason for us to do Ramal [fast and vigorous walking] (in Ṭawāf [circumambulation of the Ka'ba]) except that we wanted to show off before the pagans, and now Allah has destroyed them."[23] Its origin sprang from the rumor by the pagan Meccans that the Muslims visiting from Medīna in AD 628 were afflicted with Yathrib fever. Muhammad ordered his men to perform Ramal to dispel this suggestion of weakness.[24] Despite these reservations, 'Umar continued the practice because "the Prophet did that and we do not want to leave it."[25] Even today, Muslim pilgrims vigorously perform this obsolete custom for the same nonexistent audience.

Sometimes 'Umar followed precedent. When the Caliph considered distributing all the gold and silver stored in the Ka'ba among the Muslims, Abū Wail objected: "'You cannot do that.' 'Umar said, 'Why?' I said, 'Your two (previous) companions (the Prophet and

Abū Bakr) did not do it.' 'Umar said, 'They are the two persons whom one must follow.'"[26]

Yet 'Umar was clearly unhappy with the inability of his fellow believers to think independently or speak their minds. He once asked them what they thought about a particular Qur'anic verse. Their response was the typical one given whenever Muhammad had asked them a question. They replied, "Allah knows best."[27] 'Umar became angry and said, "Either say that you know or say that you do not know!"[28]

'Umar then began to drive a wedge between Qur'anic teaching and prophetic practice in a variety of ways. He said to Muslims: "If you follow the Holy Book then it orders you to remain in the state of Iḥrām till you finish from Ḥajj; if you follow the Prophet then he did not finish his Iḥrām till the Hādi (sacrifice) had reached its place of slaughtering (Ḥajj-al-Qiran)."[29] He introduced other changes. For the first time, arms were permitted in the sanctuary at Mecca.[30] Captured land was not immediately distributed to the fighters, as Muhammad had done, due to "those Muslims who have not come to existence yet."[31] 'Ali reports that Muhammad and Abū Bakr both applied forty lashes as a penalty for drinking while 'Umar applied eighty. In the words of the tradition, "All this is sunnah." Abū Yūsuf adds: "Our companions are agreed that the punishment for drinking wine is 80 stripes."[32]

'Umar introduced variation in the worship rubric handed down from Muhammad. He

> recited *Surat-an-Nahl* [a chapter from the Qur'an] on a Friday on the pulpit and when he reached the verse of *Sajda* [prostration] he got down from the pulpit and prostrated and the people also prostrated. The next Friday 'Umar bin Al-Khattab recited the same Sura and when he reached the verse of Sajda he said, "O people! When we recite the verses of *Sajda* (during the sermon) whoever prostrates does the right thing, yet it is no sin for the one who does not prostrate." And 'Umar did not prostrate (that day).[33]

In the Prophet's time, the evening *nawāfil* (non-compulsory) prayers were performed individually or in small groups. 'Umar now ordered them to gather behind one *imām*, pronouncing: "What an excellent *bid'a* (innovation) is this!" However he also cast doubt on the efficacy of such prayer with the comment: "The prayer which they do not perform, but sleep at its time is better than the one they are offering."[34] 'Umar's use of the term "innovation" was in clear contravention to the teaching of the Prophet (see Sidebar *Opposing Innovation*).

"Innovation" has been a pejorative term since the early days of Islam. The scholar Ibn al-Waddāh (d.286/899) wrote a small book, *Kitāb al-bid'a*, warning against the heresy of innovation.[39] However, soon after Muhammad's death, emulating the example of the Prophet was listed as only one of several options in decision making. "'Umar b. Al-Khaṭṭāb, when asked about appointing a successor, replied that he could either follow the Prophet and leave the matter open or follow 'Abū Bakr and make an appointment; either course of action would be sunnah."[40] In fact, 'Umar used a method different to either of these, by choosing a panel of six men to determine the next Caliph.

> ### OPPOSING INNOVATION
>
> Muhammad said: "If somebody innovates something which is not in harmony with the principles of our religion, that thing is rejected."[35] He denied that he had brought any innovation,[36] and it was said that "the worst matters are the heresies (those new things which are introduced into the religion)."[37] The introduction of such changes is condemned as *bid'a* (innovation). Seda comments: "The changing of God's laws is forbidden in Islam. God condemns religious leaders who alter divine principles. One who attempts to make changes places him or herself on the same level with God, committing polytheism....The laws of God are perfect and do not need to be 'modernized' by anyone."[38]

3. 'UTHMĀN BIN 'AFFĀN (R.23/644–35/656)

'Abdul-Raḥmān, 'Umar's son, took upon himself the role of king-maker and selected 'Uthmān as the next Caliph, but with a condition. "I gave the oath of allegiance to you on condition that you will follow Allah's Laws and the traditions of Allah's Apostle and the traditions of the two Caliphs after him."[41] Despite now having three previous leader models to follow, Uthman developed some innovations of his own and increased the number of *adhān* (calls to ritual prayer) on Fridays to three, even though Muḥammad had sanctioned only one.[42]

It is small wonder that during the time of the third Caliph, open tensions appeared. 'Ali, Muhammad's son-in-law, defied 'Uthmān over his newly introduced Ḥajj rules, declaring, "I will not leave the tradition of the Prophet on the saying of somebody."[43] No doubt he recalled the statement of Muhammad: "What is wrong with some people who stipulate things which are not in Allah's laws? Any condition which is not in Allah's laws is invalid even if there were a hundred such conditions. Allah's rules are the most valid and Allah's conditions are the most solid."[44]

When people complained about the "alms" *(zakat)* distribution by Uthman's officials, Ali sent him a copy of Muḥammad's orders regarding the "free-will offering" *(ṣadaqa)*. 'Uthmān's response seemed dismissive: "Take it away, for we are not in need of it."[45] Such responses caused some to consider 'Uthmān unapproachable. A slanderous adage by Muḥammad was applied to the Caliph, hinting at his duplicity. 'Uthman was compared to a man who "will be brought on the Day of Resurrection and thrown in the (Hell) Fire, so that his intestines will come out, and he will go around like a donkey goes around a millstone." The reason for this state of affairs was given. The man would admit that "I used to order you to do good deeds, but I did not do them myself, and I used to forbid you to do bad deeds, yet I used to do them myself."[46] Significantly, it was 'Uthman's unjust appointments of his relatives to high positions throughout the rapidly expanding Islamic empire and the widespread corruption of this nepotism that led to his undoing. He was confronted about this by a group of Muslims from Egypt. "Uthman, taken by surprise, pretended to meet their grievances, but was then caught red-handed going back on his assurances. The Egyptians, outraged by his double-dealing, laid siege to his house, stormed it, and hacked him to death."[47]

4. LATER CALIPHS AND RULERS

As time went by, some were grieving the loss of prophetic *sunnah*. 'Anas lamented, "I do not find (now-a-days) things as they were (practiced) at the time of the Prophet." The wealth flowing into public coffers due to taxes on conquered lands even affected spiritual matters. One commented wistfully: "Our companions who died (during the lifetime of the Prophet) left (this world) without having their rewards reduced through enjoying the pleasures of this life, but we have got (so much) wealth that we find no way to spend it except on the construction of buildings."[48] Sometimes the alterations were simply dress or ritual matters,[49] but other changes were deep and noticeable. "Narrated Az-Zuhri that he visited 'Anas bin Mālik at Damascus and found him weeping and asked him why he was weeping. He replied, 'I do not know anything which I used to know during the lifetime of Allah's Apostle except this prayer which is being lost (not offered as it should be).'"[50]

Of course the early Caliphs could claim Qur'anic sanction for their actions. Did not Islam's holy scripture itself say: "O you who believe! Obey Allah and obey the Messenger and those in authority among you"?[51] Likewise the Prophet had said, "Listen and obey (your chief) even if an Ethiopian whose head is like a raisin were made your chief."[52] Similarly, "whoever obeys the ruler, obeys me and whoever disobeys him, disobeys me."[53] Leaders saw themselves as the holders of power originating from Allah himself and passed on to them through the Prophet. However, their critics read the next part of that verse: "Then if you quarrel about anything, refer it to Allah and the Messenger."[54] This should have sent the Caliphs back to the example of Muhammad whenever differences arose in the Muslim community. There was no place for *bid'a*. Nor was there any place for rebellion or schism, for Muhammad said: "If somebody sees his Muslim ruler doing something he disapproves of, he should be patient, for whoever becomes separate from the Muslim group even for a span and then dies, he will die as those who died in the Pre-Islamic period of ignorance."[55]

However, if a leader's order required one to disobey Allah, then the order should be ignored.[56] Troops who disobeyed an unreasonable command by their military commander had been commended by Muhammad.[57]

'Ibn 'Abbās commented on a prophetic ruling regarding inheritance: "Some people claim that the order in the above verse is cancelled; by Allah, it is not cancelled, but the people have stopped acting on it."[58] Novel practices were developed. Muhammad's favorite wife, 'A'isha, for example, broadcast the fact that she offered the midmorning prayer (duha), despite never having seen the Prophet doing so.[59] Later such variations were used against her. When she gathered her forces to oppose 'Ali's son al-Ḥassan, he was advised: "By Allah! She is the wife of your Prophet in this world and in the Hereafter. But Allah has put you to test whether you obey Him (Allah) or her."[60]

Even rulings with a social justice aspect were ignored. Although Muhammad had ordered that meat from sacrifices not be kept for more than three days "so that the rich would feed the poor," 'A'isha notes: "But later we used to keep even trotters to cook, fifteen days later."[61] Marwān, the governor of Medīna during 'Umar's caliphate, changed the order of service for Friday prayers after Muhammad's death, because people would leave the mosque straight after the prayers instead of staying to listen to the sermon.[62] Actions such as this prompted Hudhaifa to observe: "In fact, it was hypocrisy that existed in the lifetime of the Prophet but today it is *Kufr* (disbelief) after belief."[63] Muhammad promised at the last judgment to refute those who did not follow his example: "I will say, 'Far removed (from mercy), far removed (from mercy), those who changed (the religion) after me!'"[64] How far removed they are from mercy will be clearly revealed. "Then will be brought some men of my followers who will be taken towards the left (i.e., to the Fire), and I will say: 'O Lord! My companions!' Whereupon Allah will say: 'You do not know what they did after you left them.'"[65] for "they innovated (new things) after you"[66] or "introduced new things into the religion"[67] and consequently "they turned apostate as renegades (reverted from Islam)."[68]

5. EARLY UNEVEN ADOPTION OF THE SUNNAH

The adoption of prophetic *sunnah* during the early years of Islam was apparently uneven, and clearly open to negotiation and adaptation by those who knew it well.

> Associating position with Muhammad directly was not always felt to be necessary, because companions of the Prophet or otherwise individuals were also considered authoritative sources for determining proper behavior and policies during much of the first century following his death. But as controversies between different Muslim approaches developed along with the community's growing interest in uniformity, the need to ground positions in the person of the Prophet became paramount.[69]

One Hadith records a man swearing allegiance to the Caliph 'Abdul Mālik bin Marwān (r.65/685–85/705) with the form: "I swear allegiance to you in that I will listen and obey what is in accordance with the Laws of Allah and the Tradition of His Apostle."[70] Others claim that the acceptance of *sunnah* as authoritative for all Muslims to imitate was an even later adoption, suggesting that it did not develop until after the demise of the 'Umayyad caliphate in 132/750. "Under the early 'Abbāsid caliphs the 'ulamā' became a professional elite of religious leaders …. It was they who established that the sunnah (way, example) of Muhammad should become the key reference point for determining what should and should not be sanctioned under Islam. This led to the codification of *Sharīʿa* (Islamic law)."[71]

The uniformity of Islam is proposed by Jordan's King Abdullah II: "There is no such thing as extremist Islam and no such thing as moderate Islam, for Islam is one."[72] Despite this claim, a single interpretation of Islam did not emerge in early Islam and has not persisted. The diversity within the four orthodox schools (Hanafi,

Hanbali, Maliki, and al-Shāfiʿī) and the Jaʿfari school of Shia Islam indicates that the behavior of Muhammad and his first followers was not unvarying.

Hassan al-Turabi, the leader of the Sudanese Muslim Brotherhood and Speaker of the Sudanese Parliament, points out how this eclectic approach has operated throughout Islamic history and up to the present day.

> Any form or procedure for the organization of public life that can be ultimately related to God and put to his service in the furtherance of the aims of Islamic government can be adopted unless expressly excluded by the Sharia. Once so received, it is an integral part of Islam whatever its source may be. Through the process of Islamization, the Muslims were always very open to expansion and change. Thus, Muslims can incorporate any experience whatever if not contrary to their ideals. Muslims took much of their bureaucratic forms from Roman and Persian models. Now much can be borrowed from contemporary sources, critically appreciated in the light of Sharia values and norms, and integrated into the Islamic framework of government.[73]

It seems that no single standard way of being a Muslim has ever existed, even from the earliest days. So how did the Hadith come into being? That is the subject of the next chapter.

NOTES

1   B.3:284.

2   B.3:283.

3   B.3:285.

4   B.7:297, 332; 8.464.

5   B.3:787; 7:294.

6   B.4:394; 7:669.

7   Q.93:8; B.3:495.

8   B.3:519; 4:263; 5:365, 366, 406.

9   Q.59:5.

10   Ibn Ishaq, *Sira*, 589.

11   Malik bin Anas *Al-Muwatta of Imam Malik Ibn Anas,* 174, cited by
     Saeed, "Jihad and Violence," 79.

12   Ibid.

13   B.4:257, 258.

14   Ibn Ishaq, *Sira*, 675–76.

15   Ibid., 551.

16   Ibid. This implacable attitude toward enemies of Islam and critics of
     Muhammad even extended to family members. Abū Bakr fought in
     almost all the battles along with the Prophet. "In the first battle of
     Islam at Badr he was with the Holy Prophet like a shadow. His own
     son (Abdullah), who had not embraced Islam by that time, was fight-
     ing on the side of Quraish. After he accepted Islam he said to Bakr
     one day, "Dear father! I found you twice under my sword at Badr
     but I could not raise my hand because of my love for you." "If I had
     got a chance,"Abū Bakr replied, "I would have killed you" Ahmed,
     Encyclopaedia, vol.1, 224). Umar ibn al Khattāb said of his daughter:
     "By God, if he [Muhammad] were to ask me to strike off her head, I
     would do so without hesitation" (Haykal, *Life*, 439).

17   Abū Dawud 4348–49 from CD-ROM *The Islamic Scholar,* Hadith/
     Abū Dawud.

18   Ibn Ishaq, *Sira*, 664–65.

19   Ibn Ishaq, *Sira*, 675 and Dashti, *Twenty Three Years*, 100.

20   B.5:60; 8:718.

21   B.4:325.

22   B.4:406; 6:367.

23   B.2:675.

24   B.2:672; 5:557, 558.

25   B.2:675.

26   B.9:380; 2:664.

27   Cf. B.6:297.

28   B.6:62.

29   B.3:21; also 2:630, 782.

30   B.2:83.

31   B.4:354; also 5:542, 543.

32   Brown, *Rethinking*, 10.

33   B.2:183.

34   B.3:227. 'Umar felt free to abolish other accepted practice. "Abu Nadrah reported: While I was in the company of Jabir, a person came and said: 'There is difference of opinion among Ibn Abbas and Ibn Zubayr about two *Mut'ahs* (benefits, *Tamattu'* in Hajj and temporary marriage with women)', whereupon Jabir said: 'We have been doing this during lifetime of Allah's Messenger (peace be upon him)', and then Umar forbade us to do so, and we never resorted to them" (Muslim Bk.7 no. 2874 from CD-ROM *The Islamic Scholar,* Hadith/ Muslim).

35   B.3:861. Ibn Ishaq suggests that the prohibition of innovation was a pre-Islamic concept in Mecca. He states that previously the city "was called Bakka because it used to break the necks of tyrants when they introduced innovations therein" (Ibn Ishaq, *Sira,* 47).

36   Q.46:9.

37   B.9:38.

38   Seda, *Islam,* 12. Muhammad specifically denied that he was an innovator (Q.46:9).

39   Brown, *Hadith,* 36.

40   Brown, *Rethinking,* 10 c.f. B.9:325.

41   B.9:314.

42   B.2:35, 36, 38, 39. Khan suggests that "fabrication in the Prophetic tradition began in the middle of 'Uthmān's Caliphate." Others claim that it may have even occurred in Muhammad's lifetime (Khan, *Authentification,* 2).

43   B.2:634. Ali did, however, reject a Hadith reported to him because it contradicted a Qur'anic verse (Khan, *Authentification,* 20).

44   B.3:364, 377, 735, 737, 886, 889, 893.

45   B.4:343.

46   B.4:489; 9:218.

47   Holland, *In the Shadow of the Sword,* 361.

48   B.7:576.

49   B.7:742.

50   B.1:507. Seda, *Islam,* 12. Muhammad specifically denied that he was an innovator (Q.46:9).

51   Q.4:59a.

52   B.1:662, 664; also 2:488; 9:256.

53   B.9:251; 4:204.

54 Q.4:59b.

55 B.9:257, 176.

56 B.4:203; 9:258.

57 B.5:629; 9:259.

58 B.4:21.

59 B.2:228, 273. Ibn 'Umar agreed (B.2:271). Anas suggested that Muhammad may have done so on one occasion (B.2:275.1), but some attested other occasions (B.2:268, 272, 274; 5:587).

60 B.9:220.

61 B.7:349.

62 B.2:76.

63 B.9:230.

64 B.9:174.

65 B.8:533, 578.

66 B.8:584.

67 B.9:173.

68 B.8:585, 586.

69 Firestone, *Jihad*, 162 n. 8.

70 B.9.377.

71 Riddell and Cotterell, *Islam in Conflict*, 87.

72 Sookhdeo *Global Jihad*, 430.

73 al-Turabi "The Islamic State," 249–50.

7

COMPILATION OF THE HADITH

THE CONCEPT OF THE HADITH was hotly debated during the Prophet's era and soon afterward.

1. ORIGIN

Some in the earliest days of Islam felt that the Hadith should never have been recorded in the first place. This is based on Muhammad's command to his Companions: "Do not write what I say. Anyone who has written from me anything other than the Qur'an, let him blot it out."[1] The community became divided about this (see Sidebar *The Recording of Hadiths*).

The Shia scholar Tabataba'i claims that since "the Caliphs had prohibited the writing down of the tradition, they were handed down by word of mouth by the companions and their followers ... [until] the beginning of the second century when the prohibition was lifted, allowing Scholars to record the traditions."[2]

He claims that this prohibition held force for about ninety years. "The effect of this prohibition was that the narrators and scholars of sayings were free to make small additions or changes during oral transmission of the saying. These additions gradually accumulated until the original meaning of the saying was lost."[3] It also opened

THE RECORDING OF HADITHS

"Many of the leading Companions including 'Umar b. al-Khattāb, 'Abd Allah b. Mas'ud, Zayd b. Thabit, Abū Mūsa al-'Ash'ari, and Abū Sa'id al-Khudri were against the writing of Hadith whereas 'Ali b. Abi Talib, his son, al-Hasan, Anas b. Malik, 'Abd Allah b. 'Amr b. al-'As considered it to be permissible."[4] Abū Dā'ūd records two traditions on this matter, one after the other. The first states that Muhammad commanded the writing of traditions, and the second that he forbade it.[5] The Damascene commentator al-Nawāwī (d.676/1277) reconciled the two by suggesting that early on Muhammad was concerned that confusion between his words and Allah's words in the Qur'an might occur, but later allowed the writing of his words when the Qur'an was more settled in people's minds.[6]

the door for totally spurious hadiths. "False sayings were not only introduced by attributing them to respected narrators but also by the hypocrites. Their sayings soon became part of the main body of sayings."[7] A frequently quoted hadith is "Seek knowledge, even if you have to go to China." According to an important Islamic website on the Hadith, this account is forged. "This additional statement is found in a few of the (weak) narrations of the previous hadith, and is declared as maudu' by Ibn Hibban, Ibn al-Jauzi, al-Sakhawi and al-Albani (Al-Da'ifah, no. 416; Da'if al-Jami' al- Saghir, nos. 1005-6)."[8]

But the view that writing hadiths was forbidden has been challenged by others. Al-Bukhāri, for example, was decidedly pro-Hadith. He included accounts suggesting that prophetic traditions be preserved,[9] and confirming that this was done.[10] When a man requested a copy of a saying of the Prophet, Muhammad ordered one of his companions to write it down.[11] Abū Hurayra described how Muhammad helped him to memorize hadiths.[12]

It could also be assumed that there was an element of self-censorship by the Hadith collectors, as can occur with any historical writing. Ibn Hishām, in his recension of Ibn Isḥāq's *Sīrat rasūl Allah* (biography of the Prophet of Allah), mentions that he omitted, among other features, "things which it is disgraceful to discuss [and] matters which would distress certain people."[13] He admits that he had changed the words in a derogatory poem by one of Muhammad's enemies "because he casts aspersions on the prophet in them."[14] The desire to preserve or even enhance the reputation of the Prophet may have been a factor in the minds of al-Bukhāri and others.[15]

2. COLLECTION OF THE HADITH

From the beginning, there were gaps in the knowledge of the Companions. The Caliph 'Umar admitted ignorance about one of Muhammad's commands, saying, "This tradition of the Prophet remained hidden from me. Business in the market kept me busy."[16] Another man admits that his runaway camel sidetracked him when someone said: "'O 'Imrān! Your she-camel has run away!' (I got up and went away), but I wish I had not left that place (for I missed what Allah's Apostle had said)."[17]

Even a single absence from a rare or unique event could result in error. When a man performed an incorrect number of *raka'at* (bowings) during an eclipse prayer, someone else excused him: "Yes, for he missed the Prophet's tradition (concerning this matter)."[18] Sometimes the omissions were culpable. On his deathbed Muhammad requested writing materials "so that I may write to you something after which you will never go astray." An argument broke out among those present. "Umar said, 'The Prophet is seriously ill, and we have got Allah's Book with us and that is sufficient for us.' But the companions of the Prophet differed about this and there was a hue and cry. On that the Prophet said to them, 'Go away (and leave me alone). It is not right that you should quarrel in front of me.'" A final opportunity to receive insight and perhaps inspiration looked like it might be lost. Ibn 'Abbās called it "most unfortunate, a great disaster."[19] But the dying Muhammad persisted, and "he ordered them to do three things. He said, 'Turn the pagans out of the Arabian Peninsula; respect and give gifts to the foreign delegations as you have seen me dealing with them.' (Sa'īd bin Jubair, the sub-narrator said that 'Ibn 'Abbās kept quiet as regards the third order, or he said, 'I forgot it.')."[20] Despite the Prophet's desperate determination, his followers either disregarded or failed to pass on what he had told them—possibly his last instructions. Rather than "hanging off his every word" and storing these things in their hearts,[21] his followers sometimes took a casual approach to his sayings. The reason for such an attitude might be found in the comment of Ali when 'Abbas suggested that they ask the dying Prophet who should replace him. 'Ali's response was clear: "By Allah, if we asked Allah's Apostle for it (i.e. the Caliphate) and he denied it us, the people will never give it to us after that. And by Allah, I will not ask Allah's Apostle for it."[22] Some uncertainty about the leadership succession would allow potential candidates room to maneuver when Muhammad did eventually die.

The Hadith testify to many of these gaps. Over 130 of al-Bukhāri's hadiths detail possible transmission discrepancies. There are a variety of terms and phrases (see Table 10) used by the narrators throughout al-Bukhāri's hadith collection which convey some uncertainty about details of the accounts they are passing on.

"I've forgotten"	1:340, 469,516,522,573,669,738; 4:393; 5:189, 571,701,716; 8:328
"I can't remember"	1:135,241,266,489,770; 3:617; 5:2,103; 6:368; 7:84; 9:426,532.1
"I'm not sure"	1:86,184; 3:568,671,701; 4:47,812; 5:193; 6:429; 8:36,187,822; 9:9,390
"is in doubt"	1:21,112; 2:392; 3:441; 4:670,781; 5:124,730; 6:130; 7:515; 8:364,551,583
"I don't know"	1:394,434; 2:162b; 3:608,610,752,819; 4:80.2; 5:503; 8:665
"it may be"	2:141; 4:766
"perhaps"	1:306; 3:255
"I think/thought"	1:64,361,441; 2:321,373,735; 3:17,204,214, 259,473,539,593; 4:14,48,57,249,319; 5:129, 638,688,705,708; 6:97; 7:450,765; 8:203; 9:371,540
"most probably"	1:450.1; 6:223; 8:8
"He said something like that" or "something similar"	B.1:140,669; 2: 544,554; 8:753
"He is reported to have said"	3:174, 207

TABLE 10: Descriptions of Uncertainty in Transmission

At other times, there are differences in what the narrators said. One may have disagreed with another narrator,[23] suggested an alternative saying,[24] or added something.[25]

On occasion these indicate words which the Prophet may or may not have said,[26] or uncertainty about time periods,[27] or quantities,[28] or even whether a particular event took place at all.[29] Eyewitnesses, including family members, dispute about publicly observed events.[30] At other times, doubt is cast on the entire account, with a statement such as, "But this report is not confirmed by an authentic narration."[31] Sometimes a Hadith is documented, along with the announcement of its later cancellation.[32] One man was told that he was out-of-date in refusing to eat meat which had been stored after sacrifice, for a "new verdict was given in your absence."[33]

At other times, parenthetic phrases are found with two different words and the comment "(the Narrator is in doubt as to which is the right term),"[34] thus indicating uncertainty on the part of the scribe. On one occasion the proposed alternative meanings were opposites: "the Prophet said, 'Bravo! It is a profitable (or perishable) property.' (Ibn Maslama is not sure as to which word is right, i.e. profitable or perishable.)"[36]

The admission of these discrepancies has caused some scholars to cast doubt on the Hadith accounts. At other times the editors were more forthcoming with their confessions. After listing four supplications of Muhammad, Sufyān added: "This narration contained three items only, but I added one. I do not know which one that was."[36]

'Ali, Muhammad's nephew and son-in-law, admitted that his own words might not always be reliable. "Whenever I tell you a narration from Allah's Apostle, by Allah, I would rather fall down from the sky than ascribe a false statement to him, but if I tell you something between me and you (not a Hadith) then it was indeed a trick (i.e. I may say things just to cheat my enemy)."[37] Transmitters differed in their recollections of rules. While Ibn 'Abbās saw "no harm" in mut'a (temporary) marriage, Ali claimed that Muhammad had forbidden it.[38] Even the narrators of the Hadith were mystified at times. Although Muhammad spoke of forty deeds which could result in Paradise for those who performed them, one chronicler struggled to identify even fifteen such deeds.[39]

3. TRANSMISSION

PROBLEMS WITH ARABIC SCRIPT

A hadith states: "One time, Muhammad addressed the people saying, "Allah held back the killing from Mecca. (The sub-narrator is in doubt whether the Prophet said "elephant or killing," as the Arabic words standing for these words have great similarity in shape)."[40] The earliest Arabic script had no dots above or below the letters, even though these dots are necessary for readers to distinguish between many letters. The example given in this hadith is the difference between 'elephant' fīl فـيل and 'killing' qatal قـتل. Of the twenty-eight letters in the Arabic script, only six are unambiguous in the absence of dots.[41] The remaining twenty-two letters all require dots above or below to distinguish between them.[42]

An editorial note in the Hadith demonstrates a problem in the transmission of revelation based on the way that the Arabic script was written (see Sidebar *Problems with Arabic Script*).

If transmission and editorial inconsistencies were occurring at this early stage, it could throw doubt on the preservation of Muhammad's actual words as they were committed to writing. This doubt must be compounded by the relatively large time gap between Muhammad's death in 10 AH/632 AD and the earliest available manuscripts of his sayings. Although Maududi claims that Hajjāj-bin-Yūsuf chose scholars to assign dots and vowel pointing to distinguish between similar letters during the reign of 'Abdul-Mālik (r.65/684–85/704),[43] there are no verifiable Muslim documents prior to 132/750 regarding this formative period of Islam.[44] Crone claims that the extant primary sources are from 150 to 300 years after the events which they describe.[45]

Moreover, as Islam spread into new regions, it encountered new thought forms which challenged Arab views. These highlighted the Muslim community's lack of resolution of some of its internal philosophical issues and debates.

4. THE ACCEPTANCE OF THE HADITH WAS SLOW AND UNEVEN

The two hundred-year period following the death of Muhammad was a time of debate on how to best to follow him. Three opposing groups arose (see Illustration 7).

Hadith mostly accepted	Some Hadith accepted	Hadith often rejected
'Ahl al-Hadith	*Ahl al-Ra'y*	*Ahl al-Quran*
or 'Ashāb al-Hadith		*or Ahl al-Kalam*

ILLUSTRATION 7: Three Early Schools of Thought

The *Ahl al-Qur'ān* were best represented by the comment of 'Umar bin al-Khaṭṭāb when asked to bring writing materials requested by the dying Muhammad: "The Prophet is seriously ill, and we have got Allah's Book with us and that is sufficient for us."[46] Muhammad had earlier proclaimed to the Muslims: "This day have I perfected your religion for you, completed my favor upon you, and have chosen for you Islam as your religion,"[47] and some Muslims believed they needed no further revelation.[48] This group, called the *ahl al-kalām* ("people of the speculative theology"), "rejected Hadith altogether in favour of reliance on the Qur'an alone."[49] According to al-Shāfiʿī, they "could not accept the idea of taking their religion and its laws from reports transmitted merely from 'so-and-so, from so-and-so.'"[50]

Yet even this interpretation was seen as too narrow by some. On his deathbed in 23/644, 'Umar outlined to his hearers the possible sources of guidance as "the Qur'an, the Muslims who emigrated to Medina with Muhammad *(muhājirūn)*, those in Medina who welcomed the Muslims *(anṣār)*, the people of the desert, and finally the protected communities of Jews and Christians *('ahl al-dhimma).*"[51] Brown comments that "its absence here tells us that even though the idea of Prophetic sunnah may have existed from the earliest years of Islam, it had not yet achieved universal acceptance as an indispensable source of religious authority."[52]

Such approaches as these may have contributed to the rise of the second group. The *'Ahl al-Ra'y* (literally "people of the opinion") were influential in the Iraqi cities of Kufa and Basra. They favored the use of personal reasoning, particularly in cases where the text of the Qur'an was silent. Kamali calls them "Rationalists" because they believed that "the rules of the Shariah, outside the sphere of devotional matters, pursued objectives and were founded in causes that provided the jurist and *mujtahid* with guidelines for further inquiry and research."[53] Although not rejecting the Hadith outright, they did not feel the need to slavishly follow Muhammad's example. Their quest was the identification of "overriding principles, which better represent the spirit of the prophet."[54]

Ultimately it was the third group, the *'ahl al-Hadith*,[55] which emerged victorious. For them, emulation of the Prophet was the only sure way to live a righteous life. This outcome was never certain, and was rather late in arrival. The link between the Hadith and the person, or even the time, of the Prophet "had not even been claimed in any consistent and systematic way by the Muslims until it was made the cornerstone of the polemic of the late second-century AH scholar Shāfi'ī".[56]

As scholars have studied the Hadith, they have discovered not only the internal inconsistencies outlined above but also some other problems. Internal inconsistencies are important if it is assumed that the Hadith are a true and accurate record of the sayings and actions of Muhammad and his companions. However, this assumption has been challenged. There are indications that the Hadith may be questionable from a historicocritical perspective. These require external criteria by which to assess the Hadith.

NOTES

1   Muslim no. 186 from CD-ROM *The Islamic Scholar,* Hadith/Muslim.

2   Tabataba'i, *The Qur'an in Islam,* 91. He suggests in a footnote that "this restriction was imposed by the Umayyad caliph 'Umar ibn 'Abd al-'Aziz, 99-101 AH."

3   Tabataba'i, *The Qur'an in Islam*, 92.

4   Kamali, *Textbook*, 22. The reason for such a ban may have been a concern that the Hadith might become confused with the authoritative and written Qur'ān (Tabbarah, *Spirit of Islam*, 469). The same grounds were given for the ban on writing Jewish "Oral Law," according to Rauf, "Hadith Literature," 271. The controversy over *kitāba* (writing) is discussed in detail in Siddiqui, *Hadith Literature*, 24-27.

5   *'Ilm*, 3. Robson, "Hadīth," vol. 3, 24.

6   Brown, *Hadith*, 22.

7   Ibid.

8   Source: www.islamic-awareness.org/Hadith/Ulum/aape.html (accessed July 8, 2013).

9   B.1:98.

10 B.1:113.

11 B.3:613; 9:19.

12 B.1:119, 120; B3:263, 540; 9:452.

13 Ibn Hishām's notes in Ibn Ishāq, *Sīrat*, 691.

14 Ibid., 749 n. 538.

15 It was not only Muhammad's honor that Ibn Hishām was keen to preserve. He omits two lines of a poem by 'Abū Tālib against al-Mut'im b. 'Adiy "in which he violently insulted him" (716 n. 167), as well as several "obscene" verses (726 n. 223; 749 n. 540 and n. 541; 755 n. 599; 56 n. 608, 610) (Ibn Hisham's notes in Ibn Ishaq, *Sira).*

16 B.3:277; 9:451. By contrast, Abū Hurayra explained that he had forgone employment so that he could listen to Muhammad (B.1:118; 3:263, 540). Mernissi criticized him for this (Mernissi, "Women's Rights in Islam," 112-126).

17 B.4:100, 413.

18 B.2:156; 2:172.

19 B.1:114; 5:716, 717; 9:468.

20 B.5:716.

21 c.f. Lk.2:51.

22 B.5:728; also 8:282.

23 B.1:470; 3:386, 511, 683; 4:55, 410.

24 B.1:542; 3:358; 4:124; 5:191; 6:222, 235, 294; 8:164.

25 B.1:581; 2:516; 3:205; 6:224; 7:231.

26 E.g., B.1:64, 141.

27   B.3:608.

28   E.g., B.3:568.

29   B.2:141.

30   B.5:555.

31   B.3:779

32   B.1: 291; 7:562; 1:180; 5:172.

33   B.7:475.

34   B.1:21.

35   B.4:30.

36   B.8:358.

37   B.9:64.

38   B.9:91.

39   B.3:800.

40   B.1:112.

41   They are (with their equivalent English sounds written beside them):
     a ا; k ك; l ل; m م; h ه; w و

42   They are (as written in the medial position, and bracketed with other
     letters they might be confused with if their dots were removed):

     (b ب; y ي; n ن; t ت; th ث)

     (H ح; j ج; kh خ)

     (d د; dh ذ)

     (r ر; z ز)

     (T ط; D ظ)

     (s س; sh ش)

     (S ص; Dh ض)

     ('a ع; g غ)

     (q ق; f ف)

     The ease of confusing the letters is illustrated by the story reported by
     al-Hasan b. 'Abdallah 'Askari (d.328/939) of a certain Hamrah who
     began reading an undotted version of Sura 2 as "that book *la zaita*
     زيت *fihi* (no oil in it)' instead of *la raiba* ريب *fihi* (no doubt in
     it), thus earning himself the nickname of *al-Zayyāt* (the dealer in oil)
     (Margoliouth, "Textual Variations," 157).

43   Maudūdī, "Introduction," xxxvi.

44   Wansbrough, *Sectarian Milieu*, 58, 59.

45   Crone, *Meccan Trade*, 204.

46 B.1:114.

47 Q.5:3.

48 This does not mean that Q.5:3 was the last verse revealed. According to al-Bara, it was Q.4:176 (B.6:129), but Ibn Abbas claimed it was Q.2:275-279 (B.6:69).

49 Brown, *Rethinking tradition*, 8.

50 Brown, *Hadith*, 152.

51 Brown, *Rethinking tradition*, 10.

52 Ibid.

53 *Mohammad Hashim Kamali,* "Law and Society: The Interplay of Revelation and Reason in the Shariah" in *Oxford History of Islam* (Oxford: Oxford University Press, 2000), Section 3: The History of Islamic Law. Source: http://acc.teachmideast.org/texts.php?module_id=2&reading_id=210&print=1 (accessed July 8, 2013).

54 Rami Bailony, "Finding the spirit of Muhammad." Source: www.toledomuslims.com/criterion/Article.asp?ID=199 (accessed August 24, 2011).

55 Brown refers to this group as *Aṣḥāb al-Ḥadīth* (lit. "companions of the Hadith"), *Rethinking*, 14.

56 Burton, *Introduction*, x. He bases this on the work of Schacht.

8

ISNĀD AND TRANSMITTER
PROBLEMS

1. THE RELIABILITY OF
ISNĀDS IN THE HADITH

Muslims are often proud of the apparently strong historical scaffold-ing that supports the Hadith due to the *isnāds* (lists of transmitters). Assad Rustom, former professor of history at the American University of Beirut, said: "Had the European chroniclers studied the works of the scholars of *Hadith*, they wouldn't have been delayed in founding the 'science' of methodology till the later part of the eighteenth cen-tury."[1] It was key in anchoring the history of Islam. The early Sunni Abū Naṣr al-Wā'ilī suggested that "the Sunna of the Messenger of God is not known by reason, but by transmission."[2]

(a) Origin of the isnād *system*

Some scholars claim that the isnādic system of recorded transmit-ters is unique to Islam,[3] while others recognize the concept in other earlier non-Arab cultures.[4] Danner asserts: "The isnādic principle is characteristically Arab (with) direct connections with the pre-Islamic transmission of oral literature."[5] One source gives a definite, and later,

starting date: Imām Mālik (d. 179/795) said: "The first one to uti-
lise the *isnād* was Ibn Shihāb al-Zuhri" (d. 124/741).[6] Wansbrough
suggests its origin was even later: "The supplying of isnāds, whether
traced to the prophet, to his companions, or their successors, may be
understood as an exclusively formal innovation and cannot be dated
much before 200/815."[7] Holland claims that the *isnād* system was
modeled on the similar method used by the Jewish scholars of Sura,
Iraq, to authenticate the Torah.[8]

(b) Questioning the isnāds

Whatever their view on its origins, Muslims typically place great
confidence in the historiography of the Hadith, referring to the
"strict scientific methods with which fraud and forgery became
impossible."[9] Others are dismissive. Muhammad Aslam Jayrapūri
(d.1955) mocked the science of isnāds as senseless "narration worship" (*rivāyat parastī*).[10]

Isnādic studies have brought the authenticity of the Hadith into
question. Typical of this approach is the comment by Guillaume:
"Of the resultant mass of tradition few can be confidently regarded
as emanating from the authorities whose names they bear."[11] Much
of the research, started by Goldziher[12] and carried on by Schacht,[13]
has been refined by Juynboll.

(c) Classifying the isnāds

Juynboll established a method of assessing the historicity and connections between a Hadith originating from the Prophet and its final
collection. It involves writing the names of the oldest transmitters
at the bottom of a sheet of paper and working upwards in time.
He noted the occasions where there was a "common link" (cl), for
example between a master and his known student (since both were
invariably male). A "seeming common link" (scl) occurs when a master had several students, and the next transmitter above may have
been one of them. When the master's alleged students in turn had
more than one pupil, each of these is called a "partial common link"
(pcl).

Based on these categories, Juynboll classifies *isnāds* in three ways.

1. Single strand *isnāds* **(ss)** (see Illustration 8).[14]

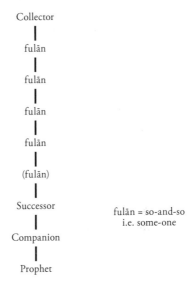

Collector

|

fulān

|

fulān

|

fulān

|

fulān

|

(fulān)

|

Successor

|

Companion

|

Prophet

fulān = so-and-so
i.e. some-one

ILLUSTRATION 8: Single Strand (ss) *Isnāds*. These have a single informant in each generation passing the information on to another single informant.

Juynboll casts doubt on such transmissions. Those traditions "linking just one master with one pupil and then with one pupil and so on, traversing at least two hundred years cannot lay claim to any acceptable historicity: in all likelihood they are the handiwork of the collectors in whose collections they are found."[15]

Abdulaziz Sachedina observes that "transmission by a single authority, to the exclusion of others, is considered to be an indication of falsehood or error on the part of the narrator."[16] Moreover, such Hadith form the bulk of those that have been passed on. "The vast majority of traditions in the Six Books are supported by *isnād* structures in the form of ss's."[17]

Juynboll specifically mentions those Hadith attributed to Ibn Abbas (d.69/687), Muhammad's nephew, who was aged between ten and fifteen years when the Prophet died. "The vast majority have only single strands as authentication…. But this has never prevented the Islamic world, or indeed a fair number of western scholars, from regularly dubbing Ibn 'Abbās the 'father of Muslim Qur'an exegesis.'"[18]

2. "Spider" isnāds (see Illustration 9).[19] These occur when "several ss's seem to come together in a seeming cl, which does not have the required minimum of believable pcl's."[20]

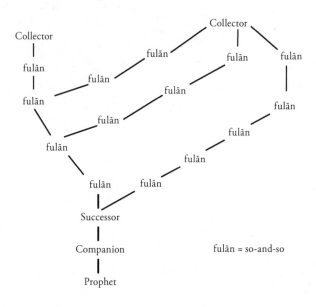

ILLUSTRATION 9: "Spider" *Isnāds*

Juynboll notes: "In Muslim tradition literature we find thousands upon thousands of ss's, a good many of which form into otherwise undatable spiders."[21]

From a Western historical perspective, there is much to warrant suspicion based on methodological grounds. The strength of any list of isnāds depends on the integrity of each one of its constituents. If only one element of a chain of authorities can be shown to be fabricated, then the whole line must be thrown into doubt. As scholars have assessed the *isnāds*, they have found that this is a common scenario. In al-Bukhāri's *Tārīkh* "History," the biographies for those responsible for the isnāds lack key details. "Less than 7 per cent of the biographies are provided with the dates of death, less than one-half of 1 per cent of them give an indication of the date of birth, and only a little more than one-half of 1 per cent contain, in addition, some date which fixes the time of their subject."[22]

3. *Isnād* bundle with one single strand (see Illustration 10).[23]
This schema has a network of informants feeding to a mixture of
collectors.

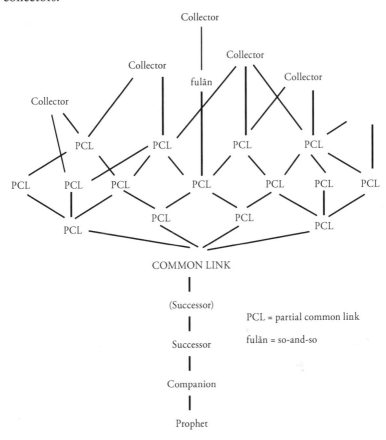

ILLUSTRATION 10: *Isnād* Bundle with One Single Strand

Where that single strand (ss) branches out first, we find a
man whom we call the common link (cl), and when his
alleged pupils have themselves more than one pupil we call
each one of such pupils a partial common link (pcl). All
these branches together constitute a so-called *isnād* bundle.
The more transmission lines there are, coming together in
a certain transmitter, either reaching him or branching out
from him, the greater the claim to historicity that moment

of transmission, represented in what may be described as a "knot," has..... Traditions supported by *isnād* bundles that deserve that qualification are rather rarer [than the other two types], but do seem to contain data that may point to a more or less tenable chronology, provenance and even authorship.[24]

Mernissi agrees with this in principle: multiple citations each with a different transmission chain "generally strengthens a *Hadith* and gives the impression of consensus concerning it."[25]

One of Schacht's main hypotheses was that Companion-supported reports were more likely to be of later origin than Successor-supported reports.[26]

(d) Charting isnāds

With such a methodology, it is possible to chart the links (and therefore possible authenticity) of any particular Hadith. For example, Hadiths reporting the efforts by Abū Bakr and 'Umar to gather up the fragments of the Qur'an and organize them into orderly chapters[27]

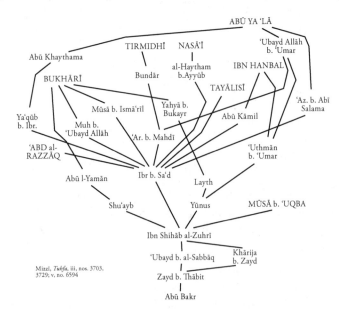

ILLUSTRATION 11: Series of Transmission Chains

Although this appears to be well supported, Juynboll is not convinced. If a chain is only as strong as its weakest link, then a chain of transmitters is only as reliable as each reporter.

"The totally obscure, and therefore probably fictitious, transmitter ʿUbayd b. al-Sabbāq, may conceivably be held responsible for the skeleton of the wording as well as for this strand, *if* that is not the handiwork of an unidentifiable transmitter higher up in the bundle who is evidently responsible for the Khārija b. Zayd strand. As for the historicity of details, one does well to treat the report with caution."[28]

By contrast, the report on ʿUthmān's attempts at collating the Qurʾanic text look like this (see Illustration 12).[29] Juynboll comments that this "is even more swamped by typically ahistorical or, differently put, topical embellishments."[30]

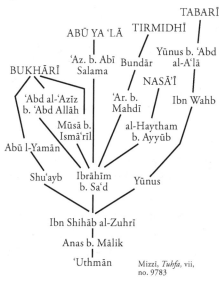

ILLUSTRATION 12: Transmission Chains for a Hadith about Collating the Quʾan

In the eyes of Juynboll, at least, the *isnāds* have questionable reliability. He echoes the earlier assessment of Margoliouth: "In spite … of the conscientious labours of those who had collected the saying of the Prophet and ultimately perpetuated them in canonical digests, it is doubtful whether we can in any case be confident that the sayings attributed to the Prophet were actually his."[31]

Perhaps later manuscript discoveries may throw more light onto this complex question. Of course, establishing a definitive list of *isnāds* could be a two-edged sword. "Once highly credible chains of authorities were universally accepted, it was not difficult to fabricate 'proper' or 'sound' traditions that led all the way back to the Prophet."[32]

(e) Positive assessments of the isnāds

Not all scholars are as negative as Juynboll and Margoliouth. To those who suggest a wholesale rejection of all Hadith, Burton cautions: "If ... the counterfeit testifies to the existence of the genuine coin, pseudo-*Hadith* imitates real *Hadith*, otherwise the exercise is pointless."[33] The two following issues must be considered.

1. Linguistic considerations

Some find some encouragement about the reliability of the Hadith in the Arab attitude toward language. Names in particular and language in general appear to have a deep significance for Arab culture. Other cultures, particularly modern Western culture, may see the relationship between an entity (e.g., an object or a concept) and its name as quite arbitrary—simply an accident of history or a literary convention. Watt cites the story in the Qur'an of how Adam gave names to things.[34] In the biblical story, Adam allocated the names himself,[35] but in the Qur'anic version Allah has to teach these names to Adam before he can tell them to the angels. Yusuf Ali comments in a footnote: "'The names of things:' according to commentators means the inner nature and qualities of things."[36] Watt concurs: "It seems to be presupposed here that knowledge of the name includes a knowledge of the real nature of a thing and that there is a closer link than mere convention between the name and nature of the thing."[37] He goes on to draw a conclusion for the transmission of Hadiths. "[This] led later Muslim scholars to insist on adherence to the precise verbal form in Traditions; they held it unsatisfactory to give the sense of an anecdote in other words ... there was always something God-given about language."[38] It implies that those who heard Muhammad's words, and then passed them on to others, would have been meticulous in preserving the identical terms.

And the Companions of the Prophet, who first heard him, were so highly regarded. Muhammad had told the early Muslims that "you are the best community brought out of mankind"[39] and "the best of my followers are those living in my generation (i.e., my contemporaries), and then those who will follow the latter."[40] The ninth-century hadith critic Abū Zurʿa al-Rāzī extrapolated this to state that anyone who criticized a Companion was a heretic.[41]

2. Recent Western scholarship
Some more recent Western scholarship has been less dismissive of the *isnād* system. In 1997, Madelung noted that "work with the narrative sources, both those that have been available to historians for a long time and others which have been published recently, made it plain that their wholesale rejection as late fiction is unjustified."[42] A year later, Donner questioned the ability of the early Muslim community to secretly engineer "a comprehensive redaction of the tradition as a whole into a unified form," declaring that no evidence of such a united effort exists.[43]

Harald Motzki has challenged the argument *e silentio* used by the Orientalist and Revisionist scholars. If the earliest sources did not quote a certain hadith, we cannot automatically assume that it did not exist, as Schacht, Juynboll, and Crone had concluded. He used a wider range of sources, dating the common links to the period of the Companions, and concluded that the major hadith transmitters reliably passed on what they had heard.[44] Not all observers, however, have held such a high view of those responsible for transmitting the Hadith.

2. THE RELIABILITY OF THE TRANSMITTERS

(a) The main contributors

The Hadith collections did not have a wide base of contributors (see Table 11). Sixty percent of al-Bukhārī's Hadith came from only four individuals, and seventeen narrators provided eighty-three percent of its content:[45]

NAME OF NARRATORS	NO. OF HADITHS	% OF TOTAL
'Ā'isha	1250	17.68%
Abu Hurayra	1100	15.56%
Ibn 'Umar	1100	15.56%
'Anas Ibn Mālik	900	12.73%
'Abdullāh Ibn 'Abbās	700	9.9%
Zubair Ibn 'Abdullāh	275	3.89%
Abu Mūsa al-'Ash'ari	165	2.33%
Abu Sa'īd al Khudri	130	1.84%
'Ali Ibn Abu Tālib	79	1.11%
'Umar Ibn Khattāb	50	0.71%
Umm Salāmah	48	0.68%
'Abdullāh Ibn Mas'ūd	45	0.64%
Mu'āwiyah Ibn Abu Sufyān	10	0.14%
Hassan Ibn 'Ali	8	0.11%
'Ali Ibn Husayn	6	0.08%
Husayn Ibn 'Ali	2	0.03%

TABLE 11: Main Narrators Cited in al-Bukhāri's Hadith

What is remarkable about this list is the absence of many of those who were closest to Muhammad, such as the first three rightly guided Caliphs Abū Bakr, 'Umar, 'Uthmān, and others such as Zaid bin Thābit, Bilāl bin Rabāḥ, and Salmān al-Farsi. Brown notes that they contributed to the other major collections of the Hadith, but only in small numbers: Abū Bakr was the source of 142, 'Umar of 537, and 'Alī of 536 hadiths.[46]

Although the collectors of the Hadith had strict criteria regarding acceptable sources, their assessments were not always accepted by others. Siddiqui notes: "All the Islamic authorities agree that an enormous amount of forgery was committed in the *Hadith* literature." However he rejects the suggestion that the whole Hadith corpus was due to later redaction. "It is more likely … that it originated during the lifetime of the Prophet himself."[47]

(b) Challenging individual transmitters

Even when an early date for transmission is accepted, the reliability of the main transmitters of al-Bukhārī's Hadith have been questioned. Mernissi has disputed the reliability of the Companion Abū Hurayra,[48] who is the source of 5,300 Hadith in the six collections. He had only known Muhammad for the last three years of the Prophet's life.[49] He contributed too many accounts which she considers anti-women.[50] The commentator Imām Muhammad ibn Bahādur al-Zarkashi (d.794/1392) recorded the following:

"They told Aisha that Abu Hurayra was asserting that the Messenger of God said: 'Three things bring bad luck: house, woman, and horse.' Aisha responded: 'Abu Hurayra learned his lessons very badly. He came into our house when the Prophet was in the middle of a sentence. He only heard the end of it. What the Prophet said was: 'May God refute the Jews; they say three things bring bad luck: horse, woman, and house.'"[51]

Abū Hurayra reported only the last part. This is not a "single-strand" Hadith, for it is reported by two informants, 'Abdullāh bin 'Umar and Sahl bin Sa'd Sa'īdi,[52] but this does not obviate the possibility of Abū Hurayra's mishearing of the Prophet's words. Abū Hurayra was not the only Companion who allegedly misheard the Prophet. Reporting on Rafi' bin Khadij's transmission of Muhammad's statement about non-rental of farms, Zaid b. Thābit said, "May Allah forgive Rafi'! I am more aware of the Hadith than he; what happened was that two of the Ansar (Helpers) had a dispute, so they

> **MUHAMMAD AND DOGS**
>
> Ibn 'Umar reported that, to Muhammad's statement about a Muslim's loss of reward for owning dogs except sheep dogs and hunting hounds,[53] Abū Huraira had added the words "or field-dogs" *au zar'in*.[54] This caused Ibn 'Umar to observe that "Abu Huraira owned cultivated land."[55] A farmer would use guard dogs for protecting his fields and crops. Yet the Prophet's anti-canine bias was reported elsewhere. In Tirmidhi's collection of the Hadith, 'Abdullāh ibn Mughaffal relates Muhammad's saying: "Were dogs not a species of creature I should command that they all be killed; but kill every pure black one."[56]

came to the Prophet (may Allah bless him and grant him peace), who said after listening to their cases, 'If this is your position, then do not rent the farms.' Rafi' has only heard the last phrase, i.e., 'Do not rent the farms.'"[57]

Al-Zuhri also reported: "Rafi' is mistaken."[58]

It is not only modern commentators who have criticized Abū Hurayra: one of his contemporaries referred to him as a "guinea pig who has come down ... from the mountain."[59] He was described by 'Umar as "the worst liar among the muḥaddithūn ('narrators of Hadith')."[60] When Abū Hurayra claimed that Muhammad said that the impurity of sex meant a person could not fast after dawn without a wash, he was challenged by the Prophet's wives. "Abu Hurayra then confessed, under pressure, that he had not heard it directly from the Prophet, but from someone else. He reconsidered what he had said, and later it was learned that just before his death he completely retracted his words."[61]

Yet he did not like to be challenged by others. When Abū Saʿīd al-Khudri corrected Abū Hurayra's recollection of a Prophetic saying they had both heard, Abū Hurayra retorted: "That man will be the last person of the people of Paradise to enter Paradise."[62]

Apparently additions were made betraying the bias of the transmitters (see Sidebar *Muhammad and Dogs*).

One time this same transmitter admitted that he had fabricated or at least added to a saying of Muhammad's. After he had quoted a supposed maxim of the Prophet about giving alms and financial support, "The people said, 'O Abu Hurayra! Did you hear that from Allah's Apostle?' He said, 'No, it is from my own self.'"[63]

Questions have also been raised about Muhammad's cousin Ibn ʿAbbās, who was only thirteen at the time of the Prophet's death, and ʿAnas Ibn Mālik, who was nineteen. These two were the sources of the "miracle" hadiths attributed to Muhammad.[64]

Other possible significant contributors, such as Muhammad's earliest biographer, Ibn Isḥāq, were notable by their absence. Guillaume notes that "al-Bukhāri, though he often mentions [Ibn Isḥāq] in the headings of his chapters, hardly if ever cites him for the matter of a tradition, unless that tradition is supported by another *isnād*. Muslim [the Hadith collector], who classifies traditions as genuine,

good, and weak, puts [Ibn Isḥāq] in the second category."
Guillaume continues: "To anyone with an historical sense this
was a monstrous injustice, but it must be remembered that by the
middle of the third century the form of a Hadith mattered more
than its substance, and provided that the chain of guarantors was
unexceptionable anything could be included."[65]

Others have differed about Ibn Isḥāq. Brown notes that he "was
a very controversial figure. Mālik, Ibn al-Qattān, Ibn Hanbal, and
others rejected him because he accepted hadiths from questionable narrators as well as Christians and Jews. But Shuʿba felt he was
impeccably reliable."[66]

Criticism of the isnād system was neatly sidestepped by the mystic
Bāyazīd al-Bistāmi (d.260/874). Like many Sufis he believed that
information, including hadiths, could be received by adepts directly
from Allah through *kashf* (unveiling) instead of unreliable human
transmission methods. He retorted to his critics: "You take your
knowledge dead from the dead, but I take my knowledge from the
Living One who does not die."[67]

While the historian Edward Gibbon characterized the first statement of the *shahāda* ("There is no god but God") as an "eternal
truth," he classified the Hadith collections as a "necessary fiction."[68]

The historical reliability of the Hadith will continue to be the
subject of scholarly debate. How the content of the Hadith accounts
differs from biblical presentations of the same or similar topics is our
next subject.

NOTES

1 Tabbarah, *Spirit of Islam*, 472.

2 Brown, *Hadith*, 174.

3 E.g., M. S. M. Saifullah and Elias Karim, "Explosive Increase of
Isnad & Its Implications" from www.islamic-awareness.org/
Hadith/exisnad.html cited on July 8, 2013. Also Assad Rustom,
quoted Tabbarah, *The Spirit of Islam: Doctrine and Teachings*, 472.

4 ʿAbdur-Raheem Green, "The history of isnad," http://thetruereligion.
org/modules/wfsection/article.php?articleid=259&page=10, cited
January 31, 2007.

5   Danner, *Islamic Tradition*, 116.

6   Based on Ibn Abi Hatim al-Razi, *Al-Jarh wa l-Ta'dil* (8 vols, Hyderabad, 1360-1373), 1:20. Cited in www.islamic-awareness.org/Hadith/Ulum/aape.html (accessed July 8, 2013).

7   Wansbrough, *Quranic Studies*, 179.

8   Holland, *In the Shadow of the Sword*, 407.

9   Tabbarah, *Spirit of Islam*, 472.

10   Brown, *Rethinking*, 98.

11   Guillaume, *Traditions*, 13.

12   Goldziher, *Muslim Studies*.

13   Schacht, *Origins*.

14   Taken from Juynboll, "Hadith and the Qur'an," 380.

15   Ibid., 379.

16   Sachedina, "The Qur'ān and other religions," 299.

17   Juynboll, 381.

18   Ibid., 389.

19   Ibid., 380.

20   Ibid., 381.

21   Ibid., 381.

22   Patai, *Arab Mind*, 71.

23   Juynboll, 379.

24   Juynboll, 379.

25   Mernissi, "Women's Rights," 123. Significantly she then goes on to question Hadiths which are supported by this principle.

26   Rubin, *Eye of the Beholder*, 233-38.

27   E.g., B.6:509.

28   Ibid., 383.

29   Ibid., 384.

30   Ibid., 383.

31   Margoliouth, *Mohammed*, 13.

32   Firestone, *Jihad*, 95.

33   Burton, *Introduction*, xii.

34   Q.2.30-33.

35   Gen 2:19,20.

36   Ali, *The Holy Qur'ān: English translation*, 15.

37 Watt, *Islamic Revelation*, 35.

38 Ibid., 35.

39 Q.3:110.

40 B.3:819, 820; 4:757; 5:2,3; 8:436, 437, 652, 686.

41 Brown, *Hadith,* 87.

42 Madelung, *Succession,* xi.

43 Donner, *Narratives,* 27.

44 Brown, *Hadith,* 226.

45 http://islamicsystem.blogspot.com/2007/11/refutation-of-gadaffi-others-who-reject.html (accessed May 18, 2010). Al-Bukhāri draws on about 2,000 narrators, according to Brown, *Hadith,* 32.

46 Brown, *Hadith,* 20.

47 Siddiqui, *Hadith Literature*, 31–32.

48 Also spelled "Hurayra" or "Hurairah." This is a nickname, meaning "Father of the little female kitten," since he was supposed to have carried a small cat around. His real name was 'Abd al-Raḥmān ibn Ṣakhr Al-Azdi.

49 Brown, *Hadith,* 19.

50 Mernissi, "Women's Rights in Islam," 112-126.

51 Imām Muhammad ibn Bahādur al-Zarkashi *Al-Ijaba ma istadrakathu 'A'isha 'ala al-ṣaḥaba [Collection of 'A'isha's Corrections to the Statements of the Companions]*, 2nd ed. (Beirut: Al-Maktab al-Islami, 1980), 113, cited in Mernissi, "Women's Rights in Islam," 123.

52 B.4:110, 111.

53 B.3:516.

54 B.3:515.

55 Guillaume, *The Traditions of Islam*, 78.

56 Tirmidhi Hadith no. 1109 cited in Siddiqui, *Hadith Literature,* 128.

57 Cited in www.islamic-awareness.org/Hadith/Ulum/asb6.html (accessed July 8, 2013).

58 B.5:349.

59 B.4:80.2; 5:544, 545.

60 Bennett, *In Search of Muhammad*, 26.

61 Mernissi, "Women's Rights in Islam," 122.

62 B.9:532.1.

63 B.7:268.

64   Bennett, *In Search of Muhammad*, 46. See ch. 4, part 4, section (l).

65   Ibn Ishaq, *Sira*, xxxv.

66   Brown, *Hadith*, 86.

67   'Abd al-Wahhāb al-Sha'rānī *Al-Tabaqāt al-kubrā*, 11, cited in Brown, *Hadith*, 195.

68   Edward Gibbon, *Decline and Fall of the Roman Empire*, vol. III, 488, cited in Zwemer, *The Muslim Doctrine of God*, 16.

II

CONTRASTS WITH
BIBLICAL TEACHING

While the Bible and Hadith appear to share much in common, it would be naive in the utmost to simply stop at the similarities. Tariq Ramadhan cautions against drawing facile conclusions based on perceptible parallels. "One should nevertheless beware of apparent analogies. Indeed, the prophets' stories, and in particular Abraham's, are recounted in an apparently similar manner in the Jewish, Christian, and Muslim traditions. Yet a closer study reveals that *the accounts are different and do not always tell the same facts nor teach the same lessons.*"*

---

*   Ramadhan, *The Messenger*, 6 (emphasis mine).

9

DIFFERING VIEWS OF GOD

THERE ARE SOME SIGNIFICANT DIFFERENCES in the percep-
tions of God presented in the Hadith and those found in the Bible.

1. THE LOVE OF GOD

The Hadith displays a deity whose *ḥubb* (love) seems limited to particular individuals. It appears that this love is a rare enough event to
warrant a heavenly proclamation:

"If Allah loves a person, He calls Gabriel saying, 'Allah loves so
and-so; O Gabriel! Love him.' Gabriel would love him and make an
announcement amongst the inhabitants of the Heaven. 'Allah loves
so-and-so, therefore you should love him also,' and so all the inhabitants of the Heaven would love him, and then he is granted the
pleasure of the people on the earth."[1]

Consequently Muhammad often invoked Allah to love his grandson al-Ḥasan, e.g., "O Allah! I love him, so please love him and love
those who love him." Divine love for everyone is not assumed. This
contrasts with the New Testament view of God's indiscriminate love
to all, including sinners.[2]

From a broader Islamic perspective, Christian love toward others also reaches into uncharted territory. German diplomat and convert to Islam Murad Hoffman reports that love for one's fellow man is not as absolute. "Islam teaches that the love of God must translate into compassion for man. However, Muslims are a bit more hesitant when it goes to use the word 'love'. In general they prefer to designate the same attitude as brother- and sisterhood."[3] Mahally arrives at the same result based on a statistical analysis of the Arabic version of the Hadith collections.

> Bukhāri lists 95 uses of *love* and 36 of *loved*. Muslim lists 22 usages of *love* and 4 for *loved*. Abū Dawud lists only 10 for *love*, one for *loved*. Malik's Muwatta lists *love* 12 times and *loved* 4 times. Considering the substantial amount of material in their texts, even in abbreviated form, this seems rather limited. Most of these have to do with human love or love of things and only a limited number referring to God's love. This is in distinct contrast with the Bible, which list 409 uses of *love*. The New Testament alone lists 223 uses.[4]

This difference is reflected in the Hadith's teaching, tentatively echoing (but certainly limiting) the Golden Rule: "The Prophet said, 'None of you will have faith till he wishes for his (Muslim) brother what he likes for himself.'"[5] The use of the adjectival modifier "(Muslim)" is significant. Muhsin Khan's translation of al-Bukhāri's Hadith occasionally contains such bracketed insertions. Through their use, he differentiates between possible meanings. In this particular case, the term "brother" is judged to apply only to fellow Muslims. In most of its 219 occurrences in al-Bukhāri's Hadith, "brother" refers to a male sibling, or another Muslim. In some other cases, a brother is bracketed as "(another person)."[6] Only once does it designate a non-believer,[7] where the specific phrase "pagan brother" is used. However, it is applied to the Ethiopian Negus as well.[8] Although he was a Christian, his generous treatment of the Muslims fleeing persecution in Mecca earned him this fraternal label. But in the more general case cited above (i.e., B.1:12), the important scholar Ibn Hajar Asqalani in his commentary on al-Bukhāri's Hadith, called *Fath al-Bari* collection, specifies that only fellow Muslims should be loved. He cites the source "according to Ismaili through Roh from Husain: 'until he loves for his Muslim brother what he loves for himself of goodness,' explaining the meaning of brother-hood and pointing the direction of love."[9] Concerning the equivalent Hadith cited by ṣaḥīḥ Muslim, Al-Nawawi in his commentary *Al Minhaj bi Sharh ṣaḥīḥ Muslim* notes that the hadith variant using the word "neighbor" is of uncertain trustworthiness, and that the word "brother" is more reliable.[10]

2. THE GRACE OF GOD

The grace of God in the Hadith is more sparingly dispensed than in the Bible. The word "grace" is found in only four of al-Bukhāri's Hadith. Three of them present a positive message, using the verbs *āwa,* "he gave refuge,"[11] or *'an'am,* "he showed grace."[12] However, one is negative: Allah withholds his grace from a man who withholds superfluous water.[13] The Bible has a rich, frequently used vocabulary of "grace," including the Hebrew *chen* (occurs 70 times), *chesed* (250 times), and the Greek *charis* (156 times). In the Bible, divine grace is not restricted to believers only, but is bestowed on all humanity with-out discrimination.[14] The biblical view presents a God who is more than just beneficent, as though reactively providing life's necessities to those who need them. This may become the spiritual equivalent of a tolerance which simply accepts the existence of another, like an aloof philanthropist who gives anonymously without direct contact, fearing the demands it may make. The Christian view of God is of one who is proactive and involved, seeking out the deeper needs of humanity and responding to them personally.

3. THE PRAISE OF GOD

The Bible teaches that God is concerned for his own glory, which he will give to no other.[15] The proper human response to the glory of God is a life of praise and worship.[16] The Hadith's view is different

ILLUSTRATION 13:
Daily Worship is a Pillar of Islam[j]

and somewhat puzzling. It proclaims: "None loves to be praised more than Allah does, and this is why He praises Himself."[17]

The impression is of a deity who is searching for adoration, and will even provide himself what is lacking. Human worship is not sufficient for him, even when accompanied by the jinn.[18] Allah's desire for human recognition is presented in a widely quoted but disputed saying: "I was a hidden treasure: I wanted to be known. Hence I created the world so that I would be known."[19] Although the following terms are not applied specifically to Allah, the absolute monotheism of Islam could result in the "lonely Monad" described by Kaiser, or even "an autistic God, not a personal God who exists (primordially) in relation to other persons."[20] An alternative explanation could be the extreme decretal doctrine that all that transpires is absolutely predestined by God, making him the author of every human action. "No creature [even] partakes in the confession of God's oneness. God alone confesses the oneness of God."[21] Consequently people are told that Allah has no need of the worlds[22] and no need of you.[23]

4. EXTREME PREDESTINATION

Much has been written on the Islamic view of *qadr* (predestination), from the early Qadarites and Mu'tazilites who proposed some form of human free will, to the more orthodox and prescriptive views presented by the Ash'arites and al-Ghazāli. The Hadith present God as predetermining each person's actions even before he or she was born. After a child's conception, an angel asks four questions: "(O Lord!) Will it be a male or female, a wretched or a blessed,

---

j   http://fivepillarsofislamandwhattheydo.blogspot.com/

and how much will his provision be? And what will his age be?"[24] The divine reply comes and the angel "is ordered to write down his (i.e. the new creature's) deeds, his livelihood, his (date of) death, and whether he will be blessed or wretched (in religion). Then the soul is breathed into him…. So all that is written while the child is still in the mother's womb"[25] (see Illustration 14).

ILLUSTRATION 14: The Hadith Present a Strong View of Divine Predestination[k]

When born, each person must act out his or her written decrees, much like an actor performing to a script authored by someone else: just after he created the heavens and the earth, Allah "wrote everything in the Book."[26] This includes a person's sins, such as marital infidelity. "Allah has written for Adam's son his share of adultery which he commits inevitably."[27] Even good and generous deeds have already been decided by Allah, who said: "Vowing does not bring to the son of Adam anything I have not already written in his fate, but vowing is imposed on him by way of foreordainment. Through vowing I make a miser spend of his wealth."[28] Muhammad warned his opponent Musailama: "You cannot avoid what Allah has ordained for you."[29]

Prior to his or her birth, the person's ultimate destiny has also been determined. "There is none among you, and no created soul but has his place written for him either in Paradise or in the Hell-Fire, and also has his happy or miserable fate (in the Hereafter) written for him."[30] It is no use trying to escape this fate, for Allah "creates for Hell (Fire) whomever He will, and they will be thrown into it."[31] A person's lifestyle might prove deceptive. "A man amongst you may do good deeds till there is only a cubit between him and Paradise and *then what has been written for him decides his behavior* and he starts doing (evil) deeds characteristic

---

k   http://gambar24.blogspot.com/2010/04/we-have-indeed-revealed-this-message-in.html

of the people of the (Hell) Fire. And similarly a man amongst you may do (evil) deeds till there is only a cubit between him and the (Hell) Fire, and *then what has been written for him decides his behavior,* and he starts doing deeds characteristic of the people of Paradise."[32] Muhammad told a man: "You cannot avoid the fate you are destined to, by Allah"[33] for "He raises and lowers (whomever He will)."[34]

This led some to question the value of even trying to do good, for "there is none amongst you but has been assigned a place (either) in Paradise and (or) in the Hell-Fire."[35] A man asked Muhammad: "O Allah's Apostle! Shall we depend upon what is written for us and give up doing (good) deeds? For whoever among us is destined to be fortunate (in the Hereafter), will join the fortunate peoples and whoever among us is destined to be miserable will do such deeds as are characteristic of the people who are destined to misery."[36]

Muhammad's reply was that one should simply do what he or she found easy to do, "for that too was prepared by Allah."

He also said, "Those who are destined to be happy (in the Hereafter) will find it easy and pleasant to do the deeds characteristic of those destined to happiness, while those who are to be among the miserable (in the Hereafter), will find it easy to do the deeds characteristic of those destined to misery." Then he recited: "As for him who gives (in charity) and keeps his duty to Allah and believes in the Best reward from Allah, We will make smooth for him the path of ease. But he who is a greedy miser and thinks himself self-sufficient, and gives the lie to the Best reward from Allah we will make smooth for him the path for evil." (Q.92.5-10)

"Everybody will find easy such deeds as will lead him to his destined place."[37]

When asked about those who die young, Muhammad replied that Allah would know what they were going to do in their lives.[38] Informed that his own grandson was on the verge of death, the comfort he offered to his grieving daughter was to send back the messenger to tell her: "It is for Allah what He takes, and it is for Allah what He gives, and everything has its fixed time (limit). So (she should) be patient and look for Allah's reward."[39] A woman seeking a divorce for a complex marital situation would be advised that "she will have nothing but what Allah has written for her."[40]

This view of predestination can sometimes become a means of endorsing the status quo, leading to passivity. If the plague strikes a town, a Muslim need not leave, since "nothing will befall him except what Allah has written for him then he will get such reward as that of a martyr."[41] If a person absent-mindedly ate or drank during a fast, he should still complete the fast, "for Allah has made him eat and drink."[42]

It can also be a way of avoiding responsibility for one's actions, or inaction. When Muhammad asked 'Ali if he would join him in the optional *tahajjud* nighttime prayers, Ali responded with: "O Allah's Apostle! Our souls are in the hands of Allah and if He wants us to get up He will make us get up."[43] The Prophet was unimpressed with such logic. He left the house striking his thigh and reciting the verse: "But man is more quarrelsome than anything."[44] The same logic was used by Adam. Due to his sin of eating the forbidden fruit,[45] he was accused by Moses of causing humanity to be turned out of paradise and for making people miserable. Adam's response was clear: "Do you blame me for action which Allah had written in my fate forty years before my creation?" Muhammad concludes: "So Adam overcame Moses with this argument."[46]

Paradoxically, the application of this severe decretalism is that Muslims should be forceful rather than tentative in their demands of Allah. Muhammad said, "Whenever anyone of you invoke [sic] Allah for something, he should be firm in his asking, and he should not say: 'If You wish, give me ...' for none can compel Allah to do something against His Will."[47]

The biblical concept of predestination seems less prescriptive. Although the term "predestined" never occurs in the Old Testament, it is clear that God is sovereign over all things,[48] and that he has a plan to fulfill his purposes.[49] To carry out this program, he has chosen nations (e.g., Israel),[50] groups of people (e.g., Levites),[51] individuals such as kings[52] and prophets,[53] and even foreign leaders.[54] They are each selected for a specific task or function, but the choice is connected with the concept of love.[55]

This is never a random or purposeless choice. There is frequently an element of calling or invitation to take on the responsibility.[56]

The interplay between divine sovereignty and human choice is subtly drawn out. King Saul is described as chosen by God[57] and chosen by the people.[58] Samuel describes Saul to Israel as "the king you have chosen, the one you asked for; see, the LORD has set a king over you."[59] Even the chosen people were required to confirm their status by themselves choosing to serve the Lord.[60] Election, or being chosen, cannot lead to complacency, but should result in higher standards of righteousness. "You only have I chosen of all the families of the earth; therefore I will punish you for all your sins."[61]

The chosen ones may fail to fulfill their calling and lose their chosen status, as did King Saul,[62] for there is usually a standard of performance expected in each role. A failure to reach such a standard is not due to a lack of ability or willingness on God's part, but is the result of human intransigence.[63] In the face of such human inability, God himself became involved and "his own arm worked salvation."[64] Although the chosen ones (whether an individual or a nation) may suffer temporary setbacks and even apparent defeat, they are promised eventual victory and success if they persevere and are faithful.[65] But the glory will go to the Lord who has facilitated this outcome by divine preparation[66] or a promise of divine provision, protection, or enabling.[67]

Most of these themes are continued in the New Testament. Jesus, God's chosen one,[68] designates the Twelve (representing a New Israel)[69] and declares them the light of the world.[70] The church is called "the chosen people"[71] whom God predestined "in love"[72] and "included in Christ."[73] They are called to live holy lives in response.[74] Yet this divine choice can appear counterintuitive,[75] often bringing pain and suffering to those who are chosen.[76] The word "predestined" and its cognates occur in only six verses of the New Testament.[77]

Zwemer finds the difference between biblical and Islamic views in their understanding of God. "Mohammedan Fatalism is distinguished, still more radically, from even ultra-Calvinistic views of predestination, when we consider in each case the *source* of the decrees and their ultimate *object*. IN ISLAM THERE IS NO FATHERHOOD OF GOD AND NO PURPOSE OF REDEMPTION TO SOFTEN THE DOCTRINE OF THE DECREES."[78]

We also find a dissimilarity in depth and scope. The Bible does not present God's decrees as dictating the minutiae of existence, as in the Hadith, but the Bible concerns itself with significant earthly roles and eternal salvation. According to Sedgwick, the response of the recipients of divine election should differ greatly. "The Pauline note would always be 'Rejoice in your salvation', whereas the Islamic note would be 'Submit yourself to your destiny.'"[79]

5. ANTHROPOMORPHISMS

In accord with Bible and the Qur'an (see Table 12), the Hadith mention several parts of the body attributed to God. His right hand is described as "full ... not affected by the continuous spending night and day"[80] and his other hand as holding "the balance of justice."[81] He holds the heavens and the earth between His hands. He is also depicted as writing in "His Book which is with Him on His Throne."[82] The throne of Allah is also mentioned over thirty times, implying a sitting action.[83] After the judgment, Allah will put his foot on hell to make it smaller.[84] Allah is said to "turn his face" from those who turn their faces from him.[85] He is one who "sees and hears."[86]

At the judgment, the part of Allah's body which Muslims recognize will be his "shin" *sāq*, which he will uncover at their request.[87] Muslims are almost encouraged to speculate or visualize how Allah may appear, for Allah's form will be "a shape nearest to the picture they had in their minds about Him."[88]

GOD ...	OLD TESTAMENT	NEW TESTAMENT	QUR'AN
has a hand	Ex.7:4	Mk.16:19	Q.3:26
has a face	2.Chr.7:14	Mt.18:10	Q.18:28
sees (eyes)	Gen.16:13	Mt.6:4	Q.3:163
hears (ears)	Ex.3:7	1.Jn.5:14	Q.34:50
speaks (mouth)	Ex.20:1	Heb.1:1	Q.2:253
sits on the throne	Ps.47:8	Rev.6:16	Q.7:54

TABLE 12: Anthropomorphic Language in the Bible and Qur'an

The references to God's bodily parts have created a dilemma for Islamic scholars. The heterodox Kurdish group known as the *Kakai* or *Ahl-e Haqq* believes that "God has appeared in human form at different times since the beginning of creation."[89] The Karramiyah sect advocated that God is a substance, and some believed that he even had a body.[90] Its founder was alleged to hold "the doctrine of anthropomorphism (*tajsīm, tashbīh*) to an extreme degree"[91] based on Muhammad's apparently clear statements that "You will definitely see your Lord with your own eyes"[92] and "there will be no … screen to screen Him."[93] However, Muhammad then qualifies this idea: "there will be nothing to prevent the people from seeing their Lord except the Cover of Majesty over His Face."[94] Aly notes that more orthodox groups have chosen to interpret such references purely metaphorically, claiming that God's "hand" simply means his power, control, or assistance. Another school is uncertain whether the terms are metaphorical, but is still convinced that God does not resemble his creation. It is argued that "God has a hand, but it is totally unlike anything humans can understand. The precise meaning of 'Hand' is a mystery."[95] They assert that God can have a face, eyes, and hands, and sit on His throne *bila kayf wa la tashbih*, "without asking how or making comparisons,"[96] or in Imām Aḥmad's parallel terminology "without 'how' and without 'meaning' (*bi la kayfa wa la ma'na*)."[97] Allah is described in such terms without "qualification" *takyīf* or "attempting to explain how a certain attribute or quality could be, while such knowledge lies only with Allah."[98] In the Qur'an, only God knows the unseen.[99]

A classic threefold denial involves stating that these are God's qualities (*ṣifāt*) "without *Ta'wīl* (interpreting their meanings into different things) or *Tashbīh* (giving resemblance or similarity to any of the creatures) or *Ta'tīl* (completely ignoring or denying them i.e. there is no Face, or Eyes, or Hands, or Shins for Allāh). These qualities befit for Allāh alone."[100] To these, the theologian Ibn Taymiyyah added that Allah can have these characteristics without "comparison" *tamthīl*, i.e., "supposing that divine attributes resemble those of creation," and without "distortion" *taḥrīf*, i.e., "applying an allegorical meaning which will inevitably be incorrect since it is not based on knowledge."[101] The semantic hedges which later Muslim theologians have so elaborately constructed around the Islamic concept of anthro-pomorphism have cast doubt on its meaning. Muhammad's promise of clearly seeing Allah in paradise seems, in the memorable phrase of Anthony Flew, to die "the death by a thousand qualifications."[102] A reader may wonder why such human analogies were used at all.

The theologian al-Ghazāli took this a stage further, applying the "non-comparison with human categories" argument to divine actions. "Allah's justice is not to be compared with the justice of man. A Man may be supposed to act unjustly by invading the posi-tion of another, but no injustice can be conceived on the part of Allah. It is in his power to pour down torrents upon mankind and if he were to do it, his justice would not be arraigned. There is noth-ing he can be tied to, to perform, nor can any injustice be supposed of him, nor can he be under obligation to any person whatever."[103] Likewise Allah is "the Proud" *(almutakabbir),*[104] yet people who are "proud" *(almutakabbirīn)* will be cast into hell.[105] The "blasphemers" *(alladhīna kafarū)* "schemed" *(makarū),*[106] an apparently pejora-tive term, yet Allah is described as "the best of schemers" *(khayr al-mākirīn).*[107] If a word such as "justice," "proud," or "scheming" has one meaning when applied to humanity and quite a different connotation when applied to Allah, then the whole field of seman-tics is compromised.[108]

6. THE PERSON AND NATURE OF CHRIST

Of concern to some Christians is the portrayal of Christ in the Hadith. Zwemer laments that: "with regret it must be admitted that there is hardly an important fact concerning the life, person, and work of our Savior which is not ignored, perverted or denied by Islam."[109] The Qur'anic designations of Jesus as the "word" of or from God[110] and "a spirit coming from Allah"[111] are repeated in the Hadith but without any comment or explanation.[112] The prom-ising portrayal of Christ in the Qur'an as the virgin-born miracle worker is not developed in the Hadith. Jesus is cast in the image of an Islamic prophet,[113] clearly inferior to Muhammad (see Figure 8).[114] The Qur'anic miracle of the child Jesus speaking from the cradle[115] is diminished somewhat by the revelation that this was not unique—two other babies did the same thing.[116] When grown, Jesus was reported to have been of moderate height, red-faced "as if he had just come out of the bathroom" (although this is denied in another Hadith as confusing him with Al-Dajjal, for Jesus had a brown face), broad-chested, having either curly or lank hair (the accounts differ), and water dribbling from his head (there is no explanation attached to the latter phenomenon). Nor is it explained why he should be walking between two men, with his hands on their shoulders, while circumambulating the Ka'ba. Was this some depiction of weakness?[117]

The purpose of these descriptions is not certain. Perhaps they were simply to satisfy curiosity, as were the descriptions of other prophets, e.g., Moses and Abraham. They were certainly not given as a guide for artists, as physical depictions of the prophets, or any living thing, are forbidden in Islam. What is significant is how they differ from the biblical descriptions of Jesus after his ascension. The body of Christ is described in glorious terms, with noble dress, powerful voice, dazzling features, and an impressive impact which inspires worship.[118] He is reminiscent of the apocalyptic "son of man" figure of old.[119] The mundane descriptions of the Hadith imply that he was no more than a man, and this is consistent with the Islamic view of Christ. As in the Qur'an,[120] Jesus is called a "pious slave"[121] or "one of Allah's slaves"[122] (see Sidebar *Jesus is Just a Slave*).

Muhammad reported that he met Jesus during the *mi'raj*,

JESUS IS JUST A SLAVE

The Hadith are clear to limit the role of Jesus to no more than human terms. He is a "soul" or "spirit created by Allah."[126] Muhammad warned his followers: "Do not exaggerate in praising me as the Christians praised the son of Mary."[127] This appears to be a restatement or variant of some Qur'anic verses, and concurs with the Qur'anic concept: "It is not for God to take a son unto him."[128] Along with the Qur'an,[129] Ibn 'Umar specifically denies the lordship of Christ, with his saying: "I do not know of a greater thing, as regards to ascribing partners in worship, etc. to Allah, than that a lady should say that Jesus is her Lord although he is just one of Allah's slaves."[130]

his ascent to the heaven. Rather than occupying the highest place, seated at the right hand of the Majesty,[123] Jesus is encountered in the company of John the Baptist, far below in the second of the seven heavens, one heaven above Adam in the first heaven, but beneath Enoch in the third, Joseph in the fourth, Aaron in the fifth, Moses in the sixth, and Abraham in the seventh heaven nearest to the divine throne.[124]

An alternative explanation may be that Jesus was on his way back to earth.[125] It is stated that when Jesus returns, he will rule justly, break the cross, kill the pigs, and abolish the *jizya* (tax collected from non-Muslim minorities). There will be an abundance of money and no one will accept charitable gifts.[131] The Bible's promised messianic rule of justice and prosperity[132] is given an Islamic twist.

When it comes to intercession on the day of judgment as described in the Hadith, Jesus, like all the other prophets, declares his inability to mediate and sends the enquirers to Muhammad, saying: "I am not fit for this undertaking, go to Muhammad the Slave of Allah whose past and future sins were forgiven by Allah."[133] The divine sonship of Christ is specifically denied. When the Christians testify at the judgment that "'we used to worship Messiah, the son of Allah.' It will be said, 'You are liars, for Allah has neither a wife nor a son.'"[134] The picture of Christ given in the Hadith is much diminished compared with the biblical presentation. In his place, Muhammad is presented as the final prophet, the "seal" of the prophets.[135] However, the picture of Muhammad found in the Hadith is not without its problems, as the next chapter will show.

NOTES

1   B.4:431; 8:66; 9:577.

2   B.7:772; 3:333; 5:90, 92; e.g., Jn 3:16; Rom 5:8.

3   Dr. Murad Wilfried Hofmann, "Differences between the Muslim and the Christian Concept of Divine Love," The 14th General Conference, Amman, September 4–7, 2007, www.aalalbayt.org/en/respapers.html#rd20 (accessed July 8, 2013).

4   Farid Mahally, "A study of the word 'love' in the Qur'an: Hubb Allah fi al-Qur'an" from www.answering-islam.org/Quran/Themes/love.htm (accessed July 8, 2013).

5   B.1:12. In this study, these bracketed insertions will be included, and only commented upon when their interpolation appears unwarranted.

6   E.g., B.1:91; 3:403.

7   B.2:11.

8   B.2:412.

9   From www.hadith.al-islam/Loader.aspx?pageid=261, cited in www. acommonword.blogspot.com.au/2008/03/more-on-loving-ones-muslim-neighbour-in.html?m=1 (accessed June 16, 2013). This is cited from a blog by Dr. Mark Durie.

10 Ibid.

11 B.1:66.

12 B.5:719; 6:110.

13 B.3:557.

14 Mt 5:45; Acts 14:17. For a further discussion, see John S. Kselman "Grace (OT), vol. 2, 1084–6, and Gary S. Shogren, "Grace (NT)," vol. 2, 1086–8.

15 Isa 48:11. For a further discussion, see Gerhard Kittel, "δόξά", vol. 2, 233–53.

16 Deut 5:9.

17 B.6:161, 158; 7:147; 9:500. Contrast this with Yusuf Ali's statement: "Allah needs no praise, for He is above all praise." Ali, *The Holy Qur'an: English translation of the meanings and Commentary*, 3 n.18.

18 B.2:177; 6:385.

19 Nasr, "God," 321. Although Nasr describes it as "a well-known Hadith," others have questioned it. Ibn Taimiyyah says, "It is not from the words of the Prophet (may Allah bless him and grant him peace), and there is no known *isnād* for it, neither ṣaḥīḥ [authentic] nor da'if [weak]"; al-Zarkashi (d. 794), Ibn Hajar, al-Suyuti and others agreed with him." Source: www.islamic-awareness.org/Hadith/Ulum/aape.html#G3 (accessed July 7, 2013).

20 Kaiser, *The Doctrine of God*, 22, 38.

21 Gramlich, "Mystical Dimensions of Islamic Monotheism," 144.

22 Q.3:97.

23 Q.39:7.

24 B.1:315; 4:550; 8:594.

25 B.4:430,549; 8:593; 9:546.

26 B.4:414; 9:514.

27 B.8:260,609. The description in Muslim's collection of the Hadith

is even stronger. "Abu Hurayra reported Allah's Apostle (may peace be upon him) as saying: Verily Allah has fixed the very portion of adultery which a man will indulge in, and which he of necessity must commit" (Muslim bk 33 no 6421, 6422).

28 B.8: 606, 605, 683, 684, 685.

29 B.9:553.

30 B.2:444; 6:469, 473.

31 B.9:541.

32 B.4:430, 549; 8:593, 594; 9:546 (emphasis mine).

33 B.4:817.

34 B.9:508; 6:206.

35 B.8:236, 602; 9:642.

36 B.2:444; 6:469, 473.

37 B.8:236, 595.

38 B.8:597.

39 B.8:599, 649; 9:474; 2:373.

40 B.8:598.

41 B.8:616.

42 B.8:662; 3:154.

43 B.2:227; 6:248; 9:446, 557.

44 Q.18.54.

45 B.9:532.3.

46 B.6:262; 8:611; 9:606.

47 B.9:556, 569.

48 Ps 115:3; Isa 46:10.

49 Isa14:24–27.

50 Deut 10:15.

51 1 Chr 15:2.

52 1 Kgs 11:34.

53 Amos 7:15.

54 Isa 45:1–6; 48:14,15.

55 Deut 4:37; 7:5–8; 10:15.

56 Isa 41:9; 48:12.

57 1 Sam10:23; 2 Sam 21:6.

58 1 Sam 8:18.

59 1 Sam 12:13.

60   Josh 24:22.

61   Amos 3:2.

62   1 Sam 16:1.

63   Isa 59:1,2.

64   Isa 59:16.

65   Eze 20:5–8.

66   Isa 49:1–7.

67   Isa 43:7.

68   Matt 12:18.

69   Luke 6:13; Acts1:2; 10:41.

70   Matt 5:14.

71   1 Pet 2:9; Rev 17:14.

72   Eph 1:4,5.

73   Eph 1:13.

74   Eph 1:4.

75   1 Cor 1:27-29.

76   John 15:19; Acts 9:15,16.

77   Acts.4:28; Rom 8:29,30; 1 Cor 2:7; Eph 1:5,11. The Greek word is "foreordain" προοριζω *proorizō*. Another possible term related to this topic is "foreknowledge" προγνωσις *prognosis* used of God in Acts 2:23 and 1 Peter 1:2, and its verb "foreknow" προγινώσκω *proginōskō*, which is applied to God in Romans 8:29; 11:2, and 1 Peter 1:20, but also to people in Acts 26:5 and 2 Peter 3:17.

78   Zwemer, *The Muslim Doctrine of God*, 100 (italics and capitals are his).

79   Colin Sedgwick,"Predestination Pauline and Islamic," 89, www. biblicalstudies.org.uk/pdf/vox/vol26/predestination_sedgwick. pdf (accessed July 8, 2013), c.f. Isa 25:9. For a fuller treatment of predestination and the divine will, see Zaehner, *Concise Encyclopedia*, 183,184 and Rahman, *Islam*, 86–99.

80   B.6:206; 9:508,515.

81   B.9:509.

82   B.4:416; 9:501, 514, 518, 545, 643.

83   E.g., B.3:594, 595; 4:48, 413, 414.

84   B.9:481, 541; 6:371, 372, 373; 8:654.

85   B.1:66, 463.

86   B.9:484.

87   B.9:532.2 c.f. Q.68:42 "the day when the *sāq* (shin) will be laid bare."

88   B.6:105; 8:246.

89   Source: www.ahle-haqq.com/beliefs.html (accessed July 8, 2013).
     Sufism has conceived of two ways of describing the divine-human
     relationship: *wahdat al-wujuud* ("unity of presence") sees God as the
     only real existence, and all of creation is an emanation of the divine,
     and *wahdat al-shuhuud* ("unity of testimony") where God testifies
     about himself in the heart of the believer. Parsons, *Unveiling God*,
     144–46.

90   Dudley Woodberry, *Introduction to Islam* on CD "World of Islam."
     This was just one Islamic sect that held anthropomorphic views to
     a heretical extent, according to Nuh Ha Mim Keller. He lists the
     Bayaniyya, the Mughiriyya, the Jawaribiyya, and the Hishamiyya
     as well as the Karramiyya. Nuh Ha Mim Keller, "The Re-Formers
     of Islam: the Mas'ud questions," www.masud.co.uk/ISLAM/nuh/
     masudq5.htm (accessed July 8, 2013).

91   Bosworth, "The Rise of the Karāmiyyah in Khurasan," 5.

92   B.9:530.

93   B.9:535.

94   B.9:536; 6:402.

95   Aly, *People Like Us*, 220.

96   This approach probably originated with Ibn Hanbal (164/780-
     241/855) and was developed by al-'Ashari (260/874-324/936).
     Parsons, *Unveiling God*, 156.

97   Source: www.masud.co.uk/ISLAM/nuh/masudq5.htm (accessed July
     9, 2013).

98   Saheeh International, *The Qur'an*, iv.

99   Q.3:179; 6:59; 73; 10:20; 13:9 et al.

100 Al-Hilali and Khan, *Translation of the meanings of the Noble Qur'an*,
     81 n. 1.

101 Saheeh International, *The Qur'an*, iv.

102 Flew, "Theology and Falsification," 48–49.

103 Nehls, *Christians Ask Muslims*, 128.

104 Q.59:23.

105 Q.16:29; 39:60,72; 40:76.

106 Q.3:54. Pickthall translates it "schemed," but the more common
     meanings are "deceive, delude, cheat, dupe, gull, double-cross." Hans
     Wehr, *Dictionary*, 917.

107 Q.3:54; 8:30 (Pickthall translation), http://islamtomorrow.com/

downloads/QuranPikhtal.pdf (accessed July 8, 2013).

108   It calls to mind the assertion of Humpty Dumpty: "When *I* use a word, … it means just what I *choose it* to mean—neither more nor less." Lewis Carroll, *Through the Looking Glass,* ch. 6 (italic mine), www.polvoestelar.com.mx/babilonia/Libros/Lewis%20Carroll/ Lewis%20Carroll%20-%20Through%20the%20Looking-Glass.pdf (accessed August 19, 2011).

109   Zwemer, *Moslem Christ*, 7.

110   Q.3:45; 4:171.

111   B.6:3 c.f. Q.4:171.

112   B.4:644; 9:507.

113   B.4:644; 9:507 c.f. Q.5.78.

114   B.9:507, 601; 4:644.

115   Q.3:46; 19:23-33.

116   B.4:645, 236.

117   B.4:462, 607, 608, 647, 648, 649, 650; 9:153. This was certainly the case with the dying Muhammad, who asked permission from his wives to be transferred to Aisha's house. When permission was granted, "he came out leaning on two men while his feet were dragging on the ground" (B.3:761; 5:727; 1:680).

118   Rev 1.13–17.

119   Dan 7:14.

120   Q.4.172; 19.30; 43.57-61.

121   B.4:568, 656; 6:149, 150, 264; 8:533.

122   B.4:644; 7:209.

123   Phil 2:9; Heb 1:3.

124   B.1:345; 4:429, 462, 607, 640, 647, 648; 5:227.

125   Although Muslims generally believe in Christ's *parousia*, "it is by no means certain that the Qur'an itself even alludes to Jesus' return." Robinson, *Christ in Islam and Christianity*, 103. He lists the reasons why this doctrine arose on pages 104–05. The Qur'an does refer to Jesus having *ilm as-sa'a* (the knowledge of the Hour) (Q. 43:61), and that this knowledge was to be found with God alone (Q.7:187; 31:34; 33:63; 41:47; 43:85).

126   B.4:654.

127   B.4:654.

128   Q.4:171; 5:77.

129 Q.19:36.

130 B.7:209.

131 B.3:425, 656; 4:657.

132 E.g., Isa 9:7; Amos 9:13.

133 B.6:3, 236; 8:570; 9:507, 532.3, 601.

134 B.6:105; 9:532.2.

135 Q.33:40.

10

THE CHARACTER AND ACTIONS OF MUHAMMAD COMPARED WITH JESUS

1. INVITING A COMPARISON WITH JESUS

Muhammad invited an assessment of himself against Jesus when he stated: "I am the nearest of all the people to the son of Mary, and all the prophets are paternal brothers, and there has been no prophet between me and him (i.e. Jesus)." Nevertheless, an assessment reveals significant differences between Muhammad and Jesus as the Hadith present them.[1]

2. AUTHORITY OF TEACHING

When Jesus preached, the crowds "were amazed at his teaching, because his message had authority," for he brought them "a new teaching ... as one who had authority, not as the teachers of the law."[2]

Muhammad's method of instruction, however, at times seemed to lack power and impact. After he made a statement, his Companions reported that he "kept on repeating that warning till we wished he would stop saying it."[3] Another man received an admonition from Muhammad, but "the Prophet kept on repeating that so often that I wished I had not embraced Islam before that day."[4]

3. DEALINGS WITH DEMONS

Muhammad noted that Satan is active at the mosque before and during prayer times.

When the Adhan [the call to prayer] is pronounced Satan takes to his heels and passes wind with noise during his flight in order not to hear the Adhan. When the Adhan is completed he comes back and again takes to his heels when the Iqama [the repeated call to prayer just before prayers begin] is pronounced and after its completion he returns again till he whispers into the heart of the person (to divert his attention from his prayer) and makes him remember things which he does not recall to his mind before the prayer and that causes him to forget how much he has prayed.[5]

Causing people to forget was a common ploy of Satan.[6] On several occasions, Muhammad himself was apparently afflicted, as he forgot how many prayers he had prayed.[7] He also failed to recall some of the Qur'anic revelation that he had received, and needed to be reminded by others. On hearing the verses recited by someone, Muhammad exclaimed: "May Allah bestow His Mercy on him, as he has reminded me of such-and-such Verses of such-and-such Suras, which I was caused to forget."[8] The whispering of Satan causing prophets to forget had been foreshadowed in the Qur'an,[9] although God's canceling power was also promised.[10] On these occasions, and with regard to the forgotten date of the night of Qadr, Muhammad suffered from lack of recall. He said: "I came out to inform you about (the date of) the night of Al-Qadr, but as so and so and so and so quarreled, its knowledge was taken away (I forgot it)."[11] But Allah did not remind him, and the exact date remains a mystery to this day.

There were some methods of protection from satanic attack. He advised couples having sexual intercourse to recite a certain sentence, "and if it is destined that they should have a child, then Satan will never be able to harm him."[12] Although he once described overpowering a troublesome jinn,[13] and, with Allah's strength, even Satan himself,[14] at other times Muhammad succumbed to the confounding whisper of the devil. So did his followers. At the battle of Uhud, the Muslims responded to Satan's call to attack each other, with fatal results.[15]

Satan's ability to disrupt prayers was sometimes easily dismissed. When people forgot to perform ritual requirements correctly they were told by the Prophet: "There is no harm in that."[16] The devil would seemingly stop at nothing to prevent people from praying. When one man remained asleep instead of coming to the dawn prayer, Muhammad's explanation was that "Satan urinated in his ears."[17] At other times, Muhammad's relationships with the jinn were sometimes quite congenial: "How nice those Jinns were," he said after one meeting.[18] Some of the jinn embraced Islam,[19] joined him in worship,[20] and he invoked Allah to provide them food from old bones and animal dung.[21]

Jesus' dealings with evil spirits were quite different. They recognized him as the Son of God.[22] He was able to silence demons with a word[23] and cast them out.[24] This authority and power was passed on to his disciples.[25] According to the biblical account, Christ came to destroy the devil's works,[26] for Satan holds the power of death, from which people needed to be set free.[27]

4. FEARFULNESS

Muhammad was often afflicted by fear. Whenever he went out to answer the call of nature, he would pray: "O Allah, I seek Refuge with You from all offensive and wicked things (evil deeds and evil spirits).[28] He prayed for protection from demons, poisonous pests, and the evil eye.[29] His dream about wearing two golden bangles brought panic.[30] He was bewitched one time, causing him to imagine something he had not done.[31] Prompted by a revelatory dream, he tried to recover the materials of the spell from their underground hiding place, but soon retreated, claiming "(the date-palms near the well) are like the heads of the devils." He left the materials, fearful that disturbing them "may spread evil amongst the people." Later on the well was filled up with earth. This episode suggests that Muhammad was unable to confront the demonic powers that were afflicting him.[32]

Muhammad advised his followers to avoid the places and times ruled by Satan. Prayer during sunrise and sunset was forbidden to all Muslims, "for the sun rises between two sides of the head of the devil."[33] Muslims were told to pray for protection during sexual intercourse lest Satan afflict the child born,[34] and to recite a certain prayer one hundred times in order to be shielded from Satan for twelve hours.[35] At nightfall, when Satan is active, children, gates, and utensils should be secured against his influence.[36]

Islam's prophet took a pragmatic view of the handicapped and advised his followers to "run away from the leper as one runs away from a lion." Muhammad's earliest biographer records the experience of "Asma' d. al-Nu'man, the Kindite woman, whom he married and found to be suffering from leprosy and so returned to her people with a suitable gift."[37] Jesus, by contrast, touched lepers and healed them.[38] The positive outcome in the lives of the lepers who encountered Jesus was evident. Wisdom is indeed justified by her children.[39]

5. MUHAMMAD'S GREAT CLAIMS ABOUT HIMSELF

Islam's prophet incorrectly claimed six unique characteristics of his prophethood which he claimed "were not given to anyone else before me."[40]

1) He declared: "Allah made me victorious by awe, (by His frightening my enemies) for a distance of one month's journey."
2) He noted the freedom of Muslims to pray anywhere, presumably not only in a temple or church.
3) He pointed out his freedom to take booty.[41]
4) He claimed the right of intercession on the Day of 5) Resurrection.
5) He claimed his mission was universal, not restricted to one nation.
6) He further asserted that he would be "the chief of all people on the Day of Resurrection." [42]

However, none of these characteristics is unique to Muhammad as a prophet. Similar authority and rights have been granted by God to others before him.

1) Moses had previously received a divine promise to send terror ahead of him.[43]

2) Jesus had outlined the concept of private devotions centuries beforehand in the "inner room" verses,[44] and illustrated it by retreating to quiet places to pray.[45] All of the earth was a suitable place for prayer for followers of Christ.

3) Booty was collected and distributed by the Israelites in the war against the Midianites, prior to the entry into Canaan,[46] and taken from far-off nations following the conquest of Canaan.[47]

4) The right to intercede for others had been given to Jesus after his ascension.[48]

5) Jesus, calling himself the light of the world,[49] claimed a worldwide mission as well. The initial ethnically restricted mission of the apostles[50] and Jesus[51] was later universalized.[52]

6) Jesus is nominated as the one whose name is above all other names, "so that in everything he might have the supremacy," whereas Muhammad's claim to be distinctive is denied by his statement in the Qur'an: "I bring no innovation among the prophets."[53]

It is clear that Muhammad's claims to uniqueness and preeminence have little factual basis.

Muhammad arrogated great things for himself due to his prophetic calling. He refused to eat food containing onions and garlic, since he claimed that he conversed with angels.[54] Echoing Jesus' call to discipleship,[55] Islam's prophet stated: "None of you will have faith till he loves me more than his father and his children ... and all mankind."[56] Like Jesus' demand that his followers should love him more than their own lives,[57] Muhammad told 'Umar that he would not have complete faith "until I am dearer to you than your own self."[58]

Just as blasphemy against the Holy Spirit was the unforgivable sin,[59] lying against Muhammad would bring hell-fire.[60] He interpreted his own dreams,[61] and the dreams of others,[62] and asserted that Satan could never impersonate him in a dream.[63] He had a silver ring made with an inscription on it, and forbade others from making a similar ring.[64] He reported that he was taken to heaven by Gabriel where he met the other prophets.[65] He claimed that, having been called by Allah, he would be first to cross over *al-Ṣirāt* (the bridge) to Paradise accompanied by his followers.[66]

He considered himself to have a unique role with its associated privileges. Muhammad's followers looked on him with great respect. His sexual prowess was reportedly prodigious, sometimes involving all of his nine[67] or eleven wives in one night,[68] for he was said to have the strength of thirty men.[69] This was bettered by Solomon, who boasted intercourse with sixty wives[70] or ninety-nine or one hundred women[71] in one night. However, Muhammad's claims in the sexual arena may be exaggerated, for Aisha confided: "Magic was worked on Allah's Apostle so that he used to think that he had sexual relations with his wives while he actually had not."[72] On Muhammad's visions of angels, Aisha commented: "The Prophet used to see things which we used not to see."[73]

Some Hadith accounts appear legendary, and contradict what is found in the Qur'an. He claimed to be able to see those who were praying behind him.[74] This was notwithstanding his denial of knowing "the hidden things,"[75] even though he wished he did.[76]

Jesus also claimed great things for himself. He said that he was the Son of God,[77] that he was the only way to the Father,[78] and that all judgment had been entrusted to him.[79] However, this did not translate into acting in grandiose ways. He mixed with the outcasts,[80] refused to be crowned as a king,[81] rode into Jerusalem on a donkey instead of a warhorse,[82] washed his disciples' feet,[83] and humbled himself to an ignominious death on a cross.[84] He could honestly describe himself as "gentle and humble in heart."[85]

6. LACK OF CONVICTION

At times Muhammad displayed a deficiency in conviction or leadership. He was fearful of the opinions of others, a fact testified in the Qur'an when he is chided by Allah: "But you [Muhammad] hide in your heart that which Allah was about to make manifest: you feared the people but it is more fitting that you should fear Allah."[86] A similar divine rebuke accompanied his inability to deal with the disagreement with his wives. Allah reprimands him: "O Prophet! Why did you forbid what Allah has allowed for you, seeking to please your wives?"[87] He is also censured for ignoring the request of the blind man 'Amr Ibn Um Maktūm,[88] since he had been commanded to respond to the entreaties of those seeking help.[89] When the Medinan leader Abdullah bin Ubayy was sowing discord among the Muslim ranks, 'Umar bin Al-Khaṭṭāb offered to behead him. Muhammad's response was designed to preserve his own reputation: "Leave him, lest the people say Muhammad kills his companions."[90]

The Pharisees exhibited a similar concern about public reactions.[91] Isaiah challenged the anxious Israelites: "Who are you that you fear mortal men, the sons of men, who are but grass?" [92] Jesus, by contrast, was unafraid of the opinions of men. He did not seek public praise or commendation,[93] but condemned those who did so.[94] Paul spoke of the man circumcised in the heart by the Spirit, the person whose "praise is not from men, but from God."[95] The Hadith likewise condemn those who perform actions to win the praise of men.[96]

Muhammad admitted that his resolve was sometimes weak. "If I were to stay in prison for such a long time as Joseph [the son of Jacob] did," he said, "I would have accepted the offer (of freedom without insisting on having my guiltlessness declared)."[97] This lack of steadfastness extended to an inability to root out non-Muslim influences in Islam. When prompted by his wife Aisha to demolish the Ka'ba and rebuild

DEALING WITH CRITICS

Although he told his poet Hassan bin Thābit to "lampoon the pagans"[98] and "abuse them with your poems,"[99] Muhammad would allow no one to ridicule him. Those who mocked Muhammad were placed on a death list. His typical response was to announce in a meeting: "O you Muslims! Who will relieve me from this person?" mentioning the name of the person he wanted dealt with. He used this method against Ka'b bin al-Ashraf,[100] Abū Rāfi' (Sallam ibn Abu al-Huqayq),[101] Asmā' bint Marwān, Abū 'Afak,[102] and 'Abdullah bin Ubai bin Salūl, who slandered Aisha.[103] All, except the last one (who belonged to a powerful tribe), were soon assassinated by Muhammad's followers.

it on Abraham's original foundations, Muhammad declined. He explained: "Were it not for the fact that your people are close to the pre-Islamic period of ignorance (i.e. they have recently become Muslims) I would have done so."[104] He claimed that the demolition of the Ka'ba would be carried out by a thin-legged Ethiopian man.[105]

Jesus was unconcerned about offending the sensitivities of those who held a building and its commerce in high repute. He prophesied the downfall of the magnificent temple in Jerusalem[106] and upset the tables of those who were misusing its precincts.[107]

Muhammad was sometimes unwilling to confront or deal personally with those who criticized him in public (see Sidebar *Dealing with Critics*).

Jesus' response to his adversaries was quite different. He told his followers to love their enemies and to pray for them,[108] and did so himself even when he was being crucified.[109] While Jesus healed the blind[110] and extended the hand of friendship to the one who betrayed him,[111] Muhammad blinded with hot irons thrust into the eyes of those who betrayed him, as well as cutting off their hands and feet.[112]

At the signing of the treaty of Hudaibiya, the pagan Meccans rejected the written designation "Muhammad, apostle of Allah." Muhammad told Ali to cross it out, but Ali refused. So Muhammad took the pen and changed it to "Muhammad, son of Abdullah."[113] Even the threat of public stoning[114] and death by crucifixion[115] could not force Jesus to deny his title as "Son of God."[116]

7. GREED

During the battle of Badr, seventy prisoners were taken by the Muslims. 'Umar bin al-Khaṭṭāb wanted to kill them all,[117] but Muhammad decided to sell them back to the Meccans for ransom, making a considerable profit. Some asked Muhammad to set his own uncle Al-'Abbās free, since he was secretly a Muslim, but the Prophet was adamant: "Do not leave (even) a Dirham (of his ransom)."[118] Then a divine revelation came sternly criticizing Muhammad for his decision:

It is not for a Prophet that he should have prisoners of war (and free them with ransom) until he had made a great slaughter (among his enemies) in the land. You desire the good of this world (i.e. the money of ransom for freeing the captives), but Allah desires for you the hereafter…. Were it not for a previous ordainment from Allah, a severe torment would have touched you for what you took.[119]

Tariq Ramadhan comments that this revelation "was to reproach the Prophet for this choice, which indeed was mainly motivated by the desire to acquire wealth."[120] Ironically, Muhammad was "astonished at [the] greediness" of his uncle Al-'Abbās who wanted to share in some of the Muslim wealth later on, since he had been ransomed by his nephew back to the Meccans.[121] The Qur'an testifies that Muhammad had started life poor and ended it rich.[122]

For Jesus the movement was in the opposite direction. "Though he was rich, yet for your sake he became poor, so that you through his poverty might become rich."[123] He lived with no fixed abode,[124] and having traveled into Jerusalem on a borrowed donkey,[125] he died there with the clothes he was wearing as his sole possessions.[126]

8. MENDACITY

Islam's prophet may have been guilty of mendacity. When his men attacked a Meccan caravan in a sacred month (contrary to long-standing agreements and a Qur'anic injunction),[127] he justified their action as a means of bringing idolatry in the holy city to an end.[128] Despite agreeing, in AD 628, to a ten-year treaty not to enter Mecca while armed, he returned in military attire with an army of 10,000 men two years later.[129] Although this treaty had stipulated that any Muslims who came to Medina without the permission of their guardians should be returned, Muhammad broke this on the basis of a new divine revelation.[130]

Pledges of allegiance were taken,[131] and oaths were required in legal disputes,[132] invoking only the name of Allah.[133] Although

Muhammad told his followers to fulfil their oaths[134] including those
made before they accepted Islam,[135] he did not always do so himself,
claiming that "if I take an oath and later I see a better solution than
that, I act on the latter (and gave the expiation of that oath)."[136] He
gave this same advice to others.[137] This was based on a revelation
from Allah.[138] Aisha stated that her father Abū Bakr, known as the
al-ṣiddīq (the truthful one) had never broken an oath until this revelation came. He cited Muhammad's above words as justification for
failing to fulfill his promises.[139]

Muhammad condemned those who took false oaths[140] and told
his followers to help others fulfill their oaths,[141] yet he ordered
a man to break his vow to fast daily and pray nightly.[142] An
Anṣār man owned a slave to whom he had promised freedom
on the master's death. But the master had no other property, so
Muhammad broke the pledge to the slave by selling the slave for
his master.[143] The Prophet said, "The worst people in the Sight of
Allah on the Day of Resurrection will be the double faced people
who appear to some people with one face and to other people
with another face."[144] However, he indulged in the same behavior,
as the following account by Aisha shows. "A man asked permission to enter upon Allah's Apostle. The Prophet said, 'Admit him.
What an evil brother of his people or a son of his people.' But
when the man entered, the Prophet spoke to him in a very polite
manner. (And when that person left) I said, 'O Allah's Apostle!
You had said what you had said, yet you spoke to him in a very
polite manner?'" Muhammad did not respond to Aisha's question, but simply criticized the man again.[145]

After asserting that "Allah loves that one should be kind and
lenient in all matters,"[146] he responded to some Jews by covertly
turning their spoken curse directed at him back on themselves.[147] He
did not encourage people to be honest about their own shortcomings. A person who at night committed a sin which did not become
public knowledge because it was "screened by his Lord" would not
be forgiven this sin if he openly confessed it. Those secret sins confessed only to Allah on the Day of Judgment would be forgiven.[148]
Such teaching and example would do little to promote transparency
or vulnerability among his followers.

Jesus described himself as "the truth."[149] His phrase "tell you the truth" is found nearly eighty times in the Gospels. Despite the presence of spies in his entourage listening to his every word,[150] witnesses testifying against Christ at his trial could find no discrepancy in his sayings or his actions, but rather contradicted each other.[151] Jesus did not tolerate mendacity in others. He criticized as "whitewashed tombs" those who "appear to people as righteous but on the inside … are full of hypocrisy and wickedness."[152] He described them as following Satan, who is "the father of lies."[153]

9. MIRACULOUS CLAIMS

Many miracles were attributed to Muhammad in al-Bukhārī's Hadith (see Table 13).

HEALING	Muhammad cured Ali's eyes by spitting	3:891; 4:192; 5:51, 521
	Muhammad healed the broken leg of 'Abdullah bin Atik whom he had sent to kill the Jew Abu Rafi	5:371
	Water from Muhammad's ablutions was used by others (B.1:187, 195), sometimes for healing	1:193; 7:554
	Healing of Salama's wounded leg by Muhammad's saliva	5:517
	He cured Sad's liver by placing hands on abdomen	5:563
WATER	Water flowed from Muhammad's fingers, providing drink and ablutions for 1400 or 1500 people	5:473; 7:543
	Muhammad revived a dry well at Hudaybiya	3:891; 5:471, 472
	Eighty people performed ablutions from a small pot, when water flowed from the Prophet's fingers	1:170,194,199
FOOD	Food in pot multiplied to feed 1000 people	5:427,428
	Muhammad's multiplication of dates to pay the debts of Jabir bin Abdullah, a martyr's son	3:337,580, 589,773,872; 4:40,780; 5:383; 6:304; 7:354
	Muhammad used a small amount of bread (haisa) to feed 40 or 70 or 80 men at Um Sulaim's house	4:778; 7:92.2, 293,361; 8:679
	Muhammad used one sheep to feed 130 men	7:294

	Muhammad invoked evil on Suraqa, the soldier pursuing him, so his horse's legs sank into the earth	4:812; 5:250
	Miraculous provision of rain	2:123,129,135, 143
	Rain fell but not on the Muslims	2:128,130,132, 133; 8:115,353
NATURE	The sun was stopped from setting so victory was won	4:353
	A rock turned to sand when digging the Trench around Medina	5:427,428
	Muhammad comforted a tree that cried when it was no longer used as a pulpit	2:41; 4:784
	The moon was split into two pieces	5:208,209,210, 211; 4:830,832; 6:387,388,389, 390,391

TABLE 13: Miracles Attributed to Muhammad

According to the Qur'an, however, Muhammad could not perform any miracles.[154] When asked for a miracle, he said: "I am only a man, a messenger,"[155] or a warner,[156] not a miracle worker. Consequently, the only sign he would give them would be the Qur'an,[157] the like of which they could not produce.[158] He confirmed this in the Hadith: "There was no prophet among the prophets but was given miracles because of which people had security or had belief, but what I was given was the Divine Inspiration which Allah revealed to me."[159] A Muslim scholar asserts: "Muhammad ... had only one irresistible miracle–the Qur'an."[160] The unscientific nature of miracles is a potential drawback for some commentators. A contemporary Muslim writer states: "Muslims do not claim any miracles for Muhammad. In their view, what proves Muhammad's prophethood is the sublime beauty and greatness of the revelation itself, the Holy Qur'an, not any inexplicable breaches of natural law which confound human reason."[161] Others claim that Muhammad did not perform any feats "in the sense of a reversing of Nature,"[162] for "Islam relies on truth itself, without the support of miracles. The miracle of Islam is rationalism."[163]

It has been suggested that Muhammad's miracle narratives in the Hadith began to appear only after two Christian bishops, Abu Qurra from Edessa and Arethas from Caesarea, pointed out the superiority of Jesus to Muhammad by virtue of Jesus' miracles.[164] A Muslim writer affirms this view: "Later Muslims, seeing the extraordinary miracles in the Christian and Jewish scriptures, invented all sorts of extraordinary happenings and attributed them to Muhammad, all of course outside the Qur'an."[165] Zwemer suggests that these may have been converts from Christianity: "As regards Moslem traditions which give us fuller information than the Koran itself, Goldziher has shown that these were largely contributed by Christian renegades."[166]

Jesus' miracles, by contrast, were recorded or passed on by his contemporaries who were eyewitnesses [167] (see Table 14).

Jesus used his mighty works as one of the proofs of his divine sonship. "Even though you do not believe me, believe the works, that you may know and understand that the Father is in me, and I in the Father."[168]

NATURE MIRACLES	DELIVERANCE FROM DEMONS	RAISING FROM THE DEAD
Turning water into wine (Jn.2)	Man in Capernaum (Mk.1/Lk.4)	Widow's son (Lk.7)
Catching many fish (Lk.5)	Many delivered in evening (Mt.8/Mk.1/Lk.4)	Jairus' daughter (Mt.9/Mk.5/Lk.8)
Calming storm (Mt.8/Mk.4/Lk.8)	Mute man (Mt.9)	Lazarus (Jn.11)
Feeding 5000 (Mt.14/Mk.6/Lk.9/Jn.6)	Gerasene demoniac (Mt.8/Mk.5/Lk.8)	Jesus' Resurrection from the dead (Mt.28/Mk.16/Lk.24/Jn.20)
Walking on water (Mt.14/Mk.6/Jn.6)	Canaanite girl (Mt.15/Mk.7)	
Feeding 4000 (Mt.15/Mk.8)	Possessed boy (Mt.17/Mk.9/Lk.9)	
Fish with a coin (Mt.17)	Possessed blind and mute man (Mt.12/Lk.11)	
Cursing the fig-tree (Mt.21/Mk.11)		
Catching 153 fish (Jn.21)		

HEALING MIRACLES	
Capernaum official's son (Jn.4)	Woman with bleeding (Mt.9/Mk.5/Lk.8)
A leper (Mt.8/Mk.1)	Man born blind (Jn.9)
Simon's mother-in-law (Mt.8/Mk.1/Lk.4)	Many in Gennesaret (Mt.14/Mk.6)

TABLE 14: Jesus' Miracles

NOTES

1 B.4:651, 652. The question of comparing Jesus and Muhammad is discussed in more detail in chapter 7. In a misunderstanding of the text and a misplaced attempt to magnify Muhammad, al-Kalby claims that Jesus prophesies the coming of Muhammad. "Jesus is saying that he does not have to explain much of God's law to the people because the next prophet, 'the prince of the world' (Muhammad) will teach you everything. Jesus also says that this future prophet is not him ('and hath nothing in me')" (pp.521, 522). Unfortunately, the term "prince of this world" in John14:30 refers to Satan, not to Muhammad.

2 Luke 4:32; Mark 1:22,27/Matt 7:29.

3 B.9:54; 8:7,291; 3:822.

4 B.5:568; 9:11.

5 B.1:582; 4:505.

6 B.1:74,78.

7 B.1:394, 398, 469, 682, 683; 8:77, 663, 664.

8 B.3:823; 6:556, 557, 558, 562; 8:347.

9 In Q.6:68, Satan causes Muhammad to forget the Qur'anic verses, and in Q.58:19, Satan causes people to forget the "remembrance" *dhikr* of Allah. In Q.18:63, Moses says of his goal in seeking the fish: "Satan made me forget." Allah also causes people to forget (Q.2:106).

10 Q.22:52. The commentators Al-Waqidi and Al-Tabari claim that this verse was a response to the "Satanic verses" which justified worship of the goddesses Al-Lat, al-'Uzza and Manat. See "Al-Lat" in Hughes, *Dictionary*, 285.

11   B.1:46, 777; 3:240, 244. In Q. 87:6-7, God declares to Muhammad:
      "We shall teach thee to declare (the Message) so thou shalt not forget,
      except as Allah wills." Yusuf Ali comments on this last phrase: "There
      can be no question of this having any reference to the abrogation of
      any verse of the Qur-an…. It is one of the beneficent mercies of God
      that we should forget some things of the past, lest our minds become
      confused and our development is retarded." Ali, *The Holy Qur-an:
      Text, Translation and Commentary*, 1724.

12   B.7:94.

13   B.1:450.2.

14   B.4:504.

15   B.4:510; 5:161, 394; 8:661; 9:22, 28.

16   B.1:83, 84, 126.

17   B.2:245; 4:492.

18   B.5:200.

19   B.6:238, 239.

20   B.2:177; 6:385.

21   B.5:200.

22   Matt 8:29.

23   Mark 1:35; Luke 4:35.

24   Matt 8:16; 9:33; 12:28; Mark 1:26, 34, 39; Luke 11:20.

25   Matt 10:1; Mark 6:13; Luke 9:1.

26   1 John 3:8.

27   Heb 2:14.

28   B.1:144.

29   B.4:590.

30   B.9:158, 160.

31   B.4:400.

32   B.4:490.

33   B.4:494.

34   B.4:493,503.

35   B.4:514.

36   B.4:500; 7:527.

37   B.7:608. Ibn Ishaq, *Sira*, 794.

38   Matt 8:3; Mark 1:41; Luke 5:13.

39   Matt 11:19; Luke 7:35.

40　B.1:331.

41　This may have been in apposition to the restrictions on Joshua, who was forbidden to take booty (Josh 6:24), and as the general rule for nearby nations (Deut 13:16). The payment to Muhammad of *khumus* (one fifth of all booty) by Bedouin tribes during their raids was the fifth pillar of earliest Islam: see B.1:50, 87, 501. This was later replaced by the *Hajj*, pilgrimage to Mecca. A tax of 20 percent in Pharaoh's favor was set by Joseph and is "still in force today" (Gen 47:23-26).

42　B.4:556; 6:236. The Qur'an asserts that there will be no intercession, except by God (Q.32:4), and particularly not for those who did not fulfill all Islam's requirements (Q.74:48). However, it also states that no intercession will avail "except by him who has permission from the Most Gracious and whose word is acceptable to Him" (Q.20:109). Muhammad may have been applying this verse to himself in this Hadith.

43　Ex 23:27, 28; Deut 2:25 c.f. Deut 28:10.

44　Matt 6:5-8.

45　E.g., Mark 1:35.

46　Num 31:25-54.

47　Deut 20:14.

48　Rom 8:34; Heb 7:25.

49　John 9:5.

50　Matt 10:5.

51　Matt 15:24.

52　Matt 28:19,20.

53　Col 1:18; Q.46:9.

54　B.1:814; 7:362, 363; 9:458.

55　Matt 10:37.

56　B.1: 13,14.

57　Luke 14:26.

58　B.8:628.

59　Matt 12:31,32; Mark 3:22-30.

60　B.1:106, 107, 108, 109.

61　B.1:22, 82; 9:159,161,162,163,164.

62　B.9:155,156.

63　B.1:110; 8:217.

64   B. 7:763, 766.

65   B.1:345.

66   B.1:770.

67   B.3:283.

68   B.1:268, 270, 282; 7:142; 8:711.

69   B.1:268.

70   B. 9:561.

71   B.4:74.1; 7:169; 8:634.

72   B.7:660; 8:89; 4:490.

73   B.8:220.

74   B.1:410-411, 708, 709; 8:639.

75   Q. 6.50, c.f. Deut 29:29.

76   Q.7:188. By contrast, it is claimed Jesus was able to see things that were concealed (Q.3:49), an attribute described as unique to Allah (Q.3:5,29; 27:65).

77   John 10:36.

78   John 14:6.

79   John 5:22.

80   Luke 15:2.

81   John 6:15.

82   Matt 21:2-7.

83   John 13:2-17.

84   Phil 2:5-8.

85   Matt 11:29.

86   Q.33.37.

87   Q.66:1.

88   Q.80:1-10. He is also called Abdullah ibn Um Maktum.

89   Q.93:10.

90   B.6:430.

91   Matt 21:26.

92   Isa 51:12.

93   John 5:41.

94   John 12:42,43.

95   Rom 2:29.

96   B.8:506; 9:266.

97   B.4:591, 601.

98   .4:435,731; 8:171, 174.

99   B.5:449.

100   B.5:369.

101   B.5:370.

102   These two are mentioned in Ibn Ishaq, *Sira*, 675, 676.

103   B.5:462; 8:655; 3:829; 6:274.

104   B.2:653-656; 4:587; 6:11; 9:349.

105   B.2:661, 665, 666.

106   Matt 24:2; Mark 13:1,2; Luke 21:6.

107   John 2:13-16; Mark 13:15; Matt 21:12.

108   Matt 5:44; Luke 6:27, 35.

109   Luke 23:34.

110   E.g., Matt 11:5.

111   John 13:25; Luke 22:21; Matt 26:23.

112   B.1:234; 2:577; 5:505; 7:589, 590.

113   B.5:553.

114   John 10:31-39.

115   Matt 26:64; Luke 22:70.

116   Mark 14:62.

117   Ramadhan, *The Messenger,* 106.

118   B.3:714; 4:284; 5:353.

119   Q.8:67,68.

120   Ramadhan, *The Messenger,* 106.

121   B.1:413.

122   Q.93:8.

123   2 Cor 8:9.

124   Matt 8:20; Luke 9:58.

125   Matt 21:1-3.

126   John 19:23,24.

127   Q.9:5.

128   Q.2.214; 9.36.

129   B.7:699. It was claimed that the Quraysh had aided the tribe of Bani Bakr against the tribe of Khuza'a, who had a treaty with the Muslims. Ibn Ishaq, *Sira,* 542.

130   Q.60:10. B. 3:874; 7:211; 3:891; 5:496; 6:414, 415, 416, 417, 418; 8:775; 9:321.

131   B.3:840.

132   B.3:691, 835; 4:398; 6:74.

133   B.3:844; 5:177.

134   B.2:331.

135   B.4:372.

136   B.4:361; 5:668; 8:619, 620, 671. The psalmist suggests an alternative approach (Ps 15:4).

137   B.9:260,261.

138   Q.5:89.

139   B.6:138; 8:618.

140   B.3:557, 599, 692, 834, 836, 838, 839, 841, 842; 6:73.

141   B.3:625.

142   B.3:197.

143   B.3:351,588; 8:707; 9:80.

144   B.8:84; 9:290.

145   B.8:80, 59.1, 152. Such behavior is criticized in Jer 9:8,9 and Ps 28:3.

146   B.8:273.

147   B.8:95.

148   B.8:96.

149   John 14:6.

150   Luke 20:20,21.

151   Mark 14:56.

152   Matt 23:27,28.

153   John 8:44.

154   Q.3:181-84; 6:8,9,109; 17.90-93; 29:50.

155   Q.17:93.

156   Q.13:7; 7:188; 11:12; 25:7.

157   Q.21.3,5,10.

158   Q.2:23;10:38;11:13; 17:88.

159   B.6:504; 9:379.

160   Haykal, *The Life of Muhammad*, xxvi.

161   Al-Faruqi, *Islam*, 20.

162   Ali, *The Holy Qur'an: Text, Translation and Commentary*, 10.

163   Azhar, *Christianity in History*, 55, 173.

164   Daniel J. Sahas "The Formation of Later Islamic Doctrines as a
        Response to Byzantine Polemics: The Miracles of Muhammad"
        in *The Greek Orthodox Theological Review*, vol. 27, nos. 2 and 3
        (Summer-Fall 1982) cited in Geisler and Saleeb, *Answering Islam*,
        166.

165   Abu-Hamdiyyah, *The Qur'an*, 46.

166   Goldziher, *Muhammedanische Studien*, vol 2, 268 cited in Zwemer,
        The Moslem Christ, 14.

167   Luke 1:2; 2 Pet 1:16; 1 John 1:1.

168   John10:38.

11

MUHAMMAD AND JESUS, VENGEANCE AND VIOLENCE

1. CURSING OTHERS

Muhammad lived in a matrix of conflict. He sometimes reacted violently against those who resisted or insulted him, and those who did not live up to Islamic law.[1]

He was commanded not to curse the idols lest the pagans in response curse Allah,[2] and one Companion claimed that Muhammad "was not one to curse others,"[3] yet we find imprecations against others flowing freely from his lips throughout the Hadith record[4] (see Table 15).

CATEGORY			DETAILS	REFERENCES IN AL-BUKHĀRI
THOSE WHO OPPOSED MUHAMMAD AND THE MUSLIMS	INDIVIDUALS		Abu Lahab, his uncle (see Q.111.1)	2:477
			Suraqa, the soldier pursuing him, so the legs of his horse sank into the earth	4:812; 5:250; 7:512
			Khosrau, for tearing up Muhammad's letter	1:64; 4:190; 5:708; 9:369
			A jinn he caught in the mosque	4:634

CATEGORY		DETAILS	REFERENCES IN AL-BUKHĀRI
THOSE WHO OPPOSED MUHAMMAD AND THE MUSLIMS	SPECIFIC GROUPS OF PEOPLE	Shaiba bin Rabi'a and 'Utba bin Rabi'a and Umaiya bin Khalaf "because they turned us out of our land to the land of epidemics."	3:113; 5:297
		Abu Jahl, Ṣafwan bin Umaiya, Suhail bin 'Amr and Al-Harith bin Hisham.	4:409; 5:397
		Those who put camel intestines on his back he was while praying	1:240,241,499; 4:185, 409; 5:193
		Enemies during battle of al-Ahzab	4:184
		Those enemies who prevented the Muslims from praying during a battle	4:182
		The murderers from the tribe of Ral, Dhakwan, Bani Lihyan and Bam Usaiya who disobeyed Allah and his Apostle.	4:57,69,299; 5:414, 420
		Unnamed persons i.e. "so-and-so" (during his prayers)	6:82; 9:445
	WHOLE TRIBES	The (tribes of) Ril, Dhakwan, Bani Lihyan and Usaiya	5:417
		Enemy tribes to be afflicted with famine	2:120,121; 4:183,184,185,186; 6:333,346,347
		The tribe of Mudar	1:768; 2:120; 4:183; 6:122; 9:73
		Unnamed Arab tribes	5:441; 6:83
JEWS AND CHRISTIANS		those who are cursed in Allah's Book	6:408; 7:815,816, 822,826,832
		Jews to be afflicted with famine	4:183,184,185,186
		the Jews for saying that Muslims would replace them in hellfire	4:394
		the Jews for selling forbidden animal meat	3:426,427,438; 4:666; 6:157
		Jews and Christians for building places of worship over graves of their prophets	1:427,428; 2:414,472; 4:660; 5:725,727; 7:706

CATEGORY	DETAILS	REFERENCES IN AL-BUKHĀRI
WOMEN	Women who use false hair	6:409
	Women who artificially lengthen their hair	7:816,817,818,819, 820,823,824,825,831
	Women who tattoo and get tattooed	3:440; 7:259,820, 823,825,831,845; 6:408; 7:815,816, 822,826,832
	Women who remove the hair from their faces	6:408; 7:815,816, 822,826,832
	Women who make artificial spaces between their teeth to look more beautiful	6:408; 7:815,816, 822,826,832
	Women who assume the manners of men	7:773,774; 8:820
THOSE WHO PERFORM UN-ISLAMIC PRACTICES	Those who put idols in the Ka'ba	1:391; 2:671; 4:571
	Effeminate men who assume the manners of women	7:773,774; 8:820
	The eater (consumer) of Riba (usury)	3:440; 7:259,820, 823,825,831,845
	Picture-makers	3:299; 7:259, 8453:440; 7:259,820, 823,825,831,845
	Those who cut the limbs of an animal while it is still alive	7:424
	Those who tie up chickens and shoot at them	7:423,422

TABLE 15: List of Those Cursed by Muhammad

An Iranian Muslim scholar finds a simple explanation for these shortcomings. "The Prophet Mohammad, far from claiming the infallibility and superhuman rank later attributed to him by others, knew himself to be prone to sin."[5] Dashti bases this on various Qur'anic verses.[6]

Once when he was cursing some people during his morning prayers, Muhammad was reproved by Allah when the revelation came: "Not for you (O Muhammad) is the decision, (but for Allah), whether He turns in mercy to them or punish them, for they are indeed wrongdoers."[7]

2. MUHAMMAD'S DEATH WISH

ILLUSTRATION 15:
Muhammad Contemplated
Suicide Several Times[l]

Muhammad's internal conflicts nearly destroyed him. A lack of patience on Muhammad's part to wait for further revelation had near fatal consequences. Like Elijah and 8 before him, Muhammad despaired of life itself. Although he told others not to invoke Allah for death,[9] and despite suicide being forbidden in Islam,[10] he contemplated it on various occasions (see Illustration 15).

Unlike the biblical prophets, he made specific plans and determined a means to kill himself. "The Divine Inspiration ... paused for a while and the Prophet became so sad as we have heard that he intended several times to throw himself from the tops of high mountains and every time he went up the top of a mountain in order to throw himself down, Gabriel would appear before him and say, 'O Muhammad! You are indeed Allah's Apostle in truth' whereupon his heart would become quiet and he would calm down and would return home. And whenever the period of the coming of the inspiration used to become long, he would do as before, but when he used to reach the top of a mountain, Gabriel would appear before him and say to him what he had said before."[11] This was a fortunate outcome for Muhammad, since he would later pronounce: "Whoever purposely throws himself from a mountain and kills himself, will be in the (Hell) Fire falling down into it and abiding therein perpetually forever."[12] Any person committing suicide would be continually punished in hell by the method he used to bring about his own death.[13]

One time, people surmised that Jesus might be going to kill himself, but there was no evidence for this accusation.[14]

---

l   http://maratray.perso.libertysurf.fr/religions/islam.htm

3. VENGEFULNESS

Muhammad motivated his attacking troops by reminding them of the previous actions of their enemies.[15] Even though he barred his followers from abusing the dead,[16] Muhammad loudly and mockingly addressed enemies whose bodies were dumped in a well.[17] This was in stark contrast to an unnamed prophet "whose nation had beaten him and caused him to bleed, while he was cleaning the blood off his face and saying, "O Allah! Forgive my nation, for they have no knowledge,"[18] resonating with the sayings of Jesus on the cross[19] and Stephen while being stoned.[20]

Disgusted at the spiritual indolence of his fellow Muslims, Muhammad wanted to take violent and drastic action: "By Him in Whose Hand my soul is, I was about to order for collecting firewood (fuel) and then order someone to pronounce the Adhan for the prayer and then order someone to lead the prayer then I would go from behind and burn the houses of men who did not present themselves for the (compulsory congregational) prayer." He suggested that they would come to prayers if food was offered.[21]

Even those who tried to emulate him too closely were treated in a spiteful way. When his followers copied his al-Wiṣāl (continuous fasting day and night) during Ramadan, he forbade them, claiming that he was not like them, for Allah gave him food and drink at night during his sleep.[22] "When the people refused to give up Al-Wisal, the Prophet fasted along with them for one day, and did not break his fast but continued his fast for another day, and when they saw the crescent, the Prophet said, 'If the crescent had not appeared, I would have made you continue your fast (for a third day),' as if he wanted to punish them for they had refused to give up Al-Wisal."[23] Another version of this Hadith says: "he wanted to vanquish them completely (because they had refused to give up *Al Wisal*)."[24]

Ill feeling was expressed against those whom he felt had violated him. The Prophet threatened to pierce with an iron comb the eye of a man who peeped through a hole in his house because he saw Muhammad scratching his head with the comb.[25] At another time,

Muhammad tried to stab the man with an arrowhead.[26] He told his followers: "If someone is peeping (looking secretly) into your house without your permission, and you throw a stone at him and destroy his eyes, there will be no blame on you."[27] Alternatively a poked stick may be used to injure the observer's eye.[28] Even on his deathbed, a rancorous Muhammad wanted to watch those who gave him bitter medicine being forced to drink it themselves.[29] A vindictive spirit seemed to pursue him right to the end. It appeared to be transferred to his followers. Remarkably, after having being saved from hellfire, Muslims will take retaliation on each other for "wrongs they have committed in the world against one another. After they are cleansed and purified (through the retaliation), they will be admitted into Paradise."[30] Islam's followers taking reprisal on each other as a precursor to entering heaven may reflect the extent to which Muhammad can serve as an exemplar.

On the basis of these actions, some are not surprised that Muhammad prayed for cleansing from his sins more than seventy times each day.[31] He begged Allah to forgive him.[32] His followers believed that he had been forgiven all his sins, past and future,[33] a claim which he never made for himself.

4. JESUS AND VENGEANCE

Jesus' actions and teaching reveal a different worldview. According to the New Testament, Jesus was sinless.[34] His sinlessness included forgiving those who sinned against him,[35] a concept included in the Lord's Prayer[36] and other teaching.[37] Rather than taking revenge on one's enemies, Christ's followers were called to love them, to do good to those who hated them, bless those who cursed them, and pray for those who ill treated them.[38] German diplomat and convert to Islam Dr. Murad Wilfried Hofmann, commenting on Christian and Muslim views of love, notes a "major theoretical discrepancy between the two denominations in as much as the concept of loving one's enemy is nowhere to be found in Islamic doctrine."[39]

5. ESPOUSAL OF VIOLENCE AND JIHAD

Many of the Hadith texts coming from Muhammad's lips describe and justify the use of violence to establish Islam. Recent international events have brought the concept of "jihad" to public attention.

Jihad is mentioned 199 times in al-Bukhārī's collection of the Hadith. It is rated very highly. "A man came to Allah's Apostle and said, 'Instruct me as to such a deed as equals Jihad (in reward).' He replied, 'I do not find such a deed.'"[40] Aisha reiterated this: "O Allah's Apostle! We consider Jihad as the best deed."[41] At other times, jihad is described as the most excellent action after belief in Allah,[42] but sometimes it is relegated to third place behind prayer and duty to parents.[43]

Jihad is equivalent in merit to performing prayers without ceasing and never breaking one's fast. Even the steps of a *mujāhid's* (jihad fighter's) horse while grazing, along with its fodder, water, dung, and footmarks, earn him a reward.[44] Khālid bin al-Walīd's involvement in jihad made him exempt from payment of the Zakat charity tax,[45] and jihad obviated the need for fasting.[46]

6. THE AIM OF JIHAD

The aim of jihad is to make Islam superior.[47] Muhammad declared: "I have been ordered (by Allah) to fight against the people until they testify that none has the right to be worshipped but Allah and that Muhammad is Allah's Apostle, and offer the prayers perfectly and give the obligatory charity, so if they perform that, then they save their lives and property from me except for Islamic laws and then their reckoning (accounts) will be done by Allah"[48] A letter was sent by

ILLUSTRATION 16:
Muhammad's Letter
to Omani Princes[m]

m   http://vudesk.com/profiles/blogs/
       unseen-pictures-of-hazrat-muhammad-pbuh-life-and-era-2

Muhammad to the princes of Oman inviting them to accept Islam or face invasion by his troops. A copy of this letter is found in the museum in Sohar, Oman (see Illustration 16).

He also declared: "Paradise is under the blades (or shades, or shadow) of the sword."[49] His followers from Mecca and Medina declared: "We are those who have given the Pledge of allegiance to Muhammad to observe Jihad for as long as we remain alive."[50] Others gave the pledge of allegiance for death.[51] Khubaib al Anṣāri, about to face death at the hands of the Meccans for spying for Muhammad, declared: "I don't care if I am killed as a Muslim, on any side (of my body) I may be killed in Allah's Cause; for that is for the sake of Allah's very Self; and if He will, He will bestow His Blessings upon the torn pieces of my body."[52]

Jihad was given as a means to establish Islamic belief and practice. Jihad found a place in the Islamic economic system. Land could be endowed, among other things, for raising finances for jihad. This meant that the owner would not pay *Zakat* on the land but, on the proceeds or produce of this endowed land (called *waqf)*, "he could eat in a reasonable just manner, and he also could feed his friends without intending to be wealthy by its means."[53]

There were some limits on killing. Muslims were not to kill each other,[54] and no Muslim could be killed in revenge for killing a non-Muslim.[55]

7. THE REWARDS OF JIHAD

Engaging in jihad accrues a return in this world or the next. "Allah guarantees to the person who carries out Jihad for His Cause and nothing compelled him to go out but the Jihad in His Cause, and belief in His Words, that He will either admit him into Paradise or return him with his reward or the booty he has earned to his residence from where he went out."[56]

One of the gates of Paradise is called "Jihad."[57] Paradise is said to be under the blades of the sword.[58] Wounds resulting from jihad will flow again on the day of Resurrection and the blood will smell like musk.[59] A saying of the Prophet seemed to equate those who fought in jihad with all other Muslims, since all would enter Paradise. However, he went on to elaborate: "Paradise has one-hundred grades which Allah has reserved for the *mujāhidīn* who fight in His cause, and the distance between each of two grades is like the distance between the Heaven and the earth."[60] Clearly those involved in jihad would earn a greater reward. Muhammad promised that some of his followers would continue this victorious trend right up until the Last Hour.[61]

Muhammad informed his followers of a word from his Lord that "whoever of us is martyred will go to paradise to lead such a luxurious life as he has never seen."[62] Consequently he expressed a wish for multiple personal martyrdoms, citing concern for his supporters as his only restraint. "Had I not found it difficult for my followers, then I would not remain behind any *sariya* [military expedition] going for Jihad and I would have loved to be martyred in Allah's cause and then made alive, and then martyred and then made alive, and then again martyred in His cause."[63] Such a desire was allegedly expressed by the spirits of those martyred in the battle of Uhud. Muhammad told one man: ""I will give you good news, Jabir. God has restored to life your father who was killed at Uhud.' Then He asked him what he would like Him to do for him and he said that he would like to return to the world and fight for Him and be killed a second time.... The apostle swore that there was no believer who had parted from the world and wanted to return to it for a single hour even if he could possess it with all it has except the martyr who would like to return and fight for God and be killed a second time."[64] This was no empty rhetoric. In the last ten years of his life Muhammad organized no fewer than seventy-four campaigns, leading twenty-four of them himself.[65] He declared: "I have been made victorious with terror"[66] and "Allah made me victorious by awe, (by His frightening my enemies) for a distance of one month's

ILLUSTRATION 17:
Muhammad Carving at Supreme Court [n]

---

n https://www.washingtonpost.com/news/morning-mix/wp/2015/01/16/ how-images-of-the-prophet-muhammad-became-forbidden/.

journey."[67] Consequently the carving of Muhammad amongst the world's great law-makers at the Supreme Court in the US depicts him carrying the Qur'an and a sword (see Illustration 17).

Such a violent personal history has caused one commentator to call Muhammad a "domineering, warring autocrat."[68] Increasingly, modern Muslims, seeking to present Islam as a religion of peace, are forced to deal with these texts.[69]

Yet it was not only spiritual benefit that war would bring. Muhammad promised his men that the Roman and Persian leaders Caesar and Khosrau would be "ruined" and that "you will spend their treasures in Allah's cause."[70]

8. JESUS AND VIOLENCE

The contrast with Jesus could not be clearer. He advised his followers to love their enemies, to bless those who cursed them, to pray for those who mistreated them.[71] But when the Quraish said "injurious things" against Muhammad as he prayed at the Ka'ba, he threatened them: "By him who holds my life in His hand I bring you slaughter!"[72] After these same men had been killed at the battle of Badr and their bodies thrown in a well, he mocked their corpses: "Have you found true what your Lord promised you?"[73] Christ, despite the twelve legions of angels at his disposal, repudiated the military option. [74] When his follower recklessly attacked a man who came to arrest him, Jesus rebuked him: "Put your sword back in its place," Jesus said, "for all who draw the sword will die by the sword." Then he healed the wounded man.[75] Of his own life, he said: "I have authority to lay it down and authority to take it up again."[76] Like a good shepherd, he risked his life for his sheep.[77] Rather than encouraging violence or killing others to establish the Kingdom of God, he allowed others to kill him. As they did so, he prayed for their forgiveness.[78]

NOTES

1　'Uqba b. Abū Mu'ayt was captured at the battle of Badr, and was one of the two prisoners of war beheaded–the rest were held for ransom.

"When the apostle ordered him to be killed 'Uqba said, "But who will look after my children, O Muhammad?" "Hell," he said, and 'Asim b. Thābit b. Abu'l-Aqlah al-Ansāri killed him." Ibn Ishaq, *Sira*, 308.

2 Q.6:108.

3 B.8:58.

4 A biblical comparison might be the imprecatory Psalms (e.g., Pss 69:22-28; 109:1-20; 137:9; 139:19) and the sayings of Jeremiah (Jer 12:3; 18:23) where curses are pronounced on one's enemies.

5 Dashti, *Twenty Three Years*, 50.

6 Q.80:1–11; 40:55; 48:2 ; 94:1–3.

7 Q.3.128 - B5:397; 6:82,83; 9:445.

8 1 Kgs 19:4; Jer 15:10; 20:14–18.

9 B.8:360, 361, 362.

10 B.2:445, 446; 4:297; 5:514.

11 B.9:111.

12 B.7:670.

13 B.2:445, 446; 8:73, 126, 647.

14 John 8:22.

15 B.5:221; 2:659.

16 B.2:476; 8:523.

17 B.2:452, 453.

18 B.4:683.

19 Luke 23:34.

20 Acts 7:59.

21 B.1:617, 626b; 3:602; 9:330. This was not an empty threat, according to Ibn Hisham. "The apostle heard that the hypocrites were assembling in the house of Suwaylim the Jew (his house was by Jasum) keeping men back from the apostle in the raid on Tabuk. So the prophet sent Talha b. 'Ubaydullah with a number of his friends to them with orders to burn Suwaylim's house down on them. Talha did so, and al-Dahhak b. Khalifa threw himself from the top of the house and broke his leg, and his friends rushed out and escaped." Ibn Hisham's notes in Ibn Ishaq, *Sira*, 782, n. 858.

22 B.3:182, 183, 184, 185, 187, 188; 9:347.

23 B.3:186; 8:834; 9:348.

24 B.9:402.

25 B.7:807; 8:258; 9:38.2.

26 B.8:259; 9:27,38.1.

27 B.9:26.

28 B.9:39.

29 B.7:610; 9:25,35.

30 B.8:542.

31 B.8:319. Muhammad asked for forgiveness one hundred times a day according to Muslim book 35 no. 6522.

32 B.1:711, 760, 781; 8:407.

33 B.1:19.

34 See ch. 5, part 8.

35 Luke 22:51; 23:34.

36 Matt 6:12; Luke 11:4.

37 Mark 11:25.

38 Luke 6:27; Matt 5:43–48.

39 Dr. Murad Wilfried Hofmann, "Differences between the Muslim and the Christian Concept of Divine Love," The 14th General Conference Amman, September 4-7, 2007, Amman: The Hashemite Kingdom of Jordan. Source: www.aalalbayt.org/Research documents/14.pdf (accessed June 1, 2010). A Muslim commentator notes that that the public *dua's* (extemporare prayers) which receive the loudest congregational *ameens* in mosques around the world are those which invoke "some form of curse upon another whom we consider an enemy." Afroz Ali, "Dua by the decibel" in www.alghazzali.org/resources/articles/decibel.doc (accessed July 8, 2013).

40 B.4:44.

41 B.2:595; 4:43.

42 B.1:25; 2:594.

43 B.1:505; 4:41; 8:1; 9:625; B.1:25; 2:594.

44 B.4:44, 104, 112; 3:559; 6:486; 9:454.

45 B.2:547.

46 B.4:81.

47 B.1:125; 4:65,355; 9:550.

48 B.1:24, 378. This is despite the Qur'anic injunction that there is no compulsion in religion (Q.2:256). The Qur'an's teaching on jihad is extensive. See Firestone, *Jihad.*

49 B.4:73, 210, 266.1.

50 B.4:87, 88, 208; 5:140, 425, 598, 599; 9:308.

51 B.4:207; 5:487; 9:313.

52 B.9:499.

53 B.4:33.

54 B.1:30;.4:92, 93.

55 B.1:111.

56 B.9:549, 555; 4:46, 352; 1:35.

57 B.3:121.

58 B.4:73.

59 B.1:238.

60 B.4:48; 9:519.

61 B.9:414, 561.

62 B.4:386; 9:621.

63 B.1:35; 4:54; 9:332, 333. Muhammad's death wish may have been granted. On his deathbed, he complained to Aisha about the continuing effects of some poisoned meat (B.5:713). It had been fed to him by the vanquished Jews after the Muslim attack on Khaibar (B.3:786; 4:394). Bishr b. al-Bara' b. Ma'rur, who died from the same poison, was counted as a martyr. Ibn Ishaq comments: "The Muslims considered that the apostle died as a martyr in addition to the prophetic office with which God had honoured him." Ibn Ishaq, *Sira*, 516, 518.

64 Ibn Ishaq, *Sira*, 400.

65 Eaton, "Man," 364. Ibn Ishaq, *Sira,* 659 states that Muhammad led 27 military raids. Zaid bin Al-Arqam claims the number was nineteen (B.5:285).

66 B.4:220.

67 B.1:331.

68 Hume, *The World's Living Religions*, 226.

69 One group, calling itself "Muslims against Sharia," suggests a radical solution. "Islamic religious texts, including the Koran and the Hadith contain many passages, which call for Islamic domination and incite violence against non-Muslims. It is time to change that.... While neither [Old or New] Testament calls for mass murder of unbelievers, the Koran does. Could it be possible that the Koran itself was corrupted by Muslims over the last thirteen centuries? ... We must remove evil passages from Islamic religious texts, so that future generations of Muslims will not be confused by conflicting messages. Our religious message should be loud and clear: Islam is peace; Islam is love; Islam is light. War, murder, violence, divisiveness & discrimination are not Islamic values." Source: www.reformislam.org (accessed January 28, 2008). The website lists 558 verses which "must be either removed from the Koran or declared outdated and invalid, and marked as such." This demand is not as radical as it appears, for the practice of

declaring certain verses as "abrogated" is found in the footnotes of widely accepted editions of the Qur'an, such as Al-Hilali and Khan, *Translation of the meanings of the Noble Qur'an,* e.g., 13 n. 2; 21 n.1; 36 n. 3; 45 n. 2.

70   B.4:267,349,350,793,815,816; 8:625,626.

71   Luke 6:27,28.

72   Ibn Ishaq, *Sira,* 131.

73   B.2:452; 5:314, 317, 360.

74   Matt 26:52, 53.

75   Luke 22:50-52.

76   John 10:18.

77   John 15:13.

78   Luke 23:34.

12

WOMEN IN THE HADITH

1. MUHAMMAD'S TROUBLESOME HOUSEHOLD ARRANGEMENTS

The number of women that Muhammad married is uncertain. When Muhammad arrived in Medina, following the *Hijra* ("migration") from Mecca in AD 622, the Muslims built a mosque which included accommodation for him and his family. At that time he had only two wives, and a separate room was built for each (see Illustration 18).[1]

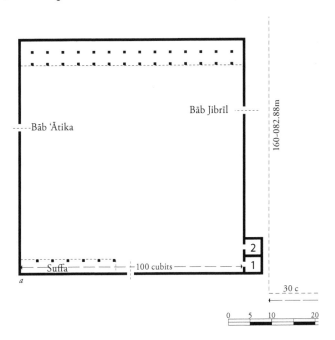

ILLUSTRATION 18: The Mosque in Medina AD 622

Sawda bint Zam'a was tall and fat,[2] older than he was, and he had married her a few days after his first wife, Khadija, died.[3] Aisha was young and pretty, and always remained Muhammad's favorite wife.[4] He was given divine permission to marry as many women as he wanted,[5] but this was later disavowed.[6]

As he married more women, extra rooms were built for each wife (see Illustration 19).

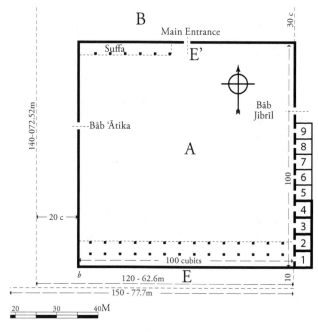

ILLUSTRATION 19: The Mosque in Medina c. AD 629

The number of women that Muhammad married is unclear, but nine and eleven have been suggested. He would spend one day, in turn, with each wife,[7] although Allah allowed him to vary their turns if he wished.[8] Ultimately Sawda gave her day to Aisha,[9] on condition that Muhammad would not divorce Sawda, but allow her to stay in the household while providing for her own support.[10] There were serious tensions in the household, and the wives formed coalitions against each other, with shouting matches. They "used harsh words" with Muhammad, demanding that he treat them all equally.[11] They argued with him about various matters,[12] and conspired together to deprive Muhammad of the sweet things he liked eating.[13]

Muhammad described his wives as "companions of Joseph,"[14] a reference to Potiphar's deceptive wife,[15] who is called Aziz's wife in the Qur'an.[16] The problems with his wives became so extreme that he considered divorcing them all,[17] on the expectation that Allah would give him better wives.[18]

2. BEATING WOMEN

The Qur'an allows a man to beat his disobedient wife under certain conditions.[19] Muhammad hit Aisha after she had followed him outside the house one night without asking his permission. She reports what happened. "He said: 'Was it the darkness (of your shadow) that I saw in front of me?' I said: 'Yes' He struck me on the chest which caused me pain, and then said: 'Did you think that Allah and His Apostle would deal unjustly with you?'"[20] Muhammad's advice about how to hit one's wife often showed a stark pragmatism. "It is not wise for anyone of you to lash his wife like a slave," he told his followers, "for he might sleep with her the same evening."[21] In another version, men were told not to beat their wives "as he beats the stallion camel."[22]

Muhammad allowed and even provoked their fathers to slap his wives in his presence. 'Umar "found Allah's Apostle (peace be upon him) sitting sad and silent with his wives around him. He (Umar) said: 'I wanted say something which would make the Holy Prophet (peace be upon him) laugh', so he said: 'Messenger of Allah, I wish you had seen (the treatment meted out to) the daughter of Kharijah when she asked me for some money, and I got up and slapped her on her neck.' Allah's Messenger (peace be upon him) laughed and said: 'They are around me as you see, asking for extra money.' Abu Bakr then got up, went to Aisha (Allah be pleased with her) and slapped her on the neck, and Umar stood up before Hafsah and slapped her saying: 'You ask Allah's Messenger (peace be upon him) for that which he does not possess.' They said: 'By Allah, we do not ask Allah's Messenger (peace be upon him) for anything he does not possess.' Then he withdrew from them for a month or for twenty-nine days."[23]

Aisha reports that her father Abū Bakr "struck me violently with his fist" while Muhammad was asleep on her lap because she had delayed their travel. But she did not move "lest I should awake Allah's Apostle although that hit was very painful."[24] The beating of women was apparently widespread among the early Muslims. Pointing out to Muhammad the deep bruises on one Muslim woman, Aisha commented: "I have not seen any woman suffering as much as the believing women. Look! Her skin is greener than her clothes!"[25]

3. STONING AND AMPUTATION

Jesus' dealing with the woman caught in adultery is well known. "Let him who is without sin cast the first stone"[26] has become proverbial in the English language. In a similar situation, Muhammad did not use his authority to protect the woman when a couple was accused of adultery. The man, being single, was flogged and temporarily banished, but Muhammad commanded that the woman be stoned to death because she was married.[27] In another case, the woman herself admitted her adultery and she was stoned for it.

> There came to him (the Holy Prophet) a woman from Ghamid and said: Allah's Messenger, I have committed adultery, so purify me. He (the Holy Prophet) turned her away. On the following day she said: Allah's Messenger, Why do you turn me away? Perhaps, you turn me away as you turned away Ma'iz. By Allah, I have become pregnant. He said: Well, if you insist upon it, then go away until you give birth to (the child). When she was delivered she came with the child (wrapped) in a rag and said: Here is the child whom I have given birth to. He said: Go away and suckle him until you wean him. When she had weaned him, she came to him (the Holy Prophet) with the child who was holding a

piece of bread in his hand. She said: Allah's Apostle, here is he as I have weaned him and he eats food. He (the Holy Prophet) entrusted the child to one of the Muslims and then pronounced punishment. And she was put in a ditch up to her chest and he commanded people and they stoned her. Khalid b Walid came forward with a stone which he flung at her head and there spurted blood on the face of Khalid and so he abused her. Allah's Apostle (may peace be upon him) heard his (Khalid's) curse that he had hurled upon her. Thereupon he (the Holy Prophet) said: Khalid, be gentle. By Him in Whose Hand is my life, she has made such a repentance that even if a wrongful tax-collector were to repent, he would have been forgiven. Then giving command regarding her, he prayed over her and she was buried.[28]

Amputation was also carried out on a female thief. "A woman from the tribe of Makhzum committed theft. She was brought to [Muhammad] and she sought refuge (intercession) from Umm Salamah, the wife of [the Prophet]. Thereupon Allah's Apostle (peace be upon him) said: 'By Allah, even if she were Fatimah [his daughter], I would have her hand cut off.' And thus her hand was cut off."[29]

Such violence against women in Muhammad's household and early Islamic society contrasts strongly with the supportive and nurturing atmosphere that typified Jesus' relationships with women.[30]

4. LACK OF EMOTIONAL SUPPORT

Jesus went to comfort Lazarus' sisters and he wept when his friend Lazarus died.[31] Although Muhammad also wept when describing the events of the battle of Mu'tah,[32] women were banned from wailing and lamenting their dead if they took the Islamic pledge of allegiance.[33] Nor were female relatives of the Muslim martyr Ja'far allowed to mourn.

A man came to him and said, 'O Allah's Apostle! The women of Ja'far are crying.' Thereupon the Prophet told him to forbid them to do so. So the man went away and returned saying, 'I forbade them but they did not listen to me.' The Prophet ordered him again to go (and forbid them). He went again and came saying, 'By Allah, they overpowered me (i.e. did not listen to me).' ... Allah's Apostle said (to him), "Go and throw dust into their mouths.[34]

5. AISHA'S JEALOUSY AND COMPLAINTS

The most outspoken among Muhammad's consorts was his child-bride Aisha, married to Muhammad when she was six years old. He consummated the marriage when she turned nine.[35] She had a caustic tongue, swearing "by the Lord of Muhammad" when she was happy with her husband, but subtly dropping his name and changing her oaths to "by the Lord of Abraham" whenever Muhammad angered her.[36] A man was considered her foster uncle according to Arab custom because his wife had breastfed Aisha as a baby. When the Prophet told her to allow this man to enter her house, Aisha sarcastically commented: "O Allah's Apostle! I have been suckled by a woman and not by a man."[37] Another time Aisha complained of a headache and Muhammad mockingly expressed a wish to pray the funeral prayer for her. The razor-tongued teenager replied: "By Allah, I think you want me to die; and if this should happen, you would spend the last part of the day sleeping with one of your wives!"[38] Despite being Muhammad's favorite wife,[39] she was clearly jealous of her competitors for his attentions.

Aisha disputed the Prophet's saying that a dog, donkey, or woman walking in front of a praying person annulled that person's prayers.[40] She retorted: "Do you make us (women) equal to dogs and donkeys?"[41] She recounted that Muhammad often prayed in her bed at night with her legs lying between him and the *Qibla* (direction of the *Ka'ba*).[42]

When a belated revelation came, exonerating Aisha from scandal-ous rumors about her relationship with the young soldier Ṣafwān, her response seemed sarcastic: "Thanks to Allah (only) and not to anybody else." Apparently she felt she had suffered public disgrace unnecessarily.[43] She did not feel valued by her husband, telling Muhammad that, if she died, "you would be busy enjoying the com-pany of one of your wives in the last part of that day."[44]

She jealously yet cleverly sought to gain more of Muhammad's attention over against his other eight wives, who had all been mar-ried before, by relating this parable to the Prophet:

"O Allah's Apostle! Suppose you landed in a valley where there is a tree of which something has been eaten and then you found trees of which nothing has been eaten, of which tree would you let your camel graze?' He said, "(I will let my camel graze) of the one of which nothing has been eaten before." (The sub-narrator added: "Aisha meant that Allah's Apostle had not married a virgin besides herself.")[45] Such efforts, and the fact that she was younger and pretti-er[46] than the other wives, made her his favorite. He claimed that "the Divine Inspirations do not come to me on any of the beds except that of 'Aisha." [47] In the face of Aisha's jealousy about Khadija,[48] Muhammad justified his frequent positive comments about his first wife with: "From her I had children,"[49] a backhanded com-ment about Aisha's inability to produce a male heir. Of course all of Muhammad's other wives had the same problem. Only Maria, the Coptic concubine, was able to produce a son for Muhammad, but Ibrahim died as an infant.[50]

Some revelations seemed to come for the Prophet's personal comfort and convenience, such as the Qur'anic prohibition against arguing in his presence[51] and the "screening" verse which was revealed when some guests stayed too long after his wedding to Zainab.[52] Since the order to marry her came to Muhammad in a revelation,[53] Zainab boasted to the other wives: "Allah married me (to the Prophet) in the Heavens."[54] Despite this, the Qur'an claims that Muhammad "does not speak of his own desire."[55]

Aisha commented: "I used to look down upon those ladies who had given themselves to Allah's Apostle and I used to say, 'Can a lady give herself (to a man)?' But when Allah revealed: 'You (O Muhammad) can postpone (the turn of) whom you will of them (your wives), and you may receive any of them whom you will; and there is no blame on you if you invite one whose turn you have set aside (temporarily),'[56] I said (to the Prophet), 'I feel that your Lord hastens in fulfilling your wishes and desires.'"[57]

Muhammad's favorite wife disputed with his one remaining daughter. Aisha asked: "'What is wrong with Fatima? Why doesn't she fear Allah?' by saying that a divorced lady is not entitled to be provided with residence and sustenance (by her husband)."[58] In dispute was the revelation regarding the husband's provision for his wife after their divorce.[59] On other occasions, Aisha "disapproved of" and "reproached" Fatima.[60] The tension between them was obvious.

Much of later Islamic history was the playing out of rivalry for power and influence between Aisha against the family of his daughter Fatima and her husband Ali.[61] Following the scandal of Aisha with Ṣafwān, Muhammad consulted Ali and Usāma about divorcing Aisha. Ali's initial advice was equivocal: "O Allah's Apostle! Allah does not put you in difficulty and there are plenty of women other than she."[62] Such comments would do little to help family relationships.

6. INFLEXIBLE RULES

Sometimes inflexible rules were enforced to the detriment of women. Women who used cosmetic treatments such as tattooing, removal of facial hair (one translation includes plucking eyebrows),[63] and artificial dental treatment "in order to look more beautiful" were cursed.[64] So were women who used hair extensions or false hair,[65] which was described by Muhammad as *az-zur* "cheating."[66] The ban was even applied to an unfortunate girl afflicted by measles[67] despite the subsequent hair loss threatening her marriage.[68]

When her second husband proved impotent, and had beaten her, a woman wanted to return to her first husband, who had divorced her.[69] "That is impossible unless [your second husband] consummates his marriage with you," the Prophet informed her.[70] This woman was now trapped in a violent and loveless relationship. Jesus' espousal

of monogamy and his teaching about
divorce, as well as Peter's and Paul's
teaching on husband-wife relationships, would seem to give far greater
protection to women in marriage.[71]

Muhammad, riding Buraq (the fly-
ing mule), is shown hell by Gabriel,
and they see a demon punishing
"shameless women" who had exposed
their hair to strangers. For this crime

ILLUSTRATION 20:
Women in Hell 1

of inciting lust in men, the women are strung up by their hair and
burned for eternity (see Illustration 20).[72]

Initially Muhammad's wives were allowed to leave their house for
necessities,[73] and were not required to be veiled. Umar urged him to
cover them. Mernissi claims that this was a capitulation to Umar,
despite Muhammad's commitment to male-female equality.[74]

Umar's strictness was legendary.[75] Even Muhammad was intimidated by him, refusing in a dream to enter 'Umar's heavenly palace for
fear of offending 'Umar's *ghira* (self-respect).[76] 'Umar put pressure on
Muhammad by calling out the names of the Prophet's unveiled wives
when they went out at night to answer the call of nature.[77] Aisha noted Umar's motive: "He said so, as he desired eagerly that the verses
of Al-Hijab (the observing of veils by the Muslim women) may be
revealed. So Allah revealed the verses of Al-Hijab" (Q.24:31).[78] From
then on, Muhammad's wives were required to veil in public. That
veiling was not freely chosen by the Muslim women seems to be
indicated in Aisha's comment during the Battle of the Ditch: "This
was before the veil had been *imposed upon us*."[79] Walking to the dawn
prayers, they covered themselves with veiling sheets so as not to be
recognized in public.[80] If they did not have enough veils, they were
told to share them.[81] These restrictions began to push the women
into more marginal roles. Sometimes they were left sleeping during
prayer times.[82] Later Aisha stated that Muhammad would have pro-
scribed his wives from attending the mosque if he had known that
Jewish women did not attend the synagogue.[83] This injunction was
then made mandatory for the Prophet's wives.[84]

After the *hijra* to Yathrib (Medina), Muhammad placed more limits on his wives' behavior, and consequently the activities of all Muslim women. This may have been a reaction to the more outspoken nature of the Medinan women: "We, the people of Quraish, used to have authority over women, but when we came to live with the Ansar, we noticed that the Ansari women had the upper hand over their men, so our women started acquiring the habits of the Ansari women."[85] By contrast, the Quraish women were lauded for their mercy, kindness, and loyalty.[86]

Some reflection of these interfamily pressures may be projected into the promise to each Muslim man of a massive pearllike tent in Paradise, "in each corner of which there are wives who will not see those in the other corners,"[87] presumably leaving the man to visit the others freely and unobserved. Muhammad's comment that "the in-laws of the wife are death itself"[88] may reflect his own bitter personal experience.

7. MUHAMMAD'S DEROGATORY STATEMENTS ABOUT WOMEN

According to Muhammad, only two women attained the standard of excellence achieved by many males. "Many men reached the level of perfection, but no woman reached such a level except Mary, the daughter of Imran, and Asia, the wife of Pharaoh."[89]

Muhammad noted: "I looked at Hell and saw that the majority of its inhabitants were women"[90] (see Illustration 21).[91]

Muhammad reported that the majority of the inhabitants of

ILLUSTRATION 21:
Women in Hell 2

hell were women. Gabriel shows Muhammad the women being tortured in hell by hanging them up by hooks through their breasts, while being burned. The women are being punished for giving birth to illegitimate children while falsely claiming the children were fathered by their husbands.

Their misdemeanor was not disbelief in Allah, but lack of appreciation toward their husbands.[92] Any woman who refused sex with her husband would be cursed by the angels until morning.[93]

In one of the most misogynistic of Hadiths, Muhammad vilifies women on the basis of their legal and physical limitations. Passing a group of women at a praying place, he commented: "'I have not seen anyone more deficient in intelligence and religion than you. A cautious sensible man could be led astray by some of you.' The women asked, 'O Allah's Apostle! What is deficient in our intelligence and religion?' He said, 'Is not the evidence of two women equal to the witness of one man?' They replied in the affirmative. He said, 'This is the deficiency in her intelligence. Isn't it true that a woman can neither pray nor fast during her menses?' The women replied in the affirmative. He said, 'This is the deficiency in her religion.'"[94] This did not stop Muhammad running to Khadija in fear when he experienced the first revelation. She devised a clever method of determining whether the spirit he had seen in the cave outside Mecca was evil or otherwise. "She disclosed her form and cast aside her veil while the apostle was sitting in her lap. Then she said, 'Can you see him?' And he replied, 'No.' She said, 'O son of my uncle, rejoice and be of good heart, by God he is an angel and not a satan.'"[95] Of course Muhammad's loss of the angelic vision in this particular situation may be capable of another, somewhat less spiritual, explanation. Some consider it ironic that a woman was called upon to authenticate Muhammad's revelation when he would later assert that "the witness of a woman [was] equal to half that of a man ... because of the deficiency of a woman's mind."[96] Consequently women should be limited in public roles. Muhammad said: "Never will succeed such a nation as makes a woman their ruler."[97] His description of them as "glass vessels"[98] implied their weakness as well as their value.[99]

This low opinion of female capabilities meant that women were not fully consulted even in decisions which directly affected them. When asked how a virgin could indicate her consent to be married, Muhammad said: "Her silence means her consent."[100] This appeared to be the situation for Muhammad's union with the six-year-old Aisha. She reported: "When the Prophet married me, my mother came to me and made me enter the house (of the Prophet) and nothing surprised me but the coming of Allah's Apostle to me in the forenoon."[101] Apparently she had not been informed about the marriage beforehand. A Medinan man offered to divide his property and share it with a poor emigrant from Mecca, adding: "and I will give one of my two wives to you."[102] It is not recorded whether the woman's permission was sought before this offer.

The Prophet of Islam declared, "After me I have not left any affliction more harmful to men than women."[103] The first woman, according to Muhammad, began the trend: "but for Eve, wives would never betray their husbands,"[104] he claimed. "An evil omen may be in three: a woman, a house or an animal," according to Muhammad.[105] This propensity toward malevolence is not peripheral to womanhood but is part of the inherent nature of each woman. Her nature cannot be changed, nor should the attempt be made, according to one Hadith. "A woman is created from a rib, and the most curved portion of the rib is its upper portion, so, if you should try to straighten it, it will break, but if you leave it as it is, it will remain crooked. So treat women nicely."[106] Muhammad advised men to exploit this defect: "So if you want to get benefit from her, do so while she still has some crookedness."[107]

8. CRITICISM OF THESE HADITHS

It is not surprising that some Muslim women have found such words offensive or condescending, and have questioned the reliability of the Hadith. The Hadith have been criticized by modern feminists, including Muslims, who do not consider that these documents further the cause of women's liberation. Their sisters of fourteen centuries ago faced similar problems. Islamic feminist theologians claim that the Hadith have an inordinate influence in Qur'anic hermeneutics.[108] "According to Riffat Hassan, it is the customary Muslim practice of interpreting the Qur'ān by way of the Hadith ... that leads to misogynistic interpretations."[109]

Hassan commented:

It is imperative for the Muslim daughters of Hawwa [Eve] to realize that the history of their subjugation and humiliation at the hands of the sons of Adam began with the story of Hawwa's creation and that their future will be no different from their past unless they ... challenge the authenticity of the *aHadith* which make them ontologically inferior, subordinate and crooked. It is gratifying to know that these *AHadith* cannot be the words of the Prophet of Islam ... regardless of how male chauvinist Muslims project their androcentrism and misogyny on their Prophet.[110]

In a section of this paper entitled "Significant *AHadith* in regard to women's creation," she critically examines the *isnād* and *matn* of some Hadiths and contrasts them with the Qur'an. Ali Asghar Engineer claims that all the anti-women Hadiths, even from the *ṣaḥīḥ* collections, were fabricated by later misogynists, who "held women in low esteem and ascribed their despicable thoughts to the Prophet."[111]

Bennett felt that the anti-women sentiments supposedly expressed in the Hadith were a reflection of Abbasid attitudes rather than the sayings of Muhammad himself.[112] Whatever their provenance, the Hadith provide much material for those who believe that women have an inferior status in Islam.

NOTES

1   The source of this diagram, and Illustration 19, is http:// thecityasaproject.org/2012/06/medina (accessed July 9, 2013).

2   B.1:148; 2:740; 6:318; 8:257.

3   Vacca, V., "Sawda Bint Zam'a," Encyclopaedia of Islam, First Edition (1913-1936). Edited by M. Th. Houtsma, T.W. Arnold, R. Basset, R. Hartmann. Brill Online, 2013. Reference. June 24, 2013. http:// referenceworks.brillonline.com/entries/encyclopaedia-of-islam-1/ sawda-bint-zama-SIM_5208.

4   B.3:755.

5   Q.33:50.

6   Q.33:52.

7   B.3:766.

8   Q.33:51.

9   B.3:766, 853; 7:139.

10   Q.4:128. See Ibn Kathir's commentary on this verse, www.qtafsir. com/index.php?option=com _content&task=view&id=599&Item id=59 (accessed July 9, 2013).

11   B.3:755.

12   B.4:635.

13   B.7:193; 9:102.

14   B.1:633, 646, 647, 650.

15   Gen 39:1–20.

16   Q.12:23–36, 50–52. The Qur'anic version has extrabiblical details, including a group of women among whom she tried to preserve her own reputation by impressing them with her slave Joseph's good looks.

17   B.1:89; 7:119.

18   Q.66:5.

19   Q.4:34.

20   Muslim Bk 4 no. 2127.

21   B.6:466.

22   B.8:68.

23   Muslim Bk 9 no. 3506.

24   B.8:828, 827.

25   B.7:715. Armstrong, *Muhammad,* 158 notes the widespread wife beating among the early Muslims.

26   John 8:7. This story is not found in the earliest manuscripts of John's gospel. This does not mean that this event did not take place. John himself admitted that his material on the life of Christ was selective (John 20:30), and that other material could have been included but was omitted due to space limitations (John 21:25). Of this account, Morris notes that "the story is true to the character of Jesus. Throughout the history of the church it has been held that, whoever wrote it, this little story is authentic. It rings true." He quotes with approval Tenney's comment on the story's "ancient character and undoubtedly historic truthfulness." Morris, *John*, 883.

27   B.3:860, 885 also 3:508; 8:629, 815, 821, 826, 842; 9:303, 365.

28   Muslim, 4206.

29   B.5:597; 4:681; 8:778, 799.

30 Examples include the woman with the flow of blood (Matt 9:20–22;
    Mark 5:25–34; Luke 8:43–48), the widow of Nain (Luke 7:11–15),
    the women who supported Jesus and his disciples (Luke 8:2,3), and
    Martha and Mary (Luke 10:38–42).

31 John 11:17–40.

32 B.5:561.

33 B.9:322.

34 B.5:562; also 2:386.

35 B.5:234, 236; 7:64, 65, 88. Permission to marry prepubescent girls
    was apparently given in Q:65:4. Ibn Kathir comments on this verse:
    "for the young who have not reached the years of menstruation,
    their 'iddah [waiting period before marriage] is three months.... This
    is the meaning of the saying 'and for those who have no courses.'"
    Muhammad's marriage to Aisha caused the Ayatollah Khomeini to
    propose nine years old to become the permissible age of marriage for
    girls in Iran (Afshar, Iran, Islam and Democracy, 7). Aisha was not the
    only child that Muhammad expressed interest in for a wife. The earli-
    est biography of Muhammad records the following. "The apostle saw
    her (Ummu'1-Fadl) when she was a baby crawling before him and
    said, 'If she grows up and I am still alive I will marry her.' But he died
    before she grew up" (Ibn Ishaq, Sira Rasul Allah, 691, 310).

36 B.7:155; 8:101.

37 B.7:166; 8:177.

38 B.7:570.

39 B.3:755; 3:648.

40 B.1:490, 493.

41 B.1:486, 498.

42 B.1:379, 380, 381, 491, 492, 494.

43 B.4:602; 5:464.

44 B.9:324.

45 B.7:14.

46 B.6:435; 7:145.

47 B.3:755.

48 B.5:164, 165, 166, 168; 7:156; 8:33; 9:576.

49 B.5:166.

50 B.2:153, 168, 170, 390, 464; 8:214, 215, 219.

51 Q.49:1; B.5:653; 6:370.

52   Q.33:53; B.8:255, 256; 9:517.

53   B. 6:310.

54   B.9:516,517.

55   Q.53:3.

56   Q.33.51

57   B.6:311

58   B.7:243

59   Q.2:236

60   B.7:244,245

61   Aisha combined with Meccan aristocrats Talha and Zubayr to oppose Ali's caliphate. Their faction was defeated by Ali's forces in AD 656 at the "battle of the Camel," so named because Aisha urged the battle on from the *howdah* (carriage) on a camel's back (Lapidus, *History*, 56).

62   B.5:462; 6:274; 9:462; 3:805.

63   It does, however, make an exception for the depilation of the beard and moustache (Al-Hilali and Khan, *Translation of the Meanings of the Noble Qur'an*, 753 n. 1).

64   B.6:408; 7:822, 826, 832.

65   B.4:674; 6:409; 7:816,821.

66   B.4:694.

67   B.7:817, 824.

68   B.7:133, 818.

69   B.7:715.

70   B.7:684; 8:107.

71   Matt 19:4–8; 5:31,32; Mark 10:2–12; 1 Pet 3:7; Eph 5:25–33.

72   Persian, 15th century, from a manuscript entitled *Miraj Nama*, which is in the Bibliotheque Nationale, Paris. Taken from *The Miraculous Journey of Mahomet*, by Marie-Rose Seguy.

73   B.1:149.

74   Mernissi, *Women and Islam*, 63, 64.

75   B.5:32; 8:108.

76   B.5:28; 7:153, 154; 9:150,151,152.

77   B.1:148; 8:257.

78   B.1:148; 6:282; 7:95. A helpful analysis of the broader history of veiling and its significance is found in Mallouhi, *Miniskirts, Mothers and Muslims*, ch. 3.

79   Ibn Ishaq, *Sira Rasul Allah*, 457 (italics mine).

80   B.1:368, 552, 826.

81   B.1:137; 2:96.

82   B.1: 821, 823.

83   B1: 828.

84   Q.33:33.

85   B.3:648; 7:119. The similarity with the concern of the courtiers at Queen Vashti's behavior toward King Xerxes cannot be overlooked: "there will be no end of disrespect and discord" (Esth 1:18).

86   B.4:643.

87   B.6:402; 4:466.

88   B.7:159.

89   B.4:643, also 4:623; 7:329. Aisha did, however, receive special mention for her superiority in this Hadith, where she is compared to a preferred type of food. Khadija was listed as the best among the Arab women (B.4:642).

90   B.4:464; also 1:28; 2:541; 7:124, 125, 126; 8:456, 554, 555.

91   Persian, 15th century, from a manuscript entitled *Miraj Nama*, which is in the Bibliotheque Nationale, Paris. Taken from *The Miraculous Journey of Mahomet*, by Marie-Rose Seguy.

92   B.1:301. Women betraying their righteous husbands (who are prophets) is a Qur'anic concept (Q.66:10), but the reverse also occurs, with a righteous wife outshining a wicked husband (Q.66:11).

93   B.4:460; 7:121, 122. This explanation of a husband's rights over his wife did not quite reach the extent outlined by Muhammad's ambassador to Yemen. "When the apostle sent Mu'adh he gave him instructions and orders and then said: 'Deal gently and not harshly; announce good news and do not repel people....' Mu'adh went off to the Yaman and did as he was ordered and a woman came to him and said, 'O companion of God's apostle, what rights has a husband over his wife?' He said, 'Woe to you, a woman can never fulfil her husband's rights, so do your utmost to fulfil his claims as best you can.' She said, 'By God, if you are the companion of God's apostle you must know what rights a husband has over his wife!' He said, 'If you were to go back and find him with his nostrils running with pus and blood and sucked until you got rid of them you would not have fulfilled your obligation.' Ibn Ishaq, *Sira Rasul Allah*, 644. The "filth from the washing of wounds" is described as the food of those in hellfire (Q.69:36), reflecting Muhammad's observation that the majority of hell's residents were women.

94 B.1:301; also 2:541.

95 Ibn Ishaq, *Sira,* 107.

96 Caner and Caner, *Unveiling Islam,* 43. Their quote is based on al-Bukhāri 1:301.

97 B.9:219. Ali Asghar Engineer challenges this Hadith which was first reported by Abu Bakr during Ali's caliphate, for Abu Bakr "was aspiring for governorship of one of the provinces and wanted to please Hadrat Ali." Ali Asghar Engineer, "Qur'an, Hadith and Women," *Islam and Modern Age,* February 2008, www.futureislam. com/20080103/insight/asgar_ali/QURAN_HADITH_AND_ WOMEN.asp (accessed December 11, 2010).

98 B8:228,229.

99 B8:230 c.f. 1 Pet 3:7.

100 B.9:79,100,101; 7:67, 68.

101 B.7:90.

102 B.7:96.

103 B.7:33.

104 B.4:547, 611.

105 B.7:649, 666.

106 B.4:548; 7:114.

107 B.7:113.

108 It is not only feminists who find a problem with interpretations of the Qur'an representing a misogynistic stance. Muslim homosexual groups report a similar distortion. One website, al-Fatiha, is "dedicated to Muslims who are lesbian, gay, bisexual, transgender, intersex, questioning [LGBTIQ], those exploring their sexual orientation or gender identity, and their allies, families and friends. Al-Fatiha promotes the progressive Islamic notions of peace, equality and justice." One of its projects is outlined: "To counter the spiritual violence that so many LGBTIQ Muslims face, which is perpetuated by anti-gay scripture and theology, Al-Fatiha has brought together LGBTIQ and queer friendly Muslim theologians and religious academics ... [to] offer alternative interpretations of the Quran." Source: www.al-fatiha. org (accessed February 12, 2008). According to the Hadith, the death penalty must be applied to both parties engaging in homosexual acts (Muslim Bk 38 nos 4447, 4448).

109 Barlas, "Women's readings of the Qur'ān," 259–60. She cites the work of Hassan, "Is family planning permitted by Islam?" 235.

110 Hassan, "Made from Adam's Rib, the Woman's Creation Question," 124.

111   Ali Asghar Engineer, "Qur'an, Hadith and Women," *Islam and Modern Age,* February 2008, www.futureislam.com/20080103/ insight/asgar_ali/QURAN_HADITH_AND_WOMEN.asp (accessed July 9, 2013).

112   Bennett, *In Search of Muhammad,* 62.

13

HISTORY, HEAVEN, AND HELL

1. CONTRASTS WITH BIBLICAL CHRONOLOGY AND NARRATIVES

Several accounts in the Hadith are not in accord with the previous biblical stories about the same characters or events. Abraham was reported to be eighty years old when he was circumcised, while the Old Testament stated that he was ninety-nine.[1] Hagar was allegedly suckling Ishmael when she took him to Mecca. However, according to the Bible, Ishmael would by then have been at least fifteen years old, hardly a suitable age to be breastfed.[2] The Hadith account claims the Arab tribe of Jurhum made Ishmael marry one of their women, while the Bible declares that his mother obtained a wife for him from Egypt.[3] Hagar, Abraham's slave wife, is said to have run between the mountains of Safa and Marwa near Mecca.[4] However, the Bible records the location of this event as "in the desert of Beersheba,"[5] near Jericho, many hundreds of kilometers to the northwest of Mecca.[6]

There are also extrabiblical stories about Old Testament prophets, including the amusing story of the stone that stole Moses' clothes while he was bathing. This forced him to run naked past a group of Israelites, while chasing the stone with a stick. Nonetheless the outcome was positive–it dispelled the public rumor that Moses had a scrotal hernia or some other defect.[7] The legend of Moses and the Jewish servant boy al-Khidr, outlined in the Qur'an,[8] is related in greater detail. In this account, Moses nearly prolonged his life by slapping the angel of death in the face,[9] but declined an opportunity to extend his life even further.[10] David, reportedly, could recite the entire book of Psalms while his horse was being saddled.[11] This would be a remarkable feat for the 2,526 verses in the book of Psalms, the longest book in the Bible.

The story of Solomon's wisdom in discovering the true mother of a disputed infant[12] is given a twist. The other baby was said to have been taken by a wolf and King David initially gave a verdict in favor of the wrong mother.[13]

One Muslim scholar applies a historicocritical approach to the Hadith. Khan identifies ten of al-Bukhāri's and Muslim's reports which do not accord with generally accepted Islamic history on various points. He says: "In a situation where a report contradicts established history, the tradition, regardless of its authenticity in terms of the chain, is to be considered dubious if not declared fabricated."[14]

2. OTHER HISTORY

The Hadith contain accounts which are historically incorrect when compared with other sources of information.

An apparent anachronism states that the world's first mosque, the Ka'ba, was built by Abraham and Ishmael in Mecca, and the second one was the Al-Aqsa mosque constructed in Jerusalem forty years later.[15] In fact the Al-Aqsa mosque began as a small *musalla* (prayer house) built by the caliph 'Umar (r. AD 634-644), and was then rebuilt and expanded by Abd al-Malik (r. AD 685-705) before being completed by his son al-Walid in AD 705.[16]

Some Hadith, although set in the Prophet's life, appear to reflect the realities of a later period. When Muhammad said of his small grandson al-Hasan, "perhaps Allah will bring about an agreement between two sects of the Muslims through him,"[17] the two main factions of Islam (Sunni and Shia) did not yet exist.

Similarly Muhammad's reported comment about the Khawarij Muslim sect in Iraq was made when Islam did not yet exist in Iraq, nor had the Khawarij group even developed.[18]

3. PARADISE AND HEAVEN

The Hadith's portrayal of paradise reveals some sharp contrasts with the biblical view of heaven. While Jesus spoke of no marriage in heaven,[19] the Islamic perception is very sensual and very detailed. Every male inhabitant of the Muslim paradise can look forward to *houri* wives,[20] who are physically desirable.[21] Some men will have two wives and "the marrow of the bones of the wives' legs will be seen through the flesh out of excessive beauty."[22] However, there will be no jealousy for, due to the large pavilion provided, the wives confined[23] to one corner will not be able to see those in the other corners; and the believers will be able to visit and enjoy each of them unhindered.[24] Paradise will be a clean place since people "will not spit or blow their noses or relieve nature ... and their sweat will smell like musk."[25] The Bible's description of heaven that "nothing impure will ever enter it, nor will anyone who does what is shameful or deceitful"[26] relates to the exclusion of moral evil[27] as opposed to the Hadith's requirement for public and personal hygiene in paradise.

4. HELL AND PUNISHMENT

Hell, as described in the Qur'an and the Hadith, is a place of agonising punishment (see Illustration 22). According to the Qur'an, there is "no way of escape" from hell.[28] Those who enter will never depart from it;[29] they will dwell in it forever[30] or "for ages."[31] Those who try to get away will be put back.[32] The Jews had claimed: "The Fire will not touch us but for a few numbered days." But this is denied.[33]

However, other Qur'anic verses suggest that some may be saved out of hell.[34] One verse states to the Muslims that "there is not one of you but will pass over it (hell) ... then We will save those who used to fear Allah and were dutiful to Him"[35] and "We shall leave the *Zālimūn*

ILLUSTRATION 22:
Gabriel Shows Muhammad
the Tortures of Hell[o]

(polytheists and wrongdoers) therein humbled to their knees."[36]

This ties in with Hadith that speak of some Muslims falling into hell before being saved by the intercession of their coreligionists and some by God himself.[37]

They will emerge from the pit due to the intercession of others.[38]

Muhammad said: "Some people will come out of the Fire after they have received a touch of the Fire, changing their color, and they will enter Paradise, and the people of Paradise will name them 'Al-Jahannamiyin' the (Hell) Fire people."[39] They will have had "a mustard seed of faith," which will be sufficient to save them.[40] Based on the mediation of Muhammad and his negotiation with Allah, some of those imprisoned in hell will be released in tranches, until only those remain "who have been destined to an eternal stay in Hell."[41] The last person to crawl out of hell will imagine heaven has been filled, but this will not be the case.[42] Interestingly he will leave the fire and enter paradise not by Muhammad's or anyone else's intercession but because of his own persistent incremental requests to Allah.[43]

The Bible suggests that no one can cross over from hell to heaven or vice versa,[44] for the punishment of hell is forever.[45]

NOTES

1   B.4:575, 576; Gen 17:24.

2   B.4:582, 583. Gen 16:16 and 17:1, 24. However, Muhammad advised a woman to breastfeed a man not related to her in order to allow him to visit her when she was alone. "The wife of Abu Hudhayfah said: 'Messenger of Allah, Salim comes to me and now he

o   http://www.floppingaces.net/2012/09/20/
distorting-a-distortion-depicting-muhammad-in-art/

is a (grown-up) person, and there is something that (rankles) in the mind of Abu Hudhayfah about him', whereupon Allah's Messenger (peace be upon him) said: 'Suckle him (so that he may become your foster-child), and thus he may be able to come to you (freely)'" (Muslim Hadith no. 700). When she objected that the man had a beard, Muhammad smiled and again ordered her to suckle him, and she did so (ṣaḥīḥ Muslim 8:3424–3428).

3   B.4:582; Gen.21:21.

4   B.4:584.

5   Gen 21:14.

6   See A. F. Rainey, "Beersheba," vol. 1, 507.

7   B.1:277; 4:616.

8   Q.18:60-82.

9   B.1:74,78,123,124; 3:467,888; 4:612,613; 6:250,251; 9:570.

10   B.2:423;4:619.

11   B.6:237.

12   1 Kgs 3:16-28.

13   B.8:760.

14   Khan, *Authentication,* 118.

15   B.4:585.

16   Source: www.noblesanctuary.com/AQSAMosque.html (accessed July 9, 2013).

17   B.5:89.

18   B.9:68.

19   Matt 22:30; Luke 20:35.

20   B.4:544.

21   B.4:53.

22   B.4:468, 469.

23   Like the "fair virgins imprisoned in tents" *hūr maqṣūrāt fī 'lkhiyām* in Q.55:72.

24   B.6:402.

25   B.4:468, 469.

26   Rev 21:27.

27   Rev 22:15.

28   Q.4:121.

29   Q.2:167; 5:37.

30   Q.2:39,81,217; 4:169; 9:68; 39:72; 40:76; 43:74,77; 72:23.

31   Q.78:23.

32   Q.32:20.

33   Q.2:80; 3:24.

34   E.g., Q.3:16, 185.

35   Q.19:71,72.

36   Q.19:72; 40:60.

37   B.9:532.

38   B.8:563.

39   B.8:564.

40   B.8:565.

41   B.6:3; 9:532.3.

42   B.8:575.

43   B.8:577.

44   Luke 16:26.

45   Dan 12:2; Jude 1:13; Rev 20:10.

III

CHALLENGES FROM OTHER PERSPECTIVES

QUESTIONS OF CONTENT

ILLUSTRATION 23:
Promoting Sharia[p]

Quite apart from the internal inconsistencies found within the Hadith and its differences from biblical accounts and teaching outlined in the previous chapter, the content of the Hadith have been queried on various other grounds. The Hadith reflect the teachings and practices of a certain society within a particular period of history. As they are read in a new context, they are assessed by the standards of that society. The Hadith have been evaluated by modern historians, feminists, ethicists, and others, and they have been foubnd wanting.

Yet it is difficult for Muslims to question well-attested Hadiths. According to Firestone, "The reason for this lack of investigation into the composition of the tradition is most likely that it was nearly impossible to establish effective universal criteria for critique. Once the message itself was open to legal or historical criticism, the entire corpus would be suspect."[**]

Despite this, the hard questions must be asked. Some Muslims are presenting Sharia as the social, economic, political, religious, and legislative future for humanity (see Illustration 23).

---

p   http://www.crossmap.com/blogs/
      belgistan-sharia-showdown-looms-in-brussels-6953

**   Firestone, *Jihad,* 95.

The Hadith form the backbone of Sharia, so they must be carefully examined to determine whether they are a suitable building block for a universal system.

14

SCIENTIFIC PROBLEMS
IN THE HADITH

SEVERAL OF THE HADITH address technical topics, but they appear to present a prescientific understanding of phenomena.

1. MEDICAL ETIOLOGY AND DEFINITIONS

Some accounts suggest medical definitions and etiological theories.

Human fevers, it is said, originated not from infection but from the hell-fire, and cooling with water particularly from the Zam-Zam well was the antidote.[1] In another comment on microbiology, Muhammad blamed food putrefaction on the Jews. He claimed: "But for the Israelis, meat would not decay."[2] Emotional states, such as gloom and depression, are attributed to the knots tied in the back of the hair by Satan during the night. These knots could be "untied" by waking up and performing ablutions and prayer, resulting in positive feelings.[3]

With some other matters, the connection seems more obvious. The prohibition against eating garlic and onion before coming to the mosque[4] may have been related to flatulence, which nullified the worshiper's ablutions.[5] Some explanations indicate a lack of physiological knowledge. The reduced appetite of a new convert to Islam was easily explained by the Prophet: "A believer eats in one intestine (is satisfied with a little food) and a Kafir [infidel] eats in seven intes-tines (eats much)."[6] His description "a tooth is a bone"[7] would be deemed scientifically inaccurate by both dentists and orthopedic specialists. One bone of the human body apparently never decom-poses: "Everything of the human body will decay except the coccyx bone (of the tail) and from that bone Allah will reconstruct the whole body."[8] No doubt this observation, if true, would result in remarkable discoveries by paleontologists, particularly with modern DNA testing.

2. CONTAGION AND CONTAMINATION

Contagion through physical contact was not understood. An uncon-ventional medical treatment is Muhammad's advice about insect contamination: "If a fly falls in the vessel of any of you, let him dip all of it (into the vessel) and then throw it away, for in one of its wings there is a disease and in the other there is healing (antidote for it) i.e. the treatment for that disease."[9] When a dead mouse was found in some ghee (butter fat), the advice was reversed: "Throw away the mouse and the portion of butter-fat around it, and eat the rest."[10] Other rulings break the most basic principles of hygiene. Although a range of infections can be conveyed by saliva,[11] Muhammad told his followers: "When you eat, do not wipe your hand till you have licked it, or had it licked by somebody else."[12] The Prophet himself engaged in the practice of *tahnik* with newborn children. "He asked for a date, chewed it, and put his saliva in the mouth of the child. So the first thing to enter its stomach was the saliva of Allah's Apostle."[13]

Muhammad claimed that "no disease was contagious without Allah's permission."[14] When challenged by an observant listener, the Prophet's reply was obtuse. "A bedouin said, 'O Allah's Apostle! What about the camels which, when on the sand (desert) look like deers, but when a mangy camel mixes with them they all get infected with mange?' On that Allah's Apostle said, 'Then who conveyed the (mange) disease to the first (mangy) camel?'"[15] He confused the ori-gin of a disease with its method of transmission. Yet at another time, he advised that diseased and healthy stock should be separated.[16]

3. MEDICAL TREATMENTS AND REMEDIES

Muhammad suggested, approved, or used a variety of remedies for various ailments (see Table 16):[17]

AILMENT	REMEDY	REFERENCE
"every sickness, except death"	placing black cumin seed in the nostrils[m]	B 7:591,592
fever	camel urine	B 1:234; 2:577; 5:505; 7:589,590
abdominal pain	honey	B 7:588
eye infections	truffle water	B 7:609
seven diseases, including throat trouble and pleurisy	an Indian incense called 'Ud al-Hindi	B 7:596, 7:447, 446; 1:236,237
eye trouble	saliva	B 4:253
battle wounds		B 5:517
snake bite		B 7:632
unspecified illness	saliva mixed with earth	B 7:641,642
poison	'ajwa dates	B 7:356
bleeding	burnt palm leaves	B 1:244; 4:152,159, 274; 5:402; 7:175,618
headaches	"cupping " i.e. using heated vessels	B 7:600,602
unspecified illness	"sea incense"	B 7:599
snake or scorpion bites	Ruqya – reciting certain verses of the Qur'an over the sick person	B 3:476; 7:632, 633,637,645
poison and ear ailments		B 7:617
the evil eye	sick person	B 7:633,634,635
other unspecified sicknesses		B 7:638,640,642

TABLE 16: Medical Treatments Recommended or Applied by Muhammad

m   This is marketed commercially as "Nature's Divine Secret" by a Muslim company http://www.habshifa.com.au/. Accessed July 9, 2013.

Some of the suggested remedies highlighted problems. Although Muhammad claimed that "he who eats seven 'Ajwa dates every morning, will not be affected by poison or magic on the day he eats them,"[18] he himself was affected by both poison[19] and magic.[20] Treatment by *ruqya* or reciting certain verses of the Qur'an over a sick person was forbidden to those who would enter Paradise without punishment,[21] yet Muhammad performed, recommended, or sanctioned it, as mentioned in Table 16. He said: "You are most entitled to take wages for doing a *Ruqya* with Allah's Book."[22]

Cultural mores sometimes superseded medical needs. A woman who wanted to use *kohl* (a type of eyeointment) to treat her infected eyes was refused permission by Muhammad as she was still in the mourning period for her dead husband.[23]

4. GENETIC ISSUES

Genetic observations by Muhammad attributed a child's phenotype to the order of emission from orgasm during sexual intercourse of the parent it most resembled.[24] When a black child was born, the concerned (presumably non-black) bedouin father was told by Muhammad: "Maybe your latest son has this color because of heredity." This was compared to a gray camel being born in a herd of red camels.[25] A man named 'Uwaimir accused his wife of adultery, so Muhammad ordered them to undergo the ritual oathtaking and cursing.[26] They did so, and the woman was acquitted. However, Muhammad said: "Watch her; if she delivers a black-eyed child with big hips and fat shins then it is Sharik bin Sahma's child [i.e. from her purported lover] but if she delivers a red child looking like a *Wahra* (a red insect or lizard) then it belongs to 'Uwaimir." She delivered a child resembling the other man, not her husband. So the Prophet said, "If the case was not settled by Allah's Law, I would punish her severely."[27] He clearly thought she was guilty based on observation and inference. The judgment of Allah's law, which set her free, conflicted with the scientifically based deduction of Allah's prophet, who would have stoned her.

According to Muhammad, congenital defects could be prevented by a prayer of protection against Satan during ejaculation,[28] and a neonate's cries upon delivery are attributed to the touch of Satan.[29] Muhammad related the extraordinary story that at the creation "the womb got up and caught hold of Allah" to extract a promise from him to favor those who keep the ties of kith and kin.[30]

5. ASTRONOMY AND METEOROLOGY

Astronomical and meteorological explanations display similar misunderstandings. In the Qur'an, the sun is described as rotating around the earth.[31] On the question of what happens after sunset, Muhammad's view was that, following its expedition across the sky, the sun spent each night in prostration under the divine throne, and would one day rise in the west.[32] Seasonal changes in temperature were described as the result of hell's request to God for an opportunity to breathe.[33] Muhammad apparently did not understand cause-and-effect as a scientific phenomenon. When an eclipse occurred, he hurried to the mosque with his clothes dragging behind him on the ground, and performed a special eclipse ritual. He told his followers to "offer the prayer and invoke Allah till He remove that state,"[34] for "Allah makes His worshipers afraid by [eclipses]."[35]

6. ANIMAL AND VEGETABLE BEHAVIOR

Some descriptions of animal behavior are curious. The tale is told of a talking wolf and cow,[36] as is the strange account of a group of monkeys stoning a she-monkey which had committed illicit sexual intercourse. The man who observed this unusual conduct felt impelled to join it. He said: "I too, stoned it along with them." [37] A tribe of ungracious people will be transformed by Allah into monkeys and pigs,[38] a fate described in the Qur'an for some of the People of the Book,[39] and for Jews who did not keep their Sabbath.[40] A peculiar story seeks to explain why some rodents prefer sheep milk to camel milk. "The Prophet said, 'A group of Israelites were lost.

Nobody knows what they did. But I do not see them except that they were cursed and changed into rats, for if you put the milk of a she-camel in front of a rat, it will not drink it, but if the milk of a sheep is put in front of it, it will drink it.'"[41]

Also quite bizarre is the image of Muhammad's food glorifying Allah while it was being eaten by the Prophet. His fellow guests reported that "we heard the meal glorifying Allah, when it was being eaten (by him)."[42] However, voluble vegetables might not have surprised Muhammad, for a talking tree had notified him about the jinn who heard the Qur'an recited and then believed in Islam. Muhammad knew about these reclusive creatures because "a tree informed the Prophet about them."[43] The Qur'an labels this as "revelation," i.e., "It has been revealed to me that a company of Jinns listened (to the Qur'an)."[44]

7. QUESTIONING THE HADITH'S SCIENTIFIC CREDENTIALS

These unusual ideas have not gone unchallenged by some Muslims. "Even before modern medicine, the Hadith of the Fly [that purportedly has disease on one wing and healing on the other] was raising skeptical eyebrows and prompting Sunni defensiveness as early as the writings of Ibn Qutayba (d.276/889)."[45] French scientist and Muslim convert Maurice Bucaille confesses that some of the Hadith contradict scientific understandings. "The difference is in fact quite staggering between the accuracy of the data contained in the Quran, when compared with modern scientific knowledge, and the highly questionable character of the statements in the Hadiths on subjects whose tenor is essentially scientific." While admitting the limited nature of early medicine, he states: "It does not seem—*a priori*—to be a very good idea, however, to suggest that people drink camel's urine."[46] This is a reference to some unusual prophetic advice: "Some people of 'Ukl or 'Uraina tribe came to Medina and its climate did not suit them. So the Prophet ordered them to go to the herd of (Milch) camels and to drink their milk and urine (as a medicine)."[47] This regimen was attested by others.[48] Although healing was claimed to be found in honey, cupping, and cauterization, the latter, though efficacious, was "forbidden."[49] However, other versions softened it to a simple personal Prophetic preference: "I do not like to be cauterized."[50]

The Bible, by contrast, is quite circumspect about medical treatments. Pain in childbirth and "painful toil" in gaining a living are seen as a result of the Fall.[51] Obedience to God's laws brought freedom from diseases for the nation.[52] Satan sometimes afflicted the righteous with sickness, within the sovereignty of God.[53] Suffering could have redemptive value,[54] as Christ demonstrated;[55] this can give meaning to other suffering.[56] God is the one who heals disease.[57] The Bible seems much more concerned with the spiritual dynamics of suffering, pain, and sickness rather than the mechanics of medicinal treatment.[58]

The scientific lapses in the Hadith of themselves would be no problem, since they clearly reflect the limited understanding of a much earlier era. No one should expect a ninth- century document to conform to twenty-first century understandings of science. However, the problem arises due to the claims of some Muslims about the applicability of every aspect of Muhammad's behavior to all times and occasions. His statement that "I only follow what is revealed to me"[59] has caused some Muslims to see every facet of his life as perfect and worthy of emulation. Clearly, from a modern scientific perspective, this is not the case. There are serious questions about the science and medicine in the Hadith and the Qur'an that must be asked before they can be accepted as mandatory for all of humanity for all time.

NOTES

1   B.4:483, 484, 485, 486; 7:619,621,622. Modern samples taken from the Zam Zam well have been found to have three times the acceptable limit of arsenic, high levels of nitrate, and potentially harmful bacteria. Guy Lynn, Contaminated Zam Zam holy water from Mecca sold in UK, BBC News, May 5, 2011 (accessed May 13, 2013).

2   B.4:547, 611.

3   B.2:243; 4:491.

4   B.1:817; 7:362, 363; 9:458.

5   B.4:452.

6   B.7:309, also 7:305-308.

7   B.3:668, 684; 4:309; 7:406, 411, 417, 451, 472.

8   B.6:33.

9   B.7:673; also 4:537.

10   B.7:448, also 7:447, 446; 1:236, 237.

11   These include gastroenteritis, hepatitis A, glandular fever, herpes, respiratory infections, and parasites such as giardia.

12   B.7:366.

13   B.7:378, also 2:578; 7:376, 377, 379.1, 450, 714; 8:31, 218.

14   B.7:608, 615,649, 665.1, 667, 768.

15   B.7:665.1; also 7:615.

16   B.7:665.2, 667.

17   This area of study has resulted in books such as Al-Jawziyaa, *Natural Healing with the Medicine of the Prophet* .

18   B.7:356, 663.

19   B. 5:713.

20   B.7:658, 660; 8:400.

21   B.7:606, 648; 8:479, 549.

22   B.7:633.

23   B.7:252, 607.

24   B.6:7; also 4:545, 546; 5:275; 8:113. One of Muhammad's wives was apparently unaware of female climax during orgasm. When the Prophet mentioned this theory of heredity, "Um Salama, then covered her face and asked, 'O Allah's Apostle! Does a woman get a discharge?'" B.1:132; 8:113. Ali, however, was no stranger to the male equivalent for he said: "I used to get emotional urethral discharges frequently and felt shy to ask Allah's Apostle about it." B.1:178, 134, 269.

25   B.7:225; 8:830; 9:416.

26   Based on the Q.24:6–9.

27   B.6:269-271; 8:837–839.

28   B.4:493, 503.

29   B.4:641, also 4:506; 7:61.

30   B.6:354; 8:16; 9:593.

31   Q.36:38.

32   B.4:421; 9:520. This is different from the observation of Zul-qarnain (probably referring to Alexander the Great) recorded in the Qur'an that the sun set in a pool of murky water (Q.18:86).

33   B.4:482.

34   B.7:676.

35   B.2:167

36   B.3:517; 5:15. The Bible contains the story of Balaam's talking donkey (Num 22:28–30).

37   B.5:188.

38   B.7:494.2.

39   Q.5:60.

40   Q.2:65; 7:166.

41   B.4:524.

42   B.4:779.

43   B.5:199.

44   Q.72:1.

45   Brown, *Hadith,* 264.

46   Bucaille, *The Bible, the Qur'an and Science,* 244–46.

47   B.1:234; 2:577; 5:505; 7:589, 590.

48   B.7:672.

49   B.7:584, 585.

50   B.7:587, 603, 605.

51   Gen.3:16, 17.

52   Ex 15:25–26; Lev 26:14–16; Deut 7:12–16 and ch. 28, especially vv. 22, 27, 58–61. McMillen and Stern, *None of These Diseases* have documented positive preventative health outcomes of the Old Testament laws.

53   Job 2:1–10.

54   Isa 53:4,5.

55   Heb 13:12.

56   1 Pet 2:21.

57   Ps 103:3; Acts 3:12–16.

58   The only biblical accounts of therapeutic medicine are "a poultice of figs" (2 Kgs 20:7; Isa 38:21) and perhaps mud made with saliva (John 9:6).

59   Q.6:50.

15

POLITICAL, SOCIAL, FINANCIAL, AND LEGAL POLICIES

THE HADITH PRESENT SIGNIFICANT differences from the political, social, financial, and legal policies presented in the Bible.

1. POWER-SHARING: AN IMPORTANT DIFFERENCE

The Israelites under Moses in the desert following their escape from Egypt show some similarities with the Muslims under Muhammad in Medina following their migration from Mecca. Both fled oppression and persecution and moved into a situation of uncertainty under a new and untried leader. In the liturgical and judicial spheres, however, there were significant differences. Unlike Moses, Muhammad seemed unwilling or unable to delegate power to others. Although he sometimes asked the opinions of others,[1] and at times gave his followers some limited choices,[2] he retained the social, political, and religious control of Islam up until his death. Muhammad maintained the right to adjudicate in a variety of cases (see Table 17).

Wells	B.8:668
Irrigation	B.3:548,549,550,871; 6:109
Crop allocation	B.3:520
Public access to land	B.3:653
Violent scuffles between men	B.4:366
Violent scuffles between women	B.7:654,655; 9:45
Theft	B.5:597
Ownership of slaves	B.3:860,885; 8:629,815,819,821,826,842; 9:303,365
Sexual infringements by men	B.3:269,421,459,603,701; 4:8; 5:596; 8:741,757; 9:293
Sexual infringements by women	B.3:860,885; 3:508; 8:629,815,821, 826,842; 9:303,365

TABLE 17: Muhammad's Areas of Legal Jurisdiction

He only relinquished the leadership of prayers to Abū Bakr due to the illness that led to his death. But when Muhammad was seen lifting the curtain beside his sickbed during prayers, Abū Bakr "retreated to join the row as he thought that the Prophet would lead the prayer."[4] Even though he was convinced that he would die soon, the Prophet did not nominate a successor. This action resulted in much heartache for the Muslim community, bringing sectarian strife. The Sunni/ Shia schism within Islam continues to this day.

Moses, however, delegated most of Israel's judicial responsibilities to selected judges,[5] and some of his executive power to Joshua.[6] Seventy elders, recognized for their demonstrated administrative abilities, were given some of the "burden" of leadership after they were Spirit-empowered for the task.[7] When some young men spontaneously prophesied at the Spirit's prompting, Moses did not follow Joshua's advice to forbid them, but replied: "Are you jealous for my sake? I wish that all the Lord's people were prophets."[8] The prophets in later years would form an important review function, seeking to ensure that even the kings of Israel obeyed God's laws. At divine command, Moses devolved the liturgical leadership to the family of his brother Aaron and the tribe of the Levites.[9] These actions by Moses opened a way for the later separation of religion and state, or at least a clear division of executive, judicial, and legislative functions with broader involvement of the people. Power and authority was intended to be devolved, not clustered in one person. The focus of control was moving away from Moses, instead of being concentrated in him.

2. DEALING WITH APOSTASY

In establishing an Islamic polity, Muhammad used methods that may be seen as controversial. Although he freely invited others (e.g., his sick Jewish servant boy) to embrace Islam,[10] a choice of belief and conviction in the opposite direction was not permitted. Killing other Muslims was *kufr* (unbelief), but this did not apply if anyone left Islam. Muhammad's teaching was clear: "Whoever changed his (Islamic) religion, then kill him."[11] This verdict was applied to a Jewish man who, after embracing Islam, returned to Judaism. Some men who "reverted to heathenism" after embracing Islam then killed a shepherd who had provided milk for them. Their eyes were gouged out, hands and feet amputated, and they were left to die.[12] Ali burnt some people who were atheists, and the text implies they had previously been Muslims.[13] Mu'ādh bin Jabal, sent by Muhammad as a missionary to Yemen, refused to dismount[14] or sit down[15] until an apostate he encountered had been executed. This was instantly carried out.

Women may have been treated more leniently, or their commitments taken less seriously. Um Atiya was among a group of women who gave the pledge of allegiance to Muhammad, but she reports that, apart from five of them, "none of those women abided by her pledge."[16] No sanctions against these women were recorded.

Those living outside Muslim territory or rule were not subject to these constraints, and their departure from it was not even acknowledged. In AH 11/AD 632, the Byzantine emperor Heraclius received the letter from Muhammad, inviting him to Islam. Heraclius sent for Abu Sufyan, one of Muhammad's relatives who was visiting Syria, and asked him: "Does anybody amongst those who embrace his religion become displeased and renounce the religion afterwards?" Abu

Sufyan's response was negative.[17] Yet it was public knowledge that Ubayd-Allah ibn Jahsh al-Asad, one of the earliest converts to Islam, and one of those who sought refuge in Abyssinia, had returned to Christianity at least twelve years earlier.[18] Abu Sufyan would have known this, since Ubayd-Allah was his son-in-law. After Ubayd-Allah's death, Muhammad paid 400 dinars as a dowry for his widow, and Ramlah bint Abu Sufyan (also called Um Habiba) became the Prophet's ninth wife.[19]

There was a special warning and instruction about recidivism during the end times. Muhammad said: "In the last days (of the world) there will appear young people with foolish thoughts and ideas. They will give good talks, but they will go out of Islam as an arrow goes out of its game, their faith will not exceed their throats. So, wherever you find them, kill them, for there will be a reward for their killers on the Day of Resurrection."[20]

Jesus lost followers due to his high claims. "From this time many of his disciples turned back and no longer followed him."[21] The early church also had to deal with those who left its fold. The New Testament speaks of the extreme spiritual danger of those who have "fallen away . ... crucifying the Son of God all over again and subjecting him to public disgrace."[22] It also mentions those who "went out from us."[23] However, neither Jesus nor the early church called for the execution of such people.

The Universal Declaration of Human Rights (UDHR) speaks to the issue of apostasy. According to Article 18: "Everyone has the freedom of thought, conscience and religion; this right includes freedom to change his religion or belief."[24] It is telling that of the then fifty-eight members of the United Nations, only Saudi Arabia, the birthplace of Islam, abstained from signing the Universal Declaration of Human Rights in 1948, claiming that the UDHR was opposed to Sharia law.[25]

3. ECONOMIC INDUCEMENTS

Potential apostasy from Islam was prevented by Muhammad through financial incentives. Justifying his decision to distribute *zakat* to some who were less committed to Islam, he stated: "I give to a person while another is dearer to me, for fear that he may be thrown in the Hell-fire on his face (by reneging from Islam)."[26]

According to the Qur'an, money collected for the indigent could also be used to entice people to Islam. "As-Sadaqat (here it means Zakat) are only for the Fuqara' (poor), and Al-Masakin (the poor) and those employed to collect (the funds); and to attract the hearts of those who have been inclined (towards Islam)."[27] "The Prophet said, "I give (them) so as to attract their hearts (to Islam)" and "I give to Quraish people in order to let them adhere to Islam, for they are near to their life of ignorance (i.e. they have newly embraced Islam and it is still not strong in their hearts."[28] This policy was contentious, and Muhammad prophesied against a man who criticized him for it: "Something was sent to the Prophet and he distributed it amongst four (men) and said, 'I want to attract their hearts (to Islam thereby).' A man said (to the Prophet), 'You have not done justice.' Thereupon the Prophet said, 'There will emerge from the offspring of this (man) some people who will renounce the religion.'"[29]

Muhammad's earliest biographer describes this approach, listing the beneficiaries. "The apostle gave gifts to those whose hearts were to be won over, notably the chiefs of the army, to win them and through them their people. He gave to the following 100 camels: Abu Sufyān b. Harb, his son Mu'awiya; Hakim b. Hizam...."[30] A complete list of the gifts and their recipients was then provided.

The Arab Hawāzin tribe had been defeated by the Muslims in battle, their goods were taken, and many of their people captured as slaves. The remainder of the tribe then converted to Islam and came to Muhammad requesting that their captives be sent back. Muhammad consulted his troops, the request was granted, and the captured people were returned to the Hawāzin tribe.[31]

For their part, the Muslims could afford to be generous and forgo the normal ransom paid for the return of captives, since "Allah made the Prophet wealthy through conquests."[32] The Qur'an records that Allah had made Muhammad and his followers rich–so do the Hadith: "you were poor and Allah made you rich through me."[33] Years of raiding caravans and wealthy towns,[34] and Muhammad's diktat that one-fifth of all booty be given to him,[35] meant that the Islamic coffers were overflowing. "People used to give some of their date palms to the Prophet (as a gift), till he conquered Bani Quraiza and Bani An-Nadir, whereupon he started returning their favors."[36]

Arab tribes realized that aligning with Islam might bring quick and disproportionate financial returns (see Sidebar *Financial Inducements for Conversion*).

The newly acquired riches were used to persuade others and to shore up the identity of new Muslims.

Interestingly, Muhammad's enemies were criticized in the Qur'an for doing the same thing: "The unbelievers spend their wealth to hinder (men) from the path of Allah and so will they continue to spend; but in the end they will have (only) regrets and sighs; at length they will be overcome: and the unbelievers will be gathered together to Hell."[39] Some former enemies were allowed to keep their property if they converted to Islam. Bani Nadir was a Jewish tribe that was attacked and expelled by Muhammad after they surrendered to him, but "two of B. al-Nadir became Muslims … in order to retain their property."[40]

Muhammad's use of monetary incentives became so well-known that some tribes demanded material reward to become Muslims. "A delegation from Banu Tamim came to the Prophet. The Prophet said, 'Accept the good tidings, O Banu Tamim!' They said, 'O Allah's Apostle! You have given us good tidings, so give us (something).' Signs of displeasure appeared on his face."[41]

A Christian equivalent is hard to identify. Although some have suggested that following

---

FINANCIAL INDUCEMENTS FOR CONVERSION

Al-Tufayl bin 'Amr al-Dausi reported: "I went to the apostle with my converts while he was in Khaybar. I arrived at Medina with seventy or eighty households of Daus, and then we joined the apostle in Khaybar and he gave us an equal share of the booty with the Muslims."[37]

When asked why he gave booty to the new Muslims from among the treacherous Meccan Quraish instead of to the faithful Medinan Ansār "in spite of the fact that our swords are still dribbling (wet) with the blood of the infidels," Allah's Apostle replied, "I give to such people as are still close to the period of infidelity (i.e. they have recently embraced Islam and faith is still weak in their hearts)."[38]

Christ will bring "prosperity," based on various verses,[42] the overall thrust of the New Testament is that Christian discipleship results in fewer financial resources, not more. "We have left everything to follow you," said Peter.[43] Jesus refused to provide miracles for those who demanded a sign.[44] He criticized those who followed him for less than spiritual motives. A rich young man was told by Christ to give away all his wealth,[45] a general command extended to others.[46] Those who followed Christ for physical benefit were reprimanded by him.[47] Paul's comment about "making many rich"[48] must be understood as spiritual riches in the context of Paul's sufferings in the second letter to the Corinthians. "Simony." the use of wealth to gain spiritual power, has long been condemned as a sin in the church.[49] Payment for people to become or remain Christians is clearly not acceptable.

4. LOWERED STANDARDS

At times the impression is given that standards were lowered to accommodate people's desires. "Whenever Allah's Apostle ordered the Muslims to do something, he used to order them deeds which were easy for them to do (according to their strength endurance)."[50] When they complained that they needed tasks burdensome enough to earn their forgiveness, Muhammad became angry and rebuked them. He told his people: "Facilitate things to people (concerning religious matters), and do not make it hard for them and give them good tidings and do not make them run away (from Islam)."[51] Religious practices such as prayer[52] and good deeds[53] should be limited for this reason and sermons shortened.[54] "You were sent to make things easy for them, and not to make them difficult."[55] Even teeth cleaning before prayers was omitted because it might be too hard to do.[56] He tried to discourage people from al-wiṣāl (continuous fasting) by extending the fast until it became like a "punishment" for them.[57] 'Umar summarized it: "We have been forbidden to undertake a difficult task beyond our capability."[58] This follows a recurring theme in the Qur'an (see Table 18).

Allah does not burden a person beyond his scope	Q.2:286
Allah intends for you ease, and does not want difficulty for you	Q.2:185
We [Allah] will make it easy for you (to follow) the simple (Path)	Q.87:8; 92:7
Whoever fears Allah and keeps his duty to Him, He will make his matter easy for him	Q.65:4
Allah will grant after hardship ease	Q.65:7;94:5,6
Allah wishes to lighten (the burden) for you	Q.4:28
Allah does not want to place you in difficulty	Q.5:6

TABLE 18: The "Ease" Motif in the Qur'an

The only suggestion that the way of Islam might be hard is the unexplained reference in the Qur'an to "the steep path" (*al-'aqaba*).[59] Yet the Qur'an itself was made easy to recite and understand,[60] and night prayers reduced to "as much as may be easy for you."[61] This became a life principle for Muhammad. "Whenever the Prophet was given an option between two things, he used to select the easier of the two as long as it was not sinful." [62]

Juynboll notes two trends:

> On the one hand, Islamic teaching in the Qur'an is based on the principle of *yusr*, ease, rather than *'usr*, hardship, leading to the alleviation of, and concessions in, several previously revealed prescripts. On the other hand, however, a hardening of a legal point of view is, for instance, discernible in Islam's increasingly outspoken disapproval of intoxicating beverages.[63]

The only evidence in the Hadith of the latter is the admission that "the (Hell) Fire is surrounded by all kinds of desires and passions, while Paradise is surrounded by all kinds of disliked undesirable things."[64] In this statement we find a parallel to the dominical teaching: "for small is the gate and narrow the road that leads to life."[65] Jesus always put forward the highest standards, even a perfection that matched God's.[66] His ethical demands were clearly beyond any person's natural capability.[67] He could do this, since human efforts alone were not sufficient, for "What is impossible with men is possible with God."[68] Those who follow him must learn the secret of dependence on him rather than themselves: "Apart from me," he told his disciples, "you can do nothing."[69]

NOTES

1 E.g., B.5:495; 6:281.

2 E.g., Q.3:503; 5:495.

3 B.1:648, 649, 721; 2:297.1; 5:729.

4 Ex 18:17–26.

5 Num 27:18–23.

6 Num 11:16–25.

7 Num 11:26–30.

8 Ex 28:1; Num 1:50–54.

9 B.2:438.

10 B.1:122.

11 B.9:57; 4:260; 9:17. Some modern apologists for Islam claim that the death penalty was applied in these cases for "treason" against the State. e.g., Saeed, *Muslim Australians*, 72. However, the terminology used in the Hadith describing the offense is clearly religious, not civil, military, or judicial: *man baddala **dīnahu** fa'aqtaluhu* (bold letters mine) Whoever changes his **religion,** kill him.

12 B.5:505; 7:623; 8:794, 797.

13 B.4:260; 9:57.

14 B. 5:630, 632; 9:58,271.

15 B.9:58, 271.

16 B.9:322.

17 B.1:6 also 1:48; 4:191; 6:75.

18 Ibn Ishaq, *Sira Rasul Allah*, 527.

19 Ibn Ishaq, *Sira Rasul Allah*, 793.

20 B.4:808; 6:577; 9:64.

21 John 6:66.

22 Heb 6:6.

23   1 John 2:19.

24   Source: www.un.org/en/documents/udhr/index.shtml#a18 (accessed July 9, 2013).

25   Abiad Sharia, *Muslim States and International Human Rights Treaty Obligations: A Comparative Study,* 60–65.

26   B.2:556.

27   Q.9:60.

28   B.4:558; 6:189.

29   B.4:374.

30   Ibn Ishaq, *Sira,* 594.

31   B.3:503,716.

32   B.3:495.

33   Q.93:8.

34   Q.9:74.

35   B.5:619.

36   B.4:357.

37   Ibn Ishaq, *Sira,* 177.

38   B.4:375; 5:620. This policy continues today. An Australian Islamic website lists among the recipients of its distribution of Zakat funds those who are "recently converted individuals." Source: http://campaign.r20.constantcontact.com/render (accessed June 1, 2013).

39   Q.8:36.

40   Ibn Ishaq, *Sira,* 438.

41   B.5:651, 669.

42   Such as Luke 6:38 and 3 John 2-4 as well as Deut 8:18, Mal 3:10.

43   Mark 10:28.

44   John 6:26.

45   Matt 19:21; Mark 10:21; Luke 18:23.

46   Luke 12:33.

47   John 6:26.

48   2 Cor 6:10.

49   Acts 8:18.

50   B.1:19.

51   B.1:69.

52   B.1:38,41.

53   B.1:41.

54 B.1:70.

55 B.1:219; 8:146,149; 9:284.

56 B.2:12; 9:346.

57 B.3:186; 8:834; 9:348.

58 B.9:396.

59 Q.90:11,12.

60 Q.19:97; 44:58 & 54:17, 22, 32, 40.

61 Q.73:20.

62 B.8:777; 4:760.

63 Juynboll, "Hadith and the Qur'an," vol. 2, 389.

64 B.8:494.

65 Matt 7:14.

66 Matt 5:48.

67 Matt 5:20–47.

68 Luke 18:27.

69 John 15:5.

16

HUMAN RIGHTS CONCERNS

THE HADITH SANCTION PRACTICES now considered human rights abuses, such as the owning and mistreatment of slaves, criminals, and women as well as encouraging anti-Semitism and violence.

1. OWNERSHIP AND TREATMENT OF SLAVES

Like many wealthy men in his society, Muhammad remained a slave owner all his life, keeping several black slaves, including women.[1] Slave owning was an ancient practice, and Muhammad did not disapprove of it in any way (see Illustration 24).

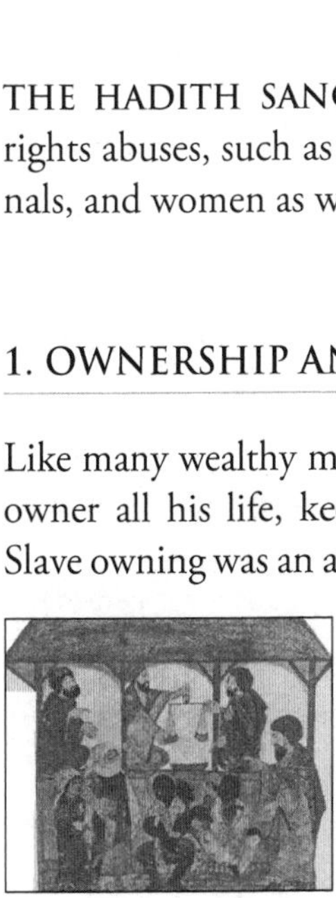

ILLUSTRATION 24:
A Slave Market in the Early Muslim Period [q]

Manumitting slaves was a pre-Islamic phenomenon.[2] One non-Muslim set free one hundred of his slaves.[3] It was also carried out by Muhammad's pagan uncle Abu Lahab, who was cursed by the Prophet.[4] Even Muhammad had freed his slave Zaid bin Haritha "before revelation came to him."[5]

---

[q] Http://islammonitor.org/uploads/pics/13thcent.jpg.

Later Muhammad recommended[6] and even ordered his Muslim followers to manumit their slaves. The following reasons were given for this practice:

- to alleviate disasters such as a solar eclipse[7]
- to pay for the owners' sins[8]
- to enable them to break vows[9]
- as an act of piety[10]
- to save the owner from the hellfire by manumitting a Muslim slave[11]

However, there were easier and less expensive ways of gaining the same benefit. Muhammad declared: "Whoever says: '*La ilaha illallah wahdahu la sharika lahu, lahu-l-mulk wa lahu-l-hamd wa huwa 'ala kulli shai'in qadir,*' [There is no god except Allah and he has no partner; His is the dominion, and his is the praise, and he is powerful over all things] one hundred times will get the same reward as given for manumitting ten slaves." [12] This five-minute recitation attracted the equivalent return as freeing ten slaves, thereby lowering a slave owner's incentive to give up his valuable assets.

The Prophet himself set free the captured Jewish girl Safiya before their marriage.[13] Her wedding gift, or *mahr*, was her freedom.[14] Not all war captives were so well treated. Muhammad challenged his soldiers when they told him that they used a form of birth control ("coitus interruptus") to prevent female war captives becoming pregnant. He said to them: "Do you really do that?" repeating the question thrice. "There is no soul that is destined to exist but will come into existence, till the Day of Resurrection."[15] Remarkably, the Prophet criticized his men for their lack of faith in the divine decrees, but not for the rape of their female prisoners. Muhammad's son-in-law indulged in this as well, for Buraida reported that "'Ali had taken a bath (after a sexual act with a slave-girl from the *Khumus*."[16] The Qur'an refers to such prisoners and slaves as "those whom your right hand possesses."[17] Muslim men were permitted to have sex with them,[18] even if the women were already married,[19] as long as the women were "good" (*ṣāliḥīn*)[20] and "believing,"[21] (i.e. Christian or Jewish).

Muhammad's slaves were not always treated gently. When Aisha was suspected of infidelity, her female slave, Burayra, was interrogated in Muhammad's presence. "The apostle called Burayra to ask her, and 'Ali got up and gave her a violent beating, saying, 'Tell the apostle the truth.'"[22]

Another time Muhammad ordered his son-in-law to flog one of his female slaves for adultery. Ali demurred because the woman "had recently given birth to a child and I was afraid that if I flogged her I might kill her. So I mentioned that to Allah's Apostle (peace be upon him) and he said: 'You have done well'."[23]

Muhammad acted as slave trader for an owner who voided an earlier commitment to free his slave. "A man decided that a slave of his would be manumitted [set free] after his death, and later on he was in need of money, so the Prophet [Muhammad] took the slave and said, 'Who will buy this slave from me?' Nu'aim bin 'Abdullah bought him for such and such price and the Prophet gave him the slave."[24] When one of Muhammad's wives set her slave girl free, he admonished her: "You would have got more reward if you had given her (i.e. the slave-girl) to one of your maternal uncles."[25]

Nor were the rights of freed slaves maintained. The Prophet ruled that owners could acquire a slave's inheritance, *al-walā'*, by releasing him or her.[26] *Al-Walā'* is "a right to inherit the property of a freed slave by the person who has freed him."[27] This practice would seem to impoverish further those who had already been oppressed.

2. TREATMENT OF CRIMINALS

Those who committed actions deemed crimes in Muhammad's time were subject to harsh penalties. A hand could be cut off for stealing an egg or a rope which cost "a few dirhams,"[28] or something worth quarter of a dinar or more,[39] or a shield worth three dinars.[30]

Although the Qur'ān prescribes only flogging for adultery,[31] a Jewish man and woman were stoned for this offense on the basis of the Torah's teachings.[32] This then became Islamic *sunna*, although it is uncertain when Muhammad began this practice.[33] Ali reported that he had stoned a lady to death on a Friday "according to the tradition of Allah's apostle."[34] When a man openly confessed to adultery, Muhammad initially tried to avoid the issue. "Then the Prophet ordered that he be stoned to death, and he was stoned to death at the Muṣalla [prayer hall]. When the stones troubled him, he fled, but he was caught and was stoned till he died. The Prophet spoke well of him and offered his funeral prayer." The Prophet's eulogy declared that the man's action had purified him from his sin, and that he had entered Paradise.[35] Another man received one hundred lashes and a year's exile for the same action, because he was unmarried and it was deemed fornication.[36]

Different punishments for the same offense brought disproportionate outcomes. Murder was described as one of the biggest sins, and was punishable by death,[37] but this law did not apply equally to Muslims and non-Muslims.[38] Muhammad declared that "a Muslim should not be killed in *Qisās* (equality in punishment) for killing a disbeliever,"[39] while "no repentance is accepted from … the murderer of a believer."[40] Similar disparities were found in cases of adultery, but here it was based on marital status. In one case, an unmarried man and a married woman engaged in an illicit sexual act together. The man suffered flogging and temporary banishment, but his female partner was stoned to death.[41] Another woman, caught with a man by her husband, was brought to Muhammad. However, she escaped stoning by invoking a curse (*lian*) on herself if she had committed adultery.[42] Even though the husband lacked the required legal proof of adultery,[43] he subsequently divorced his wife with the Prophet's approval.[44] Since the child subsequently born did not resemble her husband, the woman was allowed to keep the child.[45] This was a clear public recognition that the child was illegitimate, for Islamic law invariably grants custody to the father in cases of divorce.

Apostasy from Islam merited capital punishment. The Prophet said: "If somebody (a Muslim) discards his religion, kill him,"[46] a ruling which was carried out.[47] Amputation of hands for theft, mandated by the Qur'an,[48] was carried out at Muhammad's command on a woman.[49] In another case it was accompanied by eye branding after which the blinded amputees were abandoned, uncauterized, in a deserted place and left to bleed to death or die of thirst.[50]

3. ANTI-SEMITISM

The Hadith contain a strong anti-Jewish theme. There are nearly 180 references to the Jews, and they are overwhelmingly negative.[51] One account refers to the Jews as "the fools amongst the people."[52] Muhammad responded to them with double-meaning derogatory greetings.[53] The Prophet clearly wanted to supersede the Jews. When they told him about fasting on the day of Ashura instituted by Moses, Muhammad retorted: "We have more claim over Moses than you," and ordered the Muslims to fast.[54] He gave Jews near to Medina an ultimatum: "If you embrace Islam, you will be safe. You should know that the earth belongs to Allah and His Apostle, and I want to expel you from this land. So, if anyone amongst you owns some property, he is permitted to sell it, otherwise you should know that the earth belongs to Allah and His Apostle."[55]

Muhammad stood for a passing Jewish funeral procession,[56] which some scholars claim was a sign of respect.[57] However, the account in *Mishkat al-Masabih* gives a different reason for Muhammad standing. Hasan bin Ali reported: "A bier carrying a Jew was brought past when Allah's Messenger (peace be upon him) was sitting in its path, and just *because he did not like having a Jew's bier higher than his head* he stood up."[58] Another report claims that Muhammad later stopped this observance. "His practice had been to follow funerals and remain standing until the body was interred. This practice was changed, however, after a rabbi approached him and said: 'We do likewise, O Muhammad!' at which point he took his seat, exclaiming 'Oppose them.'"[59]

Muhammad made many accusations against the Jews as a group (see Table 19).

selling the forbidden fat of animals	B.3:426,427,438; 4:666; 6:157
making false oaths	B.3:834; 8:164; 9:36,37,302
lying	B.4:546; 5:250
deceiving	B.4:394,398; 6:91
being insincere	B.5:277
worshipping Ezra as the son of Allah	B.6:105; 9:932.2 c.f. Q.9:30

concealing their scriptures	B.4:829; 6:79; 8:809,825; 9:633
distorting their scriptures	B.6:12; 9:461
disbelieving their scriptures	B.6:229,252
disagreeing about their scriptures	B.6:510

TABLE 19: Muhammad's Accusations Against the Jews

The Jews are invariably depicted in a bad light. They asked Muhammad difficult questions,[60] and "disapproved" when the *Qibla* was changed from Jerusalem to Mecca.[61] Jews were seen as involved in crime such as cheating on land deals,[62] adultery,[63] and murder.[64] Muhammad had to mortgage his armor to a Jew to get credit to buy food,[65] and a Jew refused respite in repayment of a loan, despite Muhammad's intercession.[66] It was Jews who tried to poison the Prophet,[67] for they disbelieved him.[68] Unsurprisingly, the man who worked magic against Muhammad was Labid bin A'sam, a Jew.[69]

Muslims who go astray are depicted as following the Jews and Christians, even into the holes of sandlizards,[70] so Muslims are not to copy them. Muslims should dye their gray hair, because Jews and Christians did not,[71] but not wear false hair, because the Jews did.[72] Muhammad himself initially copied Jewish/Christian hairstyles but later reverted to a pagan coiffure.[73] The Muslim use of the voice for the call to prayer was in contradistinction to the "fire" or "horn" of the Jews and the "bell" of the Christians,[74] as was Friday for the day of prayer instead of Saturday or Sunday.[75] Muslims should not use the same hand gestures in prayer as Jews.[76]

The Jews allegedly made unjustified claims, such as, "If one has sexual intercourse with his wife from the back, then she will deliver a squint-eyed child,"[77] and it was said that the Jews had bewitched the Muslims so they could have no children.[78] They were resistant to conversion,[79] and refused to accept that any Jew could become a Muslim.[80] They are blamed for causing meat to decay.[81] They, along with the Christians, are depicted in a story as becoming angry at the generous employer who engaged Muslims late in the day for the same wages.[82]

In the first chapter of the Qur'an, described by Muhammad as the "greatest"[83] or "most superior"[84] chapter, or the *'umm* ("substance") of the whole Qur'an,[85] and recited compulsorily by Muslims every time they pray,[86] the Jews are labeled as "those who have earned [Allah's] anger."[87] One Jew apparently concurred with this view.[88]

Muhammad exiled or executed all the Jews from Medina,[89] destroying their farms during a siege,[90] and later invaded Khaybar making Jews pay yearly 50 percent of their crops.[91] A Jewish woman abused and disparaged Muhammad, but when a man killed her, the Prophet declared that no recompense was payable for her blood.[92] He sent his men to assassinate several Jews including Ka'b bin Ashraf,[93] Abu Rafi,[94] and the 120-year-old Abu Afak.[95] A Yemeni Jew who converted to Islam and then apostasized was executed.[96] Muhammad told his followers to "kill any Jew that falls in your power."[97] His enmity toward the Jews never stopped. In "the last moment of his life," Muhammad cursed the Jews and the Christians for building places of worship on the graves of their prophets.[98] 'Umar eventually expelled the Jews from their farms at Khaybar, claiming the Prophet's sanction, and calling them Islam's "enemies."[99]

Gabriel is declared as the enemy of the Jews among the angels.[100] Muhammad interpreted a dreadful noise after sunset as "the Jews being punished in their graves."[101] Every Jew and Christian must believe in Jesus before his death, for he will be a witness against them.[102] Some Jews, it is claimed, were changed into rats.[103]

Muhammad prophesied a latter-day genocide in which the rocks betray the Jews by saying: "There is a Jew hiding behind me; so kill him."[104] This Hadith was brought to the attention of the trustees of the University of Southern California, and the Provost ordered that it be removed from the online collection of Hadith placed on their server by the Muslim Students Association, since he considered it "despicable."[105]

4. LACK OF ECUMENICAL TOLERANCE

One Muslim scholar questions the Hadith because they threaten what he sees as Islam's ecumenical and pluralist nature. Sachedina declares that "spurious and politically motivated traditions ... attributed to the early community were used to defend the declaration that Islam is the only true faith, the only one that guaranteed salvation to its adherents."[106] This is a surprising admission, since the Qur'an clearly states that the only religion acceptable to Allah is Islam.[107] According to the Hadith, "None will enter Paradise but a Muslim." [108] The Islamic view of ecumenism as described by a leading Islamic scholar is based on the concept of *dīn al-fiṭrah*, or "the natural religion."

> Islam's discovery of *din al-fiṭrah* and its vision of it as base of all historical religion is a breakthrough of tremendous importance in inter-religious relations. For the first time it has become possible to hold adherents of all other religions as equal members of a universal religious brotherhood. All religious traditions are *de jure*, for they have all issued from and are based upon a common source, the religion of God which he has implanted equally in all men, upon *din al-fiṭrah*. The problem is to find out how far the religious traditions agree with *din al-fiṭrah*, the original and first religion.[109]

In a dream Muhammad saw Abraham in paradise playing with the children who died in *al-fiṭrah*.[110] Some Muslims asked the Prophet, "O Allah's Apostle! What about the children of pagans?" The Prophet replied, "And also the children of pagans." Muhammad claimed that every child is born Muslim, but its parents turn it into a Jew, Christian, or Magian.[111]

With this claim to be the original and genuine article, Islam is then able to compare other religions by how far they have deviated from their basic foundation. Few modern ecumenicists would accept such an analysis. Some Muslims reject this modern view of ecumenism. "We are not impressed by the claim of latter-day ecumenists, advocates of interreligious dialogue, toleration and co-existence, who assert the ultimacy of any religious system because it is religious. For such a claim is the absolutization of every religion's propositions, which is nothing short of cultural relativism."[112]

The Christian faith makes similar claims to universal applicability and what Greg Forbes calls "the basis for world peace." Core beliefs, he notes, include the following: "(i) all people made in the image of God, (ii) universal sinfulness, no one is better than anyone else, (iii) no place for arrogance as Christian status is not based on performance but because of God's action in Jesus, (iv) a founder who died for his enemies and prayed for their forgiveness."[113]

In general, the Hadiths do not give a strong endorsement of inclusion and tolerance. An example may be Muhammad's instruction to Muslims not to eat out of the same utensils as the people of the Scripture (Jews and Christians) unless the utensils had been washed first.[114] Likewise he told his troops not to use nails for slaughtering animals, since "the nail is the knife of Ethiopians (whom we should not imitate for they are infidels)."[115]

Muslim sources indicate that Arabic indigenous religion was very pluralistic and tolerant[116] and had been practiced for centuries before Islam.[117] No idol worshipers required Muhammad to bow down to their gods, although for twelve years as a prophet in Mecca (AD 610-622) he continued to pray to Allah at the Ka'ba when it was full of idols.[118] Apart from an eighteen-month period of praying toward Jerusalem,[119] the Muslims continued to pray toward the idol-filled Ka'ba for another eight years until it was finally cleansed.[120] Despite the injunction in the Qur'an that "there is no compulsion in religion"[121] and the command for Muslims simply to "desert the idols,"[122] rather than destroy them, Muhammad did not allow freedom of worship to these traditional religions. When he returned to Mecca with 10,000 troops in AD 630, he demolished the local religions and their artefacts[123] and sent his soldiers to raze the temples of deities in other towns.[124] He could have legislated against the excesses of their religion such as female infant exposure, or acted practically to oppose it, as the *Hanif* Zaid bin Amr bin Nufail did before him.[125]

Western societies have banned unacceptable Islamically mandated punishments such as the amputation of hands for theft[126] or stoning for adultery,[127] while still allowing mosques to be built and Muslims to practice their faith openly in Western countries. Muhammad had other options which he had seen modeled and could have chosen. He could have permitted the indigenous Arab people to maintain their traditional religions and become involved in multi-faith dialogue with them. Instead he forbade harmless traditional practices such as setting animals free, because of their cultic associations,[128] and sought to destroy all vestiges of their religious practice.

NOTES

1   B.9:368; 3:648; 6:281; 9:321.

2   B.1:430; 2:517; 3:423; 8:21.

3   B.3:715 also 2:517; 3:423; 8:21.

4   B.7:38.

5   Ibn Ishaq, *Sira Rasul Allah*, 714.

6   B.1:97.1; 3:671, 672, 681, 682, 697-702, 720, 723, 729; 4:255, 655; 7:20; 9:285.

7   B.2:163; 3:695.

8   B.3:157, 158, 772; 7:281; 8:110, 185, 700, 701, 702; 8:811.1.

9   B.4:708; 8:98.

10 B.3:707, 708, 719; 5:652, 676.

11 B.8:706.

12 B.4:514; 8:412.

13 B.1:367.

14 B.5:513; 7:23, 98.

15 B.3:432, 718; 5:459; 7:137; 8:600; 9:506.

16 B.5:637. The *Khumus* was one-fifth of all booty, given to Muhammad and his family.

17 Q.4:3,24,25,36; 16:71; 23:6; 24:31,33,58; 30:28; 33:50,52,55; 70:30.

18 Q.4:3; 23:6; 33:50; 70:30.

19 Q.4:24.

20 Q.24:32.

21 Q.4:25.

22 Ibn Ishaq, *Sira Rasul Allah,* 496. Also Haykal, *The Life of Muhammad,* 336.

23 ṣaḥīḥ Muslim no. 4224 from CD-ROM "The Islamic Scholar," Hadith/Muslim.

24 B.3:351, also 3:588, 598; 8:707; 9:296.

25 B.3:765.

26 B.1:446; 2:570; 3:364, 365, 377, 378, 713, 735, 736, 737, 738, 739, 752, 878, 886, 889, 893; 7:34, 202, 207, 341; 8:708, 743, 744, 746, 749, 750, 751.

27 Al-Hilali amd Khan, *Translation of the Meanings of the Noble Qur'an*, 889.

28 B.8:774, 791. Some, however, think that "egg" means "helmet."

29 B.8:780,781,782.

30 B.8:783, 784, 785, 786, 787, 788, 789, 790.

31 Q.24:2.

32 B.8:809, 825; 9:432, 633.

33 B.8:804, 807, 808, 816, 817, 824.

34 B.8:803.

35 B.8:810 also 7:195, 196; 8:805, 806, 813, 814; 9:281.

36 B.3:817.

37 B.9:9,10.

38 B.5:185; 6:25,26, 134; 7:216.2.

39 B.9:40,50; 4:283.

40 B.6:287.

41 B.3:860, 885 also 3:508; 8:629, 815, 821, 826, 842; 9:303, 365.

42 Based on Q.24:9. B.1:415.

43 B.3:837.

44 B.7:185, 226, 228, 229, 232, 233, 234.

45 B.7:235; 8:740, 837.

46 B.4:260, also 9:17,57, 271.

47 See B.9:58.

48 Q.5:38.

49 B.3:816.

50 B.1:234, 577; 5:505; 7:589, 590; 8:794, 795, 796, 797. Yusuf Ali was apparently unaware of Muhammad sanctioning this punishment when he claimed that, under Islam, "piercing of eyes and leaving the unfortunate victim exposed to a tropical sun, which was practiced in Arabia, and all such tortures were abolished." Yusuf Ali, *The Holy Qur'an: Text, Translation and Commentary*, 252 n.738.

51 The exceptions are (i) the account of a Jewish boy who used to serve the Prophet. When the boy was sick, Muhammad visited him, so the boy embraced Islam (B.2:438; 7:561); (ii) Muhammad exonerated a

Jew who had been slapped by a Muslim (B.3:594, 595; 4:620, 626; 6:162; 8:524; 9:52, 564); (iii) Muhammad confirmed a rabbi's assessment of the greatness of God (B.6:335; 9:510, 543, 604) and the earth becoming bread (B.8:527).

52   B.1:392.

53   B.4:186; 8:53, 57, 273, 274, 404, 410; 9:61, 62.

54   B.3:222; 4:609; 5:279; 6:202, 261.

55   B.4:392; 9:77, 447.

56   B.2:398, 399.

57   E.g., Ramadhan, *Messenger,* 90.

58   Transmitted by Tirmidhi no. 521, italics mine. CD *Islamic Scholar* Hadith/Mishkat.

59   Ward, "Funerary Practices, Jewish," vol.1, 269.

60   B.1:127; 6:245; 9:400, 548, 554.

61   B.1:39.

62   B.3:599, 834.

63   B.2:413; 4:829; 6:79; 8:809, 825; 9:432, 633.

64   B.3:596; 4:9; 4:398; 7:216.2; 8:164; 9:15, 18, 23, 24, 36, 37, 302.

65   B.3:282, 283, 309, 404, 453, 454, 571, 690; 4:165; 5:743.

66   B.3:581, 786; 7:354.

67   B. 4:394; 7:669.

68   B.6:252.

69   B.7:661, 660; 8:89.

70   B.4:662; 9:422.

71   B.4:668; 7:786.

72   B.4:649; 7:821.

73   B.7:799 also 5:280.

74   B.1:577, 578; 4:663.

75   B.2:1, 21.

76   B.4:664.

77   B.6:51.

78   B.7:378.

79   B.5:277.

80   B.5:250.

81   B.4:547, 611.

82   B.3:468, 469, 471; 4:665; 6:539.

83   B.6:170.

84   B.6:226, 528.

85   B.6:229, 529.

86   B.1:723, 726, 729, 739, 743, 745; 2:419.

87   B.1:749.

88   B.5:169.

89   B.5:148, 362.

90   B.3:519; 4:263; 5:362, 365,366, 406. This destruction of Bani Nadir's date palms is also referred to in Q.59:5.

91   1:208, 214, 367, 584, 812; 2:68; 3:405, 437, 485, 521, 524, 527, 531, 657, 678, 881; 4:195; 5:509, 510, 550; 8:169.

92   Abu Dawud no. 4349.

93   B.4:271; 3:687; 4:270: 5:369.

94   B. 5:370, 371.

95   Ibn Ishaq, *Sira Rasul Allah,* 675.

96   B.5:632; 9:58.

97   Ibn Ishaq, *Sira Rasul Allah,* 369.

98   B.1:427, 428; 2:414, 472; 4:660; 5:725, 727; 7:706.

99   B.3:485, 531, 890; 4:380.

100   B.4:546; 5:275; 6:7.

101   B.2:45.

102   B.4:657.

103   B.4:524.

104   B.4:176, 177, 791.

105   genocidal-Hadith.html (accessed July 9, 2013).

106   Sachedina, "The Qur'ān and other religions," 299.

107   Q.3:85.

108   B.4:297; 8:535.

109   Al-Faruqi, "Christian Mission and Islamic Da'wa," 396.

110   B.9:171.

111   B.6:298; 8:597.

112   Al-Faruqi, "Christian Mission and Islamic Da'wa," 396.

113   Forbes, "All Religions lead to God?" 5.

114   B.7:387, 396, 404.

115   B. 3:668, 684; 4:309; 7:406, 411, 417, 451, 472.

116   Ibn Ishaq notes that "When the apostle openly displayed Islam as
       God ordered him, his people did not withdraw or turn against him
       ... until he spoke disparagingly of their gods." Ibn Ishaq, *Sira Rasul
       Allah,* 118.

117   B.6:442.

118   B.2:413; 3:421, 860, 885; 4:829; 6:79; 7:195, 196; 8:629, 805, 806,
       809, 810, 813, 814, 815, 821, 825, 826, 842; 9:303, 365, 432, 633.

119   Ibn Ishaq, *Sira Rasul Allah,* 298.

120   B.2:671; 3:658; 5:583, 584; 6:244.

121   Q.2:257.

122   B.1:3; 6:447,448.

123   B.2:671; 3:658; 5:583; 6:244.

124   B.4:262; 5:643. Similar commands were given in Num 33:52;
       Deut 7:5; 12:3.

125   B.5:169.

126   Q.5:33.

127   B.8:804, 807, 808, 816, 817, 824.

128   B.2:303; 6:148.

IV

PRACTICAL IMPLICATIONS

The recognition that the Hadith present a world-view that is inimical to the teaching of the Bible presents a problem for Christians. Should the Hadith and the Islamic system which they support be challenged by Christians? If not, why not? And if so, then how should this be done? This section responds to these difficult questions.

17

TO CHALLENGE OR
NOT TO CHALLENGE?

THE MATERIAL IN THIS BOOK indicates that Islam and Christianity differ in significant ways. As further proof of this, Islamic apologist organizations throughout the world are very active, constantly challenging or denigrating Christian beliefs and promoting Islam as the alternative. If there is no clear Christian response to the challenges by Muslims, the conclusion may be drawn that Christians have nothing to say and that Islam has no case to answer. How should Christians respond? What should they do with this information? Is it ever justifiable to criticize others?

1. THE IRENIC APPROACH

It is easy to find faults in the teaching and documents of a thought system different from one's own, but some might believe that it is less than Christian to point them out. After all, Christians are commanded not to judge,[1] to rid themselves of slander,[2] and to avoid controversy.[3] Christians are called to be peacemakers.[4] Based on these passages, there seems to be no place for criticism of others, particularly if it results in division.

However, this is a one-sided reading of Scripture, which itself commends "the whole counsel of God."[5] According to the writer of the book of the Proverbs: "The first to present his case seems right, till another comes forward and questions him."[6] Even a superficial reading reveals that the Bible is replete with disapproval of others, whether of the same faith or a different one. Clearly there are cases and situations when even trenchant denunciation of others is acceptable.

2. CRITICISM OF MEMBERS OF ONE'S OWN RELIGION

In the Bible, criticism is often directed against those of the same fold, whether Jewish or Christian. In the Old Testament, false prophets are pilloried,[7] as are aberrant political leaders (e.g., kings)[8] and religious leaders (priests).[9] The people as a whole are criticized when they depart from Yahweh's laws.[10] Amos, for example, censures Judah for failure to follow God's revelation, and Israel for injustice and immorality.[11]

Jesus publicly opposed the Pharisees, Sadducees, Herodians, and teachers of the law, engaging them in fierce debates.[12] He referred to Jewish leaders as "blind guides," "blind fools," "wolves in sheep's clothing," "whitewashed tombs," "snakes," a "brood of vipers," and "hypocrites." He denounced their beliefs and their practices.[13] He expressed frustration toward and rebuked his own followers. Jesus' discerning approach found him rebuking his own disciples for a variety of actions and attitudes, such as sleeping,[14] being "slow of heart,"[15] denying his coming death,[16] a lack of belief,[17] spousing or involvement in violence,[18] stopping the children from coming to him,[19] and he opposed Judas about Mary wasting perfume on him.[20]

The rest of the New Testament finds all of the writers pointing out inconsistent behavior by Christians or opposing counterfeit teaching (see Table 20).

WRITER	IMMORALITY, INJUSTICE OR BACKSLIDING WITHIN THE CHURCH	ATTACKS ON FALSE TEACHERS WITHIN THE CHURCH
Paul	1 Cor 5:1–11; Gal 3:1–5	2 Cor 11:13; Gal 2:4
Hebrews	Heb 5:11–6:12; 10:19–39	Heb 13:9
James/Jude	Jam 1:19–3:2; 3:9–5:7	Jude 3–19
Peter	1 Pet 2:1,11	2 Pet 2:1–22
John	3 Jn 9,10	1 Jn 4:1–6; 2; 7–11
Revelation	Rev 2:4,5; 3:1–3,14–19	Rev 2:14–16,20-24

TABLE 20: Criticism of Unacceptable Behavior

The people of God were expected to maintain the highest standards of behavior and speech, and those who did not do so were publicly called to account. Those passages which counsel a lack of controversy relate to false Christian teachers who refuse to listen to the truth.[21] Such people are to be warned and then ignored.[22] Those who engage in destructive behavior are no longer considered members of the people of God,[23] and are to be cut off from Christian fellowship.[24]

3. CRITICISM OF MEMBERS OF OTHER RELIGIONS

Yet even those outside the people of God could be criticized. It was characteristic of the Old Testament prophets to address condemnatory messages to the nations surrounding Israel.[25] The biblical writers were keenly aware of what was occurring in foreign realms. Sometimes criticism in the Bible is directed at pagan religions, to show the people of Israel that the nations were not worth copying.[26] The first chapter of Genesis has been recognized as undermining the mythologies of the surrounding nations.[27] The ten plagues preceding the Exodus were an assault on the nature gods of the Egyptian pantheon.[28] The Old Testament mounts a consistent and sustained attack on pagan religions. Disparagement of other gods, idols, idol makers and idol worshipers is found in four books of the Pentateuch,[29] eight out of nine historical books,[30] all of the major prophets,[31] and nine of the twelve minor prophets.[32] In the New Testament, idolatry is denounced in Acts, most of Paul's letters, and the letters of Peter, John, and the book of Revelation.

It is not only the theology of other religions that is critiqued, but also their practices. Human rights abuses are censured. The prophet Amos, for example, pronounces judgment on a variety of nations for sins against humanity: Syria, for threshing Gilead with sledges of iron; Gaza (Philistines) for slave trading; Tyre, for breaking a treaty or previous understanding, and involvement in slavery; Edom, for showing no mercy; Ammon, for killing the defenseless; and Moab, for desecration of the dead.[33] The nations are also criticized for their greed[34] and national self-reliance.[35]

Although Jesus reserved his greatest condemnation for those of the Jewish faith, he also denigrated Gentile practices which were destructive,[36] oppressed others,[37] or showed self-dependence.[38] Paul points out the behavioral shortcomings of the Greeks and other non-Jews.[39] He referred to Gentiles who believed in Christ as coming "from darkness to light."[40]

It is clear that biblical ministry does not sanction simple acquiescence in the face of opposing worldviews. They must be challenged. One qualification for an elder in the first century was not only the ability to commend the gospel but also "to confute those who contradict it."[41]

This injunction has been followed throughout history. In a letter to Bernard of Clairvaux, Peter the Venerable (c.1092 -1156), the Abbott of Cluny, justified his critical work against Islam (*Liber contra sectam sive haeresim Saracenorum*). "My intention in this work was to follow the custom of the Fathers [of the Church] by which they never silently passed by any heresy of their times, not even the slightest (if I may speak in these terms) without resisting it with all the strength of faith and demonstrating, both through writings and discussions, that it is detestable."[42] The Lausanne paper on "Ministry in Islamic Contexts" suggests that "confrontation and controversy are unavoidable in a theological approach because the points on which Christianity and Islam differ have not changed."[43]

John Stott, a modern apologist for the gospel, has written: "Controversy is sometimes a painful necessity."[44]

4. WHEN TO ENGAGE IN CONTROVERSY

But when is the right time for debate and criticism of other religious systems? In the Bible, a negative approach to other religions is found when that religion starts to negatively impact the people of God, either theologically or culturally. In the Old Testament, the nations around Israel were tempting Israel to idolatry through compromise and intermarriage. The prophetic attack on idols was a response to these trends. In the New Testament, Jesus stood up to those who opposed his message and questioned his identity. Paul continued this strategy against those who sought, by various means, to hinder the spread of the gospel.

Today Islam is resurgent, presenting itself as a viable international system in the spiritual, political, social, cultural, legal, and economic realms. The slogans "Islam is the answer" or "Islam is the solution" are increasingly being heard around the world. Islam's larger design has been described by a Muslim scholar, Bassam Tibi, Professor of International Relations at Gottingen University:

> At its core Islam is a religious mission to all humanity. Muslims are religiously obliged to disseminate the Islamic faith throughout the world: "we have sent you forth to all mankind" (Saba 34:28). If non-Muslims submit to conversion or subjugation, this call (dawa) can be pursued peacefully. If they do not, Muslims are obliged to wage war against them. In Islam, peace requires that non-Muslims submit to the call of Islam, either by converting or by accepting the status of a religious minority (dhimmi) and paying the imposed tax, jizya. World peace, the final stage of the dawa, is reached only with the conversion or submission of all mankind to Islam.[45]

Such a plan places Islam at clear loggerheads with the Christian call to take the good news of Christ to the ends of the earth,[46] and the expectation that all things will be reconciled in Christ.[47] Aspects of Islamic teaching given in the Hadith must be rejected, and the alternative Christian teaching must be presented.

ILLUSTRATION 25:
Calls for Sharia in Europe[r]

In the political arena, the Muslim call for the implementation of Sharia must also be addressed (see Illustration 25).

The inconsistent behavior of Muhammad means that there is effectively no single model which can be followed. Islam itself is divided about this. Every incident, including acts of violence, becomes disputed territory within the Muslim community, with those who carried it out and their supporters claiming that it is a legitimate action according to their understanding of Sharia, and other Muslim voices disputing this. In the absence of a clear definition of Sharia, any person's opinion can be seen as possibly authoritative. This shortcoming of Sharia law, its lack of clear definition, should be discussed publicly.

5. CONTENT OF CHALLENGES AND DEBATES

The hadith are one of the major bases upon which Islam builds its edifice. As we have seen, there are many aspects of Islam outlined in the Hadith that may be debated or challenged from a Christian or other perspective. These include the inconsistencies in Muhammad's speech and actions,[48] and the results of these discrepancies among his followers.[49] A critical analysis would point out the differences between the actions of Muhammad and those of the early Muslim leaders.[50] A conversation about compilation problems of the hadith corpus could also be engaged in.[51] Scholars have identified problems

---

r   http://bulletinoftheoppressionofwomen.com and
     http://www.frontpagemag.com/fpm/190087/
     frances-growing-islamist-problem-ryan-mauro

with the isnād system and transmission in the Hadith.[52] The contrasts between the understandings of God,[53] of political, social, and financial policies,[54] and of the ultimate destinies of humanity are significant and deep.[55] Likewise, striking dissimilarities can be found between the actions and teachings of Muhammad when compared with those of Christ,[56] and their teaching on women.[57] There are elements in the Hadith which should be openly criticized. It is in the Hadith, for example, that the basis for the law of apostasy is found, preventing Muslims from making faith choices apart from Islam. This is a human rights issue.[58] The material outlined here details compelling differences between the two religions. It is neither honest nor helpful to ignore these differences.

6. HOW TO ENGAGE IN CONTROVERSY

The Bible gives guidelines on how to engage in controversy. A commitment to the ninth commandment obliges truthful speech about others, even if one disagrees with their views. At the same time, one must be aware of one's own shortcomings, being honest about "the log" in one's own eye, and be willing to make appropriate changes in one's own practices when challenged.[59] Opposition to error should not be inspired by self-aggrandizement. The early church decided in the context of persecution that "those who broke idols or insulted the gods, and thus deliberately provoked their own death, were not to be reckoned among the Church's martyrs."[60]

In engaging with others, two aspects must be kept in equilibrium (see Illustration 26).

ILLUSTRATION 26:
Balancing Truth and Love

"The apostolic command is clear," writes Stott. "We are to 'maintain the truth in love' (Eph. 4:15), being neither truthless in our love, nor loveless in our truth, but holding the two in balance."[61] The challenge for Christians is to develop ways of putting this material out into the public arena in a manner which is honest, fair, and yet still caring toward Muslim people. It is possible to criticize a system, such as Islam, and yet still love its adherents.

The model for Christians is Christ himself, who is "full of grace and truth."[62]

NOTES

1 Matt 7:1,2; Luke 6:37; Rom 2:1; 14:4, 10; 1 Cor 4:5.

2 Jas 4:11; 1 Pet 2:1.

3 Titus 3:9.

4 Matt 5:9; Rom 12:18; Ps 34:14 and 1 Pet 3:11; Jas 3:16–18.

5 Acts 20:27 (RSV).

6 Prov 18:17.

7 E.g., Jer 14:13–16.

8 E.g., Jer 21, 22.

9 E.g., Ezek 22:26.

10 E.g., Jer 14:10–12.

11 Amos 2:4–3:16.

12 Matt 15:14; 23:16,19,24,25; 7:15; 23:27; Luke 11:44; Matt 12:34; 23:33; Matt 15:7.

13 Matt 15:3–6; 23:2–35.

14 Matt 26:41.

15 Luke 24:25.

16 Matt 16:23.

17 Luke 9:19.

18 Luke 9:54,55; 22:38, 51.

19 Luke 18:15.

20 John 12:7.

21 E.g., 1 Tim 1:3,4; 6:4,5; Titus 3:9–11.

22 Titus 3:10.

23 Matt 18:17.

24 1 Cor 5:11, 13.

25 This is found in Isa 14-25, Jer 46–51, Ezek 25–32, Joel 3, Amos 1, 2, all of Obadiah (against Edom), all of Nahum (against Nineveh), and Zechariah 9,14.

26 E.g., Jer 10:1–3.

27 Hasel, "The Polemic Nature of the Genesis Cosmology," 81–102.

28 Davis, *Moses and the Gods of Egypt*, 118.

29 E.g., Ex 20:4; 34:17 (4 references); Lev 17:7; 19:4 (4 references); Num 33:52; Deut 4:6; 5:8 (13 references).

30 Only the book of Ruth lacks such references, unless Ruth 1:15 is counted as an implied criticism of other gods.

31 There are forty-one references in Isaiah, 20 in Jeremiah, 47 in Ezekiel, 12 in Daniel, but none in Lamentations.

32 Although Joel, Obadiah, and Haggai lack any references to idols and other gods, they proclaim the uniqueness and universal sovereignty of Yahweh (e.g., Joel 2:27; Obad 21; Hag 2:22). The wisdom and poetry books lack any references with the exception of the book of Psalms, which contains ten such denunciations.

33 Amos1:3–2:3.

34 E.g., Isa 23:1–9.

35 E.g., Isa 19:1–16.

36 Luke 21:22.

37 Matt 20:28; Mark 10:42.

38 Matt 6:32.

39 E.g., Rom 1:18–32.

40 E.g., Eph 5:8.

41 Titus 1:9.

42 Kritzeck, *Peter the Venerable and Islam*, 37.

43 Lausanne Committee for World Evangelization, *Ministry in Islamic Contexts* (Monrovia, CA: MARC, 1996), 16.

44 Stott, *Christ the Controversialist*, 18.

45 Tibi, "War and Peace in Islam," 130.

46 Acts 1:8.

47 Col 1:20.

48 See ch. 4, part 1.

49 See ch. 5.

50   See ch. 6.

51   See ch. 7.

52   See ch. 8.

53   See ch. 9.

54   See ch. 15.

55   See ch. 13.

56   See ch. 10 and 11.

57   See ch. 12.

58   See ch. 16.

59   Matt 7:3–5.

60   Neill, *History*, 43.

61   Stott, *Controversialist*, 18.

62   John 1:14.

18

CONCLUSION

THIS BOOK CRITICALLY ASSESSES the Hadith, both internally and externally. It questions their role and asks whether they challenge the sufficiency of the Qur'an as revelation. Muhammad's actions and words, as recorded in the Hadith, are shown to be inconsistent, and a range of reasons is suggested for this. The outcomes among his followers, including the early Caliphs, are delineated. There is also some discussion on the compilation and transmission of the Hadith, particularly in the isnād system and its reliability.

The Hadith are also used as a tool by Islamic revivalists in their new quest for power and influence in the Muslim community. They claim to call the *umma* back to the pure Islam practiced by their Prophet and his followers. In doing so they hope to remake the modern twenty-first century in the image of seventh-century Arabia.

The reality is that there was never a single way of life in early Islam. Muhammad's *sunna* was variegated, depending on his circumstances. His companions and early followers felt free to adopt, adapt, ignore, or reject his customs, based on their circumstances. There was no clearly defined list of traditions consistently performed by Muhammad and his followers that everyone must follow. This concept was a construct of the later Islamic community in an attempt to standardize practices, which in reality have varied over time and location. It is a delusion to think that there was and always has been a single set of behaviors and mores practiced by Muhammad, his followers, and every faithful Muslim society throughout history. Islam has continually been adaptive in its responses to current situations and will remain so. The modern revivalist movement is simply the latest exemplification of that process.

The Hadith often represent an earlier and now outdated worldview. Substantial scientific and hygiene concerns are raised about some of the material in the Hadith. The issues of human rights, criminal justice, and the view of and treatment of women do not accord with more modern understandings. It is problematic for Muslims to suggest that these are suitable for universal application in all times and places. In fact, many of these aspects in the Hadith have been challenged by Muslim scholars.

There are also significant differences in some of the teaching of the Hadith when compared with the Bible. Some are associated with the view of God presented, and particularly the person of Christ, when contrasted with Muhammad. Others arise from chronology and the details of events. The laws and expectations regarding political, social, and financial matters vary from biblical prescriptions, as do the rewards and punishment promised in heaven and hell.

For some people, the existence of so many disparities between the teaching of the Bible and the values and ideas presented in the Hadith indicate that that there is little or nothing in common between Islam and Christianity.[1] For others, the Hadith can provide some areas of discussion between and within the world's two largest religions. Whatever view about Islam is held, this discussion about the contents of the Hadith can and should take place in a matrix of truth and love. But take place it must.

NOTES

1   E.g., Abdullah Al Araby, "Nothing in Common," www.islamreview. com/articles/nothingincommon.shtml (accessed July 7, 2013).

APPENDIX
Qur'anic Verses Referred to in al-Bukhāri's Hadith***

QUR'ĀNIC VERSES	AL-BUKHARI'S (B) HADITH (VOLUME NO: ACCOUNT NO)
Q.1:1-6	B.1:723, 739, 743, 745, 749; 6:1,226,227
Q.1:7	B.6:2
Q.2	B.6:536.2
Q.2:75–77	B.4:829; 6:79 ; 9:633
Q.2:97	B.6:7
Q.2:102	B.4:633
Q.2:106	B.6:8, 527
Q.2:109	B.6:89
Q.2:125	B.1:395, 396
Q.2.127	B.4:583, 584
Q.2:136	B.6:12
Q.2:142, 144	B.1:392; 6:13; 9:358
Q.2:143	B.4:555; 6:13, 14; 9:448
Q.2:149	B.6:19
Q.2:150	B.6:20
Q.2:158	B.3:18; 6:22,23,384
Q.2:159	B.1:161
Q.2:159–160	B.1:118; 3:540
Q.2:178	B.6:25; 9:20
Q.2:184	B.3:170; 6:32,33,34

*** These are not *Hadith Qudsi,* which refer to Muhammad's statements from Allah reported in the Hadith but which are not found in the Qur'an.

QUR'ĀNIC VERSES	AL-BUKHARI'S (B) HADITH (VOLUME NO: ACCOUNT NO)
Q.2:187	B.6:38
Q.2:189	B.3:30; 6:39
Q.2:193	B.6:40; 9:215
Q.2:195	B.6:41
Q.2:196	B.2:598; 5:504; 6:42,43
Q.2:197	B.2:598
Q.2:198	B.2:822; 3:266, 311; 6:44
Q.2:199	B.2:726; 6:45,46
Q.2:201	B.6:47
Q.2:214	B.6:48,49
Q.2:223	B.6:50,51
Q.2:225	B.8:656
Q.2:232	B.6:52; 7:61, 248
Q.2:234	B.6:54
Q.2:235	B.7:56
Q.2:238	B.2:290, 291, 292, 307, 308; 6:58
Q.2:239	B.6:59
Q.2.240	B.6:53,54,60; 7:256
Q,2:249	B.5:293
Q.2:255	B.6:530
Q.2:260	B.4:591; 6:61, 216
Q.2:266	B.6:62
Q.2:273	B.6:63
Q.2:275,276	B.6:64
Q.2:275–279	B.6:67
Q.2:280	B.6:66
Q.2:284	B.6:54,55,60,68
Q.2:285,286	B.5:345; 6:530, 560, 571

QUR'ĀNIC VERSES	AL-BUKHARI'S (B) HADITH (VOLUME NO: ACCOUNT NO)
Q.3:7	B.6:70
Q.3:36	B.4:461; 6:71
Q.3:64	B.1:6; 6:75
Q.3:77	B.3:301, 546, 599, 692, 834, 836, 839, 841, 842; 6:72,73,74; B.8:653,668; 9:294, 537
Q.3:84	B.9:632
Q.3:92	B.2:540; 6:76; 7:515
Q.3:93	B.3:511
Q.3:122	B.5:381; 6:81
Q.3:128	B.5:397; 6:82,83; 9:445
Q.3:144	B.5:19, 733
Q.3:153	B.5:396; 6:84
Q.3:172	B.5:404
Q.3:173	B.6:86,87
Q.3:180	B.2:486 ; 6:88
Q.3:187	B.6:35
Q.3:188	B.6:90,91,92
Q.3:190	B.6:93,94,95,96; 8:234; 9:544
Q.4:3	B.3:674; 6:97,98; 7:2, 29,35, 70, 71; 9:95
Q.4:6	B.3:414; 6:99
Q.4:8	B.6:100
Q.4:11	B.6:101, 102; 7:554
Q.4:12	B.6:55
Q.4:19	B.6:103; 9:81
Q.4:23	B.7:35
Q.4:33	B.3:489; 6:104
Q.4:40	B.6:105
Q.4:41	B.6:106; 6:570
Q.4:43	B.6:107

QUR'ĀNIC VERSES	AL-BUKHARI'S (B) HADITH (VOLUME NO: ACCOUNT NO)
Q.4:59	B.6:108
Q.4.65	B.3:871; 6:109
Q.4:69	B.5:19; 5:715; 5:719; 6:110; 7:578; 8:516, 517
Q.4:88	B.3:108; 5:380; 6:113
Q.4:89	B.6:111,112
Q.4:93	B.6:114, 6:173; 6:285,286, 287, 288, 289
Q.4:94	B.6:115
Q.4:95	B.4:84; 6:116, 117, 118, 119; 6:512
Q.4:97,98	B.6:120, 121; 9:207
Q.4:102	B.6:123
Q.4:127	B.3:674; 6:97,98,124; 7:2, 59, 62, 71; 9:95
Q.4:128	B.3:630, 859; 6:124, 125; 7:134
Q.4:145	B.6:126
Q.4:159	B.4:657
Q.4:176	B.6:129; 8:736
Q.5:3	B.5:689; 6:130; 9:373
Q.5:6	B.6:131,132
Q.5:17,18	B.8:533
Q.5:24	B.6:133
Q.5:27	B.5:288
Q.5:33	B.6:134
Q.5:45	B.6:135; 9:32
Q.5:67	B.6:136, 378; 9:622
Q.5:87	B.6:139; 7:13
Q.5:89	B.6:137, 138
Q.5:90	B.6:140, 141, 142
Q.5:93	B.3:644; 6:141, 144
Q.5:101	B.6:145, 146; 8:387; 9:211,398

QUR'ĀNIC VERSES	AL-BUKHARI'S (B) HADITH (VOLUME NO: ACCOUNT NO)
Q.5:117-118	B.4:656; 6:149, 264
Q.5:120,121	B.4:568
Q.6:14	B.4:726
Q.6:65	B.6:152; 9:503
Q.6:82	B.6:153, 299; 9:53,70
Q.6:83	B.1:31; 4:580
Q.6:84-91	B.4:632; 6:156,331
Q.6:86	B.6:328, 329
Q.6:90	B.6:330
Q.6:96	B.9:111
Q.6:103	B.6:378; 9:477
Q.6.145	B.7:437
Q.6:146	B.6:157
Q.6:151	B.6:158, 161
Q.6:158	B.6:159, 160
Q.6:159	B.6:164
Q.7:161	B.6:165
Q.7:199	B.6:166, 167; 9:389
Q.8	B.6:404
Q.8:22	B.6:169
Q.8:24	B.6:1,170,226
Q.8:33,34	B.6:171, 172
Q.8:39	B.6:173,174
Q.8:65,66	B.6:175, 176
Q.8:72	B.2:658
Q.9:4	B.6:179
Q.9:12	B.6:181
Q.9:34	B.2:488; 6:182, 183

QUR'ĀNIC VERSES	AL-BUKHARI'S (B) HADITH (VOLUME NO: ACCOUNT NO)
Q.9:36	B.6:184
Q.9:40	B.6:185
Q.9:58	B.9:67
Q.9:60	B.6:189
Q.9:79	B.2:496; 6:190, 191
Q.9:80	B.6:192; 7:688
Q.9:84	B.2:359; 6:193, 194; 7:688
Q.9:94	B.6:199
Q.9:95,96	B.5:702; 6:195
Q.9:113	B.2:443; 6:197,295
Q.9:117-119	B.5:702,707; 6:200
Q.9:118	B.6:98
Q.9:128,129	B.6:509, 510, 511
Q.11:5	B.6:203, 204, 205
Q.11:102	B.6:208
Q.11:114	B.1:504; 6:209
Q.12:18	B.4:602; 6:213
Q.12:30-32	B.1:633, 647, 648 650 , 680 ,681, 684; 4:598; 599; 9:406
Q.12:110	B.4:603; 6:49,217,218
Q.14:24,25	B.6:220
Q.14:27	B.2:450, 451, 453; 6:221
Q.14:28,29	B.5:315; 6:222
Q.15:90	B.6:228,229
Q.16:29	B.6:3
Q.17	B.6:232, 233
Q.17:18	B.1:621
Q.17:33	B.6:285,286
Q.17:57,58	B.6:238, 239

QUR'ĀNIC VERSES	AL-BUKHARI'S (B) HADITH (VOLUME NO: ACCOUNT NO)
Q.17:60	B.8:610
Q.17:60	B.6:240
Q.17:78	B.6:241
Q.17:79	B.9:532.3
Q.17:81	B.6:244
Q.17:85	B.1:126; 6:245; 9:400, 548, 554
Q.17:110	B.6:246, 247; 8:339; 9:582, 616, 617, 637
Q.18	B.6:531
Q.18:54	B.2:227; 6:248; 9:446, 557
Q.18:61-82	B.6:249, 250, 251; 9:570
Q.18:62,63	B.4:498
Q.18:73	B.8:665
Q.18:72-77	B.3:888
Q.18:103	B.6:252
Q.18:105	B.6:253
Q.19:39	B.6:254
Q.19:64	B.4:441; 6:255; 9:547
Q.19:77, 78-80	B.3: 304, 475, 607; 6:256, 257, 258, 259
Q.21:104	B.4:568, 656; 6:149; 8:533
Q.22:2	B.6:265
Q.22:11	B.6:266
Q.22:19	B.5:304, 305, 306, 307, 308; 6:267, 268
Q.22:33	B.5:679
Q.24:6-9	B.6:269–272
Q.24:11	B.3:829; 5:462 (vv.11–20); 6:212, 273, 279,280
Q.24.11-20	B.6:274,275, 281; 8:670; 9:591, 635
Q.24:15	B.5:465; 6:276
Q.24:22	B.5:462; 8:670

QUR'ĀNIC VERSES	AL-BUKHARI'S (B) HADITH (VOLUME NO: ACCOUNT NO)
Q.24:27-29	B. 7:807; 8:258; 9:38.2
Q.24:31	B.1:148; 6:282; 7:95
Q.24:34	B.6:283
Q.25	B.9:640
Q.25:68-70	B.6:284,285,286, 287, 288, 289; 6:334; 8:30; 9:623
Q.25:77	B.6:290
Q.26.214	B.4:15, 727; 6:293, 294; 6:495, 496, 497
Q.28:56	B.6:295
Q.28:85	B.6:296
Q.30:1-3	B.6:297; 6:345, 350
Q.30:30	B.2:440, 441; 6:298
Q.30:52	B.5:316, 317
Q.31:13	B.1:31; 4:580, 638, 639; 6:153, 299; 9:53,70
Q.31:34	B.1:47; 6:151,219, 300, 301; 6:378
Q.32	B.2:16, 174. 182, 183
Q.32:17	B.4:467; 6:302
Q.33:5	B.5:335; 6:305; 7:25
Q.33:6	B.6:304
Q.33:10	B.5:429
Q.33:21	B.2:205, 683, 684, 685, 691, 693, 708; 5:498
Q.33:23	B.4:61, 62, 462; 6:306, 307
Q.33:28,29	B.6:308,309
Q.33.37	B.6:310; 9:516
Q.33:51	B.7:48
Q.33:52	B.6:313
Q.33:53	B.6:314, 315, 316, 317; 8:255, 256; 8:288
Q.33:55	B.6:319
Q.33:56	B.6:320,321,322

QUR'ĀNIC VERSES	AL-BUKHARI'S (B) HADITH (VOLUME NO: ACCOUNT NO)
Q.33:58	B.6:318
Q.33:69	B.4:616; 6:323
Q.34:23	B.6:223, 224; 6:324; 9:573
Q.34:49	B.6:244
Q.35:22	B.5:316
Q.36:12	B.1:625
Q.36:38	B.4:420; 6:326, 327; 9:520, 528
Q.37:102	B.1:140,818
Q.38:24	B.6:156
Q.38:30, 35	B.4:633, 634; 6:332
Q.38:86	B.6:297; 6:332,333,349
Q.39:30	B.5:19
Q.39:53	B.6:334
Q.39:67	B.6:335,336; 9:509, 510, 511, 543, 604
Q.39:68	B.6:337, 338
Q.40:28	B.6:339
Q.41:22	B.6:340, 341, 342; 9:612
Q.42:23	B.6:343
Q.42:51	B.6:378
Q.43:77	B.4:453, 488; 6:344
Q.44:10,16	B.2:121,133;6:215, 297; 6:333, 345, 346, 347, 348, 349, 350
Q.44:15	B.6:215
Q.45:24	B.6:351
Q.46:17	B.6:352
Q.46:24	B.4:428; 6:353
Q.47:22	B.6:354, 355, 356; 8:16; 9:593
Q.48	B.6:553; 9:631
Q.48:1	B.5:490, 494; 6:357, 358; 6:357-367, 532

QUR'ĀNIC VERSES	AL-BUKHARI'S (B) HADITH (VOLUME NO: ACCOUNT NO)
Q.48:5	B.5:490
Q.49.1	B.5:653; 6:370
Q.49:2	B.6:368,369; 9:405
Q.49.9	B.3:856; 6:40,173
Q.49:13	B.4:695
Q.50:30	B.6:371, 372, 373
Q.50:39	B.1:529, 547; 6:374
Q.50:40	B.6:375
Q.52	B.1:732; 6:377
Q.53	B.2:176, 177, 178, 179; 6:385, 386,
Q.53.9-10	B.4:455, 458; 6:379, 380
Q.53:18	B.4:456; 6:381
Q.53:19	B.6:38
Q.54:1	B.6:345, 350, 387-391
Q.54:15	B.4:557, 595; 6:392, 394,397
Q.54:20,21	B.6:393
Q.54:38-40	B.6:395
Q.54:45	B.5:289; 6:398
Q.54:46,47	B.6:399 400, 513
Q.54:51	B.6:396
Q.55:15	B.6:401,402
Q.55:55	B.6:401
Q.55:56	B.6:402
Q.56:30	B.4:474, 475; 6:403
Q.59	B.6:404, 405
Q.59:5	B.5:365; 6:406
Q.59:6	B.7:271
Q.59:7	B.6:408; 7:815, 822
Q.59:9	B.6:411

QUR'ĀNIC VERSES	AL-BUKHARI'S (B) HADITH (VOLUME NO: ACCOUNT NO)
Q.60:1	B.5:572; 6:412, 413
Q.60:8	B.8:9
Q.60:10-12	B.3:874; 7:211
Q.60:12	B.5:496; 6:414, 415, 416, 417,418; 8:775; 9:321
Q.61:6	B.6:419
Q.62:3	B.6:420, 421
Q.62:11	B.2:58; 3:274,278; 6:422
Q.63:1-8	B.6:423–430
Q.65:1-5	B.6:431,432
Q.66:1-4	B.7:192; 8:682 (honey); 3:648 (Maria)
Q.66:4	B.7:119
Q.66:5	B.1:395, 396; 6:433-438
Q.68:13	B.6:439
Q.72	B.1:740; 5:200; 6:443
Q.74:1-5	B.4:461; 6:444,445,446,447,448, 478, 479, 480, 481
Q.75:16	B.1:4; 6:449, 450,451, 564
Q.75:16-18	B.9:615
Q.76	B.2:16, 174
Q.77	B.5:712
Q.84	B.2: 180
Q.84:8	B.6:461; 8:543, 544, 545
Q.84:7,8	B.6:463
Q.87	B.6:517
Q.92:1-3	B.6:467, 468; 8:295
Q.92:5-10	B.6:469, 470, 471, 472, 473, 474; 8:236, 602; 9:642
Q:93:1-3	B.2:225; 6:475, 476
Q.94:1-3	B.9:608
Q.95	B.6:477; 9:636
Q.96:1-5	B.6:478, 479, 480

QUR'ĀNIC VERSES	AL-BUKHARI'S (B) HADITH (VOLUME NO: ACCOUNT NO)
Q.98	B.6:483, 484, 485
Q.99:7,8	B.6:486, 487; 9:454
Q.103	B.2:173
Q.108:1	B.6:488, 489,490
Q.110.1	B.4:821;5:713; 6:491,493, 494
Q.111:1	B.2:477; 6:293, 325; 6:495, 496, 497
Q.112	B.6:498, 499; 8:638
Q.112:1	B.6:533, 534, 536; 9:471, 472
Q.113,114	B.6:500, 501, 535, 536

BIBLIOGRAPHY

PRIMARY SOURCES

Al-Hilali, Muhammad Taqi-ud-Din and Muhammad Muhsin Khan. *Translation of the Meanings of the Noble Qur'an in the English language.* Madinah, K. S. A.: King Fahd Complex for the Printing of the Holy Qur'an, 1427 A.H.

Ali, Abdulla Yusuf. *The Holy Qur-an: Text, Translation and Commentary.* Leicester: The Islamic Foundation, 1975.

——. *The Holy Qur'ān: English Translation of the Meanings and Commentary.* Al-Madinah: King Fahd Complex for the Printing of the Holy Qur'ān, 1413 H.

Ibn Ishaq, *Sira Rasul Allah.* Translated as *The Life of Muhammad.* Translated by A. Guillaume. Karachi: Oxford University Press, 1998.

Khan, Dr. Muhammad Muhsin. Translated as *The Translation of the Meanings of ṣaḥīḥ al-Bukhāri* Arabic-English, 9 vols. Riyadh: Darussalam Publishers and Printers, 1997.

Saheeh International, ed. *The Qur'an.* Jeddah: Al-Muntada Al-Islami, 2004.

BOOKS AND ARTICLES

Aly, Waleed. *People Like Us: How Arrogance is Dividing Islam and the West.* Sydney: Picador, 2007.

Abbott, Nabia. *Studies in Arabic Literary Papyri*, 3 vols, Volume II (Qur'anic Commentary & Tradition) Chicago: The University Of Chicago Press, 1967.

Abiad, Nisrine. *Sharia, Muslim States and International Human Rights Treaty Obligations: A Comparative Study.* London: BIICL, 2008.

Abu Eid, Sheikh Muhammad. "Islamic ruling concerning music" in *Al-Firdaus Newspaper,* first edition, August 2007.

Abu-Hamdiyyah, Muhammad. *The Qur'an –An Introduction.* London: Routledge, 2000.

Afshar, Haleh. *Iran, Islam and Democracy: Fluid Identities.* Melbourne University: Centre for the Study of Contemporary Islam, 2006.

Ahmed, Mufti M. Mukarram. *Encyclopaedia of Islam,* 25 vols. New Delhi: Anmol Publications, 2005.

Al-Faruqi, Ismail. "Christian Mission and Islamic Da'wa." *International Review of Mission,* (LXV, No. 260, October 1976): 391-409.

Al-Faruqi, Ismail R. *Islam.* Beltsville, MD: Amana Publications, 1998.

Al-Jawziyaa, Ibn Qayyim. *Natural Healing with the Medicine of the Prophet,* translated by Muhamad Al-Akili. Philadelphia: Pearl Publishing House, 1993.

Al-Kalby, Kais. *Prophet Muhammad: The Last Messenger in the Bible.* Bakersfield, CA: American Muslim Cultural Association, 1991.

Al-Turabi, Hassan. "The Islamic State" in *Voices of Resurgent Islam,* edited by John Esposito. New York: Oxford University Press, 1983.

Anderson, Norman. *Islam in the Modern World: A Christian Perspective.* Leicester: IVP, 1990.

Armstrong, Karen. *Muhammad: Prophet for Our Time.* London: Harper, 2006.

Azami, Habib Ur Rahman. *The Sunnah in Islam.* London: U.K. Islamic Academy, 1995.

Azhar, Ahmad. *Christianity in History.* Lahore: Sh. Muhammad Ashraf, 1991.

Barlas, Asma. "Women's readings of the Qur'ān" in *The Cambridge Companion to the Qur'an,* edited by Jane Dammen McAuliffe. Cambridge: Cambridge University Press, 2006.

Bennett, Clinton. *In Search of Muhammad.* London: Cassell, 1998.

Bosworth, Edmund. "The Rise of the Karāmiyyah in Khurasan" in *The Muslim World,* vol. L, no.1 (January 1960).

Brown, Daniel W. *Rethinking Tradition in Modern Islamic Thought.* Cambridge: Cambridge University Press, 1996.

Brown, Jonathon A. C. *Hadith: Muhammad's Legacy in the Medieval and Modern World.* Oxford: OneWorld, 2009.

Bucaille, Maurice. *The Bible, the Qur'an and Science.* Indianapolis: North American Trust Publication, 1979. Reprinted Kazn Publications, 2002.

Burton, John. *The Collection of the Qur'ān.* Cambridge: Cambridge University Press, 1977.

Caner, Ergun Mehmet and Emir Fethi Caner. *Unveiling Islam.* Grand Rapids: Kregel Publications, 2002.

Catherwood, Christopher. *Christians, Muslims and Islamic Rage.* Grand Rapids: Zondervan, 2003.

Cook, Michael. *Muhammad.* Oxford: Oxford University Press, 1983.

Crone, Patricia. *Meccan Trade and the Rise of Islam.* Princeton: Princeton University Press, 1987. Reprinted by Gorgias Press, 2004.

Danner, Victor. *The Islamic Tradition.* New York: Amity, 1988. Reprinted by Sophia Perennis, 2005.

Dashti, Ali. *Thirty Three Years: A Study of the Prophetic Career of Mohammad.* London: George, Allen & Unwin, 1985.

Davis, John J. *Moses and the Gods of Egypt,* second ed. Grand Rapids: Baker Book House, 1986.

Doi, Abdur Rahman I. *Introduction to the Hadith.* Kuala Lumpur: A.S. Noordeen, 1991.

Donner, Fred. *Narratives of Islamic Origins.* Princeton: Darwin Press, 1998.

Eaton, Charles Le Gai. "Man" in Seyyed Hossein Nasr, *Islamic Spirituality.* London: SCM, 1985.

Esposito, John. *Islam: The Straight Path.* Oxford: Oxford University Press, 1988.

Firestone, Reuven. *Jihad: The Origin of Holy War in Islam.* Oxford: Oxford University Press, 1999.

Fischer, Michael M. J. and Mehdi Abedi. *Debating Muslims.* Madison: University of Wisconsin Press, 1990.

Flew, Anthony. "Theology and Falsification" in *Reason and Responsibility: Readings in Some Basic Problems of Philosophy,* edited by Joel Feinberg. Belmont, CA: Dickenson Publishing Company, Inc., 1968.

Forbes, Greg. "All Religions Lead to God?" in *Ambassador,* Issue 207, September 2009. Melbourne: Bible College of Victoria, 2009.

Gabriel, Mark A. *Islam and Terrorism.* Lake Mary, FL: FrontLine, 2002.

Geisler, Norman and Abdul Saleeb. *Answering Islam: The Crescent in the Light of the Cross.* Grand Rapids: Baker Book House, 1993. Updated in 2002.

Gibb, H.A.R. *Mohammedanism.* New York: Oxford University Press, 1962.

Goldziher, Ignaz. *Muslim Studies,* 2 vols. Translated by C. R. Barber and S. M. Stern. London: Curzon Press, 1971. Reprinted 2009.

Gramlich, Richard. "Mystical Dimensions of Islamic Monotheism" in *We Believe in One God* by Annemarie Schimmel and Abdoldjavad Falaturi. New York: Seabury Press, 1979.

Guillaume, Alfred. *The Life of Muhammad: A Translation of Ishaq's Sira Rasul Allah.* London: Oxford University Press, 1955. Reprinted 1998.

———. *The Traditions of Islam: An Introduction to the Study of the Hadith Literature.* Beirut: Khayats, 1966. Reprinted 2003.

Hasel, Gerhard. "The Polemic Nature of the Genesis Cosmology" in *Evangelical Quarterly* (1974), 48:81-102.

Hassan, Riffat. "Made from Adam's Rib, the Woman's Creation Question" in *Al-Mushir* vol. XXVII (124-155). Pakistan, 1985.

Haykal, Muhammad Hussein. *The Life of Muhammad.* Indianapolis: North American Trust, 1976. Reprinted by Islamic Book Trust, 1994.

Hitti, Philip K. *Islam: A Way of Life.* Minneapolis: University of Minnesota Press, 1970.

Holland, Tom. *In the Shadow of the Sword.* London: Little, Brown, 2012.

Hughes, Thomas Patrick. *Dictionary of Islam.* London: W.H. Allen, 1885. Reprinted Asian Educational Services, 2001.

Hume, Robert E. *The World's Living Religions.* New York: Charles Scribner's Sons, rev. ed. 1959.

Ibrahim, Ezzeddin and Denys Johnson-Davies. *Forty Hadith Qudsi.* Beirut: The Holy Koran Publishing House, 1980. Reprinted by Rabab, 1993.

Juynboll, G. H. A. "Hadith and the Qur'an" in *Encyclopaedia of the Qur'an,* 5 vols, edited by Jane Dammen McAuliffe. Leiden: Brill, 2002.

———. *Muslim Tradition.* Cambridge: Cambridge University Press, 1983. Reprinted 2008.

Kaiser, Christopher B. *The Doctrine of God.* Wheaton, IL: Crossway Books, 1982. Reprinted Wipf & Stock, 2001.

Kamali, Mohammad Hashim. *A Textbook of Hadith Studies: Authenticity, Compilation, Classification and Criticism of Ḥadīth.* Leicestershire: The Islamic Foundation, 2005.

Khan, Israr Ahmad. *Authentication of Hadith: Redefining the Criteria.* London: The International Institute of Islamic Thought, 2010.

Khomeini, Ayatollah. *Islamic Government.* New York: Manor Books, 1979. Translated by Joint Publications Research Service. Reprinted 2005.

Kittel, Gerhard. "δόξά" in *Theological Dictionary of the New Testament,* 10 vols, edited by Gerhard Kittel, translated by G. Bromily. Grand Rapids: Eerdmans, 1964.

Kritzeck, James. *Peter the Venerable and Islam.* Princeton: Princeton University Press, 1964.

Kselman, John S. "Grace (OT)" in *The Anchor Bible Dictionary,* 5 vols, by David Noel Freedman. New York: Doubleday, 1992.

Kuran, Timur. *The Long Divergence: How Islamic Law Held Back the Middle East.* Princeton: Princeton University Press, 2010.

Kutty, Ahmad. "The Six Authentic Books of Hadith," in *The Muslim World League Journal,* April-May 1983.

Lapidus, Ira M. *A History of Islamic Societies.* Cambridge: Cambridge University Press, 1988. Second edition 2002.

Lausanne Paper. *Ministry in Islamic contexts.* Nicosia: Lausanne Committee for World Evangelization, 1995.

Madelung, Wilferd. *The Succession to Muhammad.* Cambridge: Cambridge University Press, 1997.

Mallouhi, Christine. *Miniskirts, Mothers and Muslims.* Grand Rapids: Kregel, 2005.

Margoliouth, David. *Mohammed.* London and Glasgow: Blackie and Son, 1939. Reprinted Hyperion Press, 1982.

———. "Textual Variations of the Qur'an" in *The Origins of the Qur'an ,* edited by Ibn Warraq. Amherst, NY: Prometheus Books, 1998. Reprinted 2002.

Maudūdī, Abul A'alā. *The Islamic Law and Constitution,* sixth edition, edited by Khurshid Ahma. Lahore, Pakistan: Islamic Publications, 1977.

McMillen, S. I. and David Stern. *None of These Diseases: The Bible's Health Secrets for the 21st Century.* Michigan: Fleming Revell, 2000.

Mernissi, Fatima. "Women's Rights in Islam" in *Liberal Islam: A Sourcebook* edited by Charles Kurzman. New York: Oxford University Press, 1998.

———. *Women and Islam: An Historical and Theological Enquiry.* Oxford: Basil Blackwell, 1991.

Morris, Leon. *The Gospel According to John.* Grand Rapids: Eerdmans Publishing, 1971.

Nasr, Seyyed Hossein. "God" in *Islamic Spirituality Foundations* edited by Seyyed Hossein Nasr. New York: Crossroad, 1991.

Nehls, Gerhard. *Christians Ask Muslims.* Bellville, South Africa: Evangelical Mission Press, 1988.

Nevo, Yehuda D. and Judith Koren. *Crossroads to Islam: The Origins of the Arab Religion and the Arab State.* Amherst, NY: Prometheus Books, 2003.

Parsons, Martin. *Unveiling God: Contextualizing Christology for Islamic Culture.* Pasadena: William Carey Library, 2005.

Patai, Raphael. *The Arab Mind.* New York: Charles Scribner's Sons, 1973. Updated edition 2007.

Qutb, Sayyid. *Milestones.* Cedar Rapids, IA: Unity, 1980.

Rahman, Fazlur. *Islam,* second edition. Chicago: University of Chicago Press, 1979.)

Rainey, A. F. "Beersheba," in *The Zondervan Pictorial Encyclopedia of the Bible,* edited by Merrill C. Tenney, vol. 1, 507-08. Grand Rapids: Zondervan, 1978.

Ramadhan, Tariq. *The Messenger: The Meanings of the Life of Muhammad.* London: Penguin, 2007.

Rauf, Muhammad Abdul. "Hadith Literature: The Development of the Science of Hadith" in *Arabic Literature to the End of the Umayyad Period,* edited by A. F. L. Beeston et al. Cambridge: Cambridge University Press, 1983.

Riddell, Peter and Peter Cotterell. *Islam in Conflict: Past, Present and Future.* Leicester: IVP, 2003.

Robinson, Neal. *Christ in Islam and Christianity.* London: Macmillan, 1991.

Robson, J. "Hadīth" in *The Encyclopaedia of Islam* New Edition, 11 vols, edited by Bernard Lewis et al. Leiden: Brill, 1971.

Rubin, Uri. *The Eye of the Beholder: The Life of Muhammad as Viewed by the Early Muslims. A textual analysis.* Princeton, 1995.

Sachedina, Abdulaziz. "The Qur'ān and other religions" in *The Cambridge Companion to the Qur'an,* edited by Jane Dammen McAuliffe. Cambridge: Cambridge University Press, 2006.

Saeed, Abdullah. "Jihad and Violence" in *Terrorism and Justice: Moral Argument in a Threatened World,* edited by Tony Coady and Michael O'Keefe. Melbourne: Melbourne University Press, 2002.

——. *Muslim Australians: Their Beliefs, Practices and Institutions.* Canberra: DIMIA & Australian Multicultural Foundation, 2004.

Schacht, Joseph. *The Origins of Muhammadan Jurisprudence.* Oxford: Oxford University Press, 1959. Reprinted by ACLS, 2008.

Schimmel, Annemarie. *Islam: An Introduction.* Albany: State University of New York, 1992.

——. "The Prophet Muhammad as a Centre of Muslim Life and Thought" in *We Believe in One God,* edited by Annemarie Schimmel and Abdoldjavad Falaturi.New York: The Seabury Press, 1979.

Seda, Pete. *Islam Is ... An Introduction to Islam and Its Principles.* Ashland, OR: Al Haramain Islamic Foundation, 2002.

Shogren, Gary S. "Grace (NT)" in *The Anchor Bible Dictionary,* 5 vols, edited by David Noel Freedman. New York: Doubleday, 1992.

Siddiqui, Muhammad. Zubayr *Hadith Literature: Its Origin, Development and Special Features.* Cambridge: Islamic Texts Society, 1993. Reprinted by Suhail Academy, 2001.

Sookhdeo, Patrick. *Global Jihad: The Future in the Face of Militant Islam.* McLean VA: Isaac Publishing, 2007.

St. John, Ronald Bruce. *Libya and the United States: Two Centuries of Strife.* Pennsylvania: University of Pennsylvania Press, 2002.

Stott, John. *Christ the Controversialist.* London: Intervarsity Press, 1970. Reprinted 1996.

Tabataba'I, Allamah Sayyid M. H. *The Qur'an in Islam: Its Impact and Influence on the Life of Muslims.* London: Zahra Publications, 1987.

Tabbarah, Afif. *The Doctrine of Islam: Doctrine and Teachings.* Translated by Hassan T. Shoucair. Beirut: Dar El-Ilm Lil-Malayin, 2001.

Thomas, David. *Anti-Christian Polemic in Early Islam.* Cambridge: Cambridge University Press, 1992.

Tibi, Bassam. "War and Peace in Islam," in Terry Nardin, ed., *The Ethics of War and Peace: Religious and Secular Perspectives,* edited by Terry Nardin. Princeton: Princeton University Press, 1996.

Voll, John Obert. *Islam: Continuity and Change in the Modern World.* Essex: Longman, 1982. Second edition, 1994.

Vouwzee, Samir. "Islamic Philosophy" in *The Encyclopedia of Christianity,* 5 vols, edited by Erwin Fahlbusch et al. Grand Rapids: Eerdmanns, 2001.

Wansbrough, John. *Quranic Studies: Sources and Methods of Scriptural Interpretation.* Oxford: Oxford University Press, 1977. Updated by Andrew Rippin, Prometheus Books, 2004.

———. *The Sectarian Milieu: Content and Composition of Islamic Salvation History.* Oxford: Oxford University Press, 1978.

Ward, Seth. "Funerary Practices, Jewish" in *Medieval Islamic Civilization: an Encyclopedia,* 2 vols., edited by Josef W. Meri. New York: Routledge, 2006.

Warraq, Ibn. "Aspects of the History of Koranic Criticism" in *The Hidden Origins of Islam: New Research into Its Early History* , edited by Karl-Heinz Ohlig and Gerd-R. Puin. Amherst, NY: Prometheus Books, 2010.

Watt, Montgomery. *Islamic Revelation in the Modern World.* London: Hodder & Stoughton, 1970.

Wehr, Hans. *A Dictionary of Modern Written Arabic,* edited by J. Milton Cowan. Ithaca, NY: Spoken Language Services, 1976.

Weston, Paul. "Gospel, Mission and Culture" in *Witness to the World,* edited by David Peterson. Guildford, UK: Paternoster Press, 1999.

Wild, Stefan. "Political interpretation of the Qur'ān" in *The Cambridge Companion to the Qur'an,* edited by Jane Dammen McAuliffe. Cambridge: Cambridge University Press, 2006.

Zaehner, R. C. *The Concise Encyclopedia of Living Faiths.* London: Hutchinson, revised edition 1971. Reprinted 1988.

Zwemer, Samuel. *The Moslem Christ.* Edinburgh: Oliphant, Anderson and Ferrier, 1912. Reprinted by BiblioBazaar, 2010.

———. *The Moslem Doctrine of God.* New York: American Tract Society, 1905. Reprinted by Advancing Native Missions, 2010.

SOFTWARE

The Alim for Windows ver. 4.5, 1996. CD-ROM.

The Islamic Scholar ver.3. Johannesburg: Par Excellence, 1998. CD-ROM.

The World of Islam ver.1.0. Global Mapping Information, 2000. CD-ROM.

INDEX